Western Esotericism

GUIDES FOR THE PERPLEXED

Guides for the Perplexed are clear, concise and accessible introductions to thinkers, writers and subjects that students and readers can find especially challenging. Concentrating specifically on what it is that makes the subject difficult to grasp, these books explain and explore key themes and ideas, guiding the reader towards a thorough understanding of demanding material.

Bahá'í Faith: A Guide for the Perplexed, Robert H. Stockman
Confucius: A Guide for the Perplexed, Yong Huang
Kabbalah: A Guide for the Perplexed, Pinchas Giller
Mysticism: A Guide for the Perplexed, Paul Oliver
New Religious Movements: A Guide for the Perplexed, Paul Oliver
Zoroastrianism: A Guide for the Perplexed, Jenny Rose

A GUIDE FOR THE PERPLEXED

Western Esotericism

WOUTER J. HANEGRAAFF

Bloomsbury Academic
An imprint of Bloomsbury Publishing Plc

B L O O M S B U R Y
LONDON · OXFORD · NEW YORK · NEW DELHI · SYDNEY

Bloomsbury Academic
An imprint of Bloomsbury Publishing Plc

50 Bedford Square	1385 Broadway
London	New York
WC1B 3DP	NY 10018
UK	USA

www.bloomsbury.com

Bloomsbury is a registered trade mark of Bloomsbury Publishing Plc

First published 2013
Reprinted 2014, 2016

© Wouter J. Hanegraaff, 2013

Wouter J. Hanegraaff has asserted his right under the Copyright, Designs and
Patents Act, 1988, to be identified as Author of this work.

British Library Cataloguing-in-Publication Data
A catalogue record for this book is available from the British Library.

ISBN: HB: 978-1-4411-8713-0
PB: 978-1-4411-3646-6

Library of Congress Cataloging-in-Publication Data
Hanegraaff, Wouter J.
Western esotericism: a guide for the perplexed: / Wouter J. Hanegraaff.
p. cm. – (Guides for the perplexed)
Includes bibliographical references and index.
ISBN 978–1-4411–8713–0 (alk. paper) – ISBN 978–1-4411–3646–6
(pbk.: alk. paper) – ISBN 978–1-4411–4674–8 (ebook epub: alk. paper) –
ISBN 978–1-4411–8897–7 (ebook pdf: alk. paper) 1. Occultism. I. Title.
BF1411.H364 2013
135'.4 – dc23
2012019254

Series: Guides for the Perplexed

Typeset by Newgen Imaging Systems Pvt Ltd, Chennai, India
Printed and bound in Great Britain

CONTENTS

FOREWORD

We might as well begin by spilling the secret. The ultimate objective of this book, and of the field of study that it seeks to introduce, is to change the reader's perspective on Western culture and society. We will be concerned with basic assumptions about reality, knowledge and history that have been taken for granted by Europeans since antiquity, and more particularly since the Enlightenment, and that have spread over large parts of the world in our era of globalization. However, the perspective from which we will be looking at these issues may seem counter-intuitive at first sight: we will be concentrating precisely on those worldviews, practices and ways of knowing that have *not* succeeded in becoming dominant and have therefore been marginalized as 'rejected knowledge' since the age of Enlightenment. Under the not entirely satisfactory label of 'Western esotericism' – yes: many have complained about it, but nobody has come up with a better terminology – research in this domain has been developing quite rapidly since the 1990s. However, reliable introductions are still very rare and it remains extremely difficult for non-specialists to distinguish fiction from fact and gain some kind of overview of what the field is all about.

This Guide for the Perplexed is conceived as a practical and accessible guide into Western esotericism as a field of study, and it hopes to provide readers with the basic knowledge and tools that will enable them to explore it further. It is primarily written for students and teachers in the Humanities and the Social Sciences, but it should also be of interest to general educated readers who are curious about these topics and would like to learn more about them. While the book seeks to cover the domain in all its dimensions (of course, within the limits imposed by the modest format of an introductory textbook), it does not just repeat information already well known to specialists, but presents a deliberate agenda – a vision – of how the field should develop into the future.

Key terms in that regard are historicity, complexity, openness and inter- or transdisciplinarity. Although some of its students seem to be of a different opinion, the study of esotericism is never just about esotericism 'in itself' (whatever that may be). On the contrary, it is always about more general, larger, even universal problems and questions that should be of eminent interest to all educated persons. Therefore one could not pay a worse service to Western esotericism than by leaving it to specialized scholars of esotericism alone: on the contrary, we will see that its materials are extremely relevant to historians, philosophers, scientists, theologians, art historians, musicologists, literary scholars or students of popular culture, and even to sociologists, anthropologists, psychologists or political scientists. Like the exterritorial waters on the global map, Western esotericism does not belong to anybody in particular and can therefore be freely explored by all.

So this Guide for the Perplexed is meant as an open invitation for students and scholars to explore it. Without any exaggeration, esotericism stands for the single most neglected and misunderstood domain of research in the humanities, at least as far as Western culture is concerned, and this means that the possibility – even the probability – of new discoveries and surprising new insights is nowhere so great as precisely here. How can one possibly resist such a temptation? And why should one? The hope is that many readers will give in to it wholeheartedly, and set out on expeditions of their own. On the following pages they will find a roadmap and some good travel advice, but what they will encounter on their journey is theirs to find out.

CHAPTER ONE

What is Western esotericism?

'Esotericism' seems an elusive concept, referring to a no less elusive domain of study. The term tends to evoke strong associations in almost everybody's mind – sometimes positive, often highly negative – but nobody finds it easy to explain what it means, let alone why we should be paying serious attention to it. Nevertheless, it is a fact that 'Western esotericism' has been on the agenda of the academic study of religion for several decades now, and is attracting ever more attention in other disciplines of the humanities as well. Behind this development lies a growing recognition that, in our conventional ways of thinking about Western culture and its history, we may have been overlooking something important. Next to the well-known pillars of our official European and American cultural identity – the normative religious traditions of Judaism and Christianity, rational philosophy and modern science – yet another dimension seems to exist, about which we are usually not so well informed. Within the modest limitations imposed by an introductory textbook, this Guide for the Perplexed hopes to fill that hiatus.

As a first step towards understanding what 'Western esotericism' is all about, let us begin with a simple observation: regardless of how this field of study is defined, it clearly does not fit within any of the established disciplines and the fields that they study. Somehow it does not really look like 'religion' as commonly understood, but it does not appear to be a form of 'philosophy' either, nor would it be accepted as 'science' today. Nevertheless it participates in all these fields, as well as in the arts, and yet it cannot be reduced to either of them and has been seriously neglected by all. Prior to the watershed of the eighteenth century, when the academic disciplines began to be established in their present form, the domain in question was still widely recognized as an important, although controversial, focus of intellectual and scholarly inquiry: theologians, philosophers and practitioners of the natural sciences were seriously debating its ideas and their implications. It is only in the wake of the Enlightenment that it vanished almost completely from accepted intellectual discourse and standard textbook narratives. The field now became academically homeless, so to speak, and the level of general and expert knowledge about it declined dramatically during the nineteenth century. It is only after World War II, and increasingly since the 1990s, that this situation has begun to improve; but for the time being, popular perceptions of 'esotericism' are still dominated by the largely misleading products of amateur scholarship and the commercial media.

From a scholarly point of view it is peculiar, to say the least, that a vast and complicated domain of religious and intellectual activity that (as will be seen) has been a pervasive presence in Western culture from late antiquity to the present should have been ignored by the academy as if it did not exist – or treated as if it *should* not exist. The reasons and historical backgrounds to this phenomenon, which has no parallel in intellectual history, will be explored in Chapter Three. At this point we only need to note that the history of academic exclusion and neglect has had problematic effects even with respect to basic scholarly terminology: without exception, all the available terms or labels have their origin in heavily polemical or apologetic contexts, and are therefore loaded with pejorative connotations in general academic discourse. Although 'Western esotericism' has become the label of preference among specialists since the 1990s, among the general public it still evokes associations primarily with contemporary 'New Age' phenomena. Likewise, terms such as 'the occult' or 'occultism' have been defined in a precise sense by contemporary scholars, but carry doubtful associations in wider society. The sober truth is that all the available labels tend to create misleading images of what the field is all about. A neutral and generally accepted terminology simply does not exist; and if one were to try and remedy this situation by inventing a new label from scratch, this would not help because nobody would recognize it as pertaining to the field in question. The emerging consensus among contemporary specialists is to deal with these dilemmas by sticking to 'Western esotericism' as the overall umbrella term, in spite of its disadvantages. The hope is that as serious scholarship develops, the label will eventually lose its pejorative connotations.

From definitions to prototypes

What, then, do we mean by 'Western esotericism'? The adjective 'esoteric' first appeared in the second century CE, but the substantive is of relatively recent date: it seems to have been coined in German (*Esoterik*) in 1792, migrated to French scholarship (*l'ésotérisme*) by 1828 and appeared in English in 1883.[1] This means that 'Western esotericism' is not a natural term but an artificial category, applied retrospectively to a range of currents and ideas that were known by other names at least prior to the end of the eighteenth century. It also means that, originally, not all those currents and ideas were necessarily seen as belonging together: as will be discussed in Chapter Three, it is only as recently as the later seventeenth century that we find the first attempts at presenting them as one single, coherent field or domain, and at explaining what they have in common. In short, 'Western esotericism' is a modern scholarly construct, not an autonomous tradition that already existed out there and merely needed to be discovered by historians. This does not mean, however, that there is nothing 'real' about the field. On the contrary, the category of 'Western esotericism' emerged because intellectuals and historians became attentive to structural similarities that actually did exist between the ideas and worldviews of a wide variety of thinkers and movements. We will look more closely at those commonalities in Chapters Four and Five.

Several modern scholars have attempted to define the nature of Western esotericism by proposing sets of criteria to which one might refer in order to decide whether something does or does not belong to the field. The most famous and influential example comes from the French pioneer in this domain, Antoine Faivre, who in 1992 offered a list of four 'intrinsic' characteristics of esotericism (correspondences; living nature; imagination/mediations; transmutation) next to two non-intrinsic ones (transmission; concordance).[2] Other scholars have criticized Faivre's criteria and proposed alternative approaches, resulting in a spectrum of theories and definitions that differ considerably in how they demarcate the historical and conceptual boundaries of the field as a whole.[3]

In order to understand what is really at stake in these technical debates, let us make a brief excursion to modern theories of cognition. As pointed out by the anthropologist Tanya Luhrmann (in an entirely different context), in everyday practice we do not usually categorize things by means of formal lists of criteria but, rather, by comparing them to 'prototypes'. A prototype is a cluster of characteristics that is seen as constituting a 'good example' of a class:

> When you use prototypes in your thinking, you ask whether the item in question resembles the best example of that class, not whether it meets specified rules or criteria of that category. Is an ostrich a bird or a grazing animal? A prototype user asks himself whether the ostrich is more like a sparrow or more like a cow, relying both on what he can see and on an array of background theory and assumptions. . . . When you look at a piece of furniture to decide whether it is a table or a chair, you do not list the rules of membership in the 'table' and 'chair' categories in your mind. That takes time. It also often does not work, since many category members do not have all the apparent criteria of the class (A bird that cannot fly, like the penguin, is still a bird). . . . You do not ask yourself whether this chair meets the criteria for chairship. You look at it, and you know it's a chair.[4]

Scholars have provided various sets of formal criteria to define what should or should not fall under the category of 'Western esotericism', but in reality they are almost always reasoning by prototype. That is to say, they *already* have some 'best examples' in mind of the class that they see as Western esotericism, and then proceed to compare specific historical phenomena to that model. Depending on the models they have in mind, certain historical currents may be included by some scholars but excluded by others, and this accounts for most of the confusion about the field and its boundaries. The three most common models underlying current concepts of Western esotericism appear to be the following: (1) an 'enchanted' pre-Enlightenment worldview with ancient roots but flourishing in the early modern period, (2) a wide array of 'occult' currents and organizations that emerged after the Enlightenment as alternatives to traditional religion and rational science, (3) a universal, 'inner' spiritual dimension of religion as such.

Model 1: Early modern enchantment

If one looks more closely at the famous criteria proposed by Antoine Faivre, one will notice that they actually read like a definition of 'enchantment', set against the 'disenchanted' worldviews associated with post-cartesian, post-newtonian and positivist science. Faivre's notion of 'correspondences' has its ultimate origin in Plotinus' notion of *sympathy*:[5] it suggests that all parts of the universe are interrelated without a need for intermediary links or causal chains, and is therefore clearly meant as an alternative to linear or instrumental causality. 'Living nature' stands against mechanistic worldviews as well: it means that the world is conceived of as a living organism permeated by an invisible life force, not as a dead mechanism or clockwork. The notion of 'imagination/mediations' suggests a multi-leveled Platonic cosmology as opposed to a cosmos reducible to only matter in motion; and it suggests not only that there are various 'subtle' levels of reality intermediary between the poles of pure spirit and pure matter but also that we may gain access to them by means of the imagination (which is therefore an organ of knowledge and not just a fabricator of illusions, as held by Enlightenment rationalism). 'Transmutation', finally, refers to a process by means of which man or nature may be changed into a higher spiritual state or even attain a divine condition.

In short, esotericism according to Faivre's definition looks like a radical alternative to the disenchanted worldviews that came to dominate Western culture in the wake of the scientific revolution, the Enlightenment and positivist science. For Faivre himself, the prototypes *par excellence* of Western esotericism are to be found in a movement in early modern culture – roughly from Paracelsus in the sixteenth century to the Romantic era – that is known as Christian theosophy and *Naturphilosophie*, and to which we will return below. Accordingly, whether any other religious or intellectual currents should be seen as forms of esotericism depends on how close they are to these 'best examples' of the class. In practice, this means that the early modern period looms largest in Faivre's work, as the golden age when Western esotericism flourished like never before or after. Ancient and medieval sources are acknowledged as a necessary background, rather than as manifestations of esotericism in their own right. And most importantly, it remains somewhat questionable – and never fully explained in Faivre's oeuvre – whether the many esoteric or occultist currents that developed through the nineteenth and twentieth centuries up to the present are still close enough to the theosophical/*naturphilosophical* prototype to qualify as 'esotericism' at all. In terms of Luhrmann's analogy: if esotericism is an enchanted sparrow that clearly differs from a disenchanted cow, then these post-Enlightenment forms of esotericism seem to be hybrid animals that might easily be dismissed as pseudo-esotericisms.

Faivre is the most prominent but certainly not the only scholar who understands esotericism as a prototypical worldview of enchantment, opposed to the disenchanted worldviews of modern and contemporary society, and points to the early modern period as its golden age. From a very different perspective and with different arguments, the English historian Frances Yates created a similar perspective with her extremely influential grand narrative of the 'Hermetic Tradition' of the Renaissance.[6] As presented by Yates, this tradition emerged from the rediscovery and translation of a collection of texts from late antiquity, the *Corpus Hermeticum*, by the Florentine philosopher Marsilio Ficino (see Chapter Two). In the wake of this translation, published in 1471, Renaissance hermeticism flourished during the sixteenth and seventeenth centuries as a worldview dominated by magic, personal experience and the powers of the imagination. It promoted a world-affirming mysticism consonant with an 'enchanted' and holistic science that looked at nature as a living, organic whole, permeated by invisible forces and energies. And, still according to Yates, it reflected a confident, optimistic, forward-looking perspective that emphasized humanity's potential to operate on the world by using the new sciences, and thus create a better, more harmonious, more beautiful society.

Like Faivre's Western esotericism, Frances Yates' Hermetic Tradition flourished during the early modern period as an 'enchanted' alternative to established religion and rationalistic science. Its literary sources went back to late antiquity, but Yates drew a sharp dividing line between the 'dark' Middle Ages and the new phenomenon of a beautiful and elegant hermetic magic in

Renaissance culture. More sharply and decisively than in Faivre's narrative, she claimed that the 'Hermetic Tradition' had come to an end during the seventeenth century with the rise of modern philology and natural science. But many of her enthusiastic readers during the 1960s and 1970s went a step further. At the dawn of modernity, so they understood, the magical and enchanted worldview of the Renaissance had lost the battle against the Christian and scientific establishment, after which the very memory of its existence had been suppressed and almost destroyed. For some of them, the newly rediscovered 'Hermetic Tradition' became a source of inspiration in their own struggle with the contemporary political, religious and scientific establishment, and their attempts to 're-enchant' the world and bring 'the imagination back to power'. This made Yates' narrative highly relevant to contemporary concerns. Many of those who were involved in, or sympathetic to, the new magical or spiritual movements flourishing since the 1960s began to look at Renaissance hermeticism as their own predecessors.

Yates and Faivre are the most prominent examples of an approach that makes esotericism into the model of an enchanted worldview flourishing from the Renaissance until the Enlightenment. An important implication is that, by definition, esotericism must be at odds with the secular world and can never be seen as an integral dimension of modern culture and society. Even if it manages to survive under post-Enlightenment conditions, it can only do so as an anti-modernist 'counterculture' engaged in an ultimately hopeless 'flight from reason'.[7] This, at least, is how many sociologists during the 1960s and 1970s in fact looked at the surprising boom of new religious movements and occultist currents during that period: the dominant 'secularization thesis' claimed that religion and magic could have no future in an age of science and increasing rationalization, and so this 'Occult Revival' (along with the 'Oriental Renaissance') had to be dismissed as a manifestation of irrationalism and futile longing for a romanticized past.

Model 2: The (post)modern occult

There is no doubt that modern and contemporary manifestations of esotericism, from the eighteenth century up to the present, proclaim ideas and convictions that have their historical origins in pre-Enlightenment models. We will encounter many examples in what follows. But it would be a mistake to assume that these traditional worldviews have persisted simply as 'survivals' from the past, continuing in their original form without being affected or changed by the impact of modern trends and developments: that magical, esoteric or occultist concepts are inherently static and 'resistant to change' is a positivist cliché that has been disproved time and time again.[8] On the contrary, as will be seen in Chapter Seven, ideas and worldviews inherited from pre- and early modern periods were thoroughly *transformed* from the nineteenth century on, under the impact of new cultural and intellectual developments in secular society, with new, surprising, and unprecedented results.

As we have seen, the first model implies that such post-Enlightenment forms of esotericism can never be more than second-hand, derivative or defective deformations of the real thing: by compromising with secular thought, the integrity and authenticity of esotericism must necessarily be impaired, and so its modern and contemporary manifestations fall short of full identification with the model and its prototypical examples. But it is perfectly possible to turn the argument around. After all, or so it can be argued, it is only after the eighteenth century that esotericism or the occult began to emerge as a social phenomenon in its own right. Before that time it had been just an intellectual tradition manifested in learned and popular writings; but only now did it take the form of actual organizations and social networks that began to compete with the established churches on a pluralistic 'market' of religion. From such a perspective, precisely the occult as manifested in modern and contemporary culture is the central core phenomenon, and so it is here that we can expect to find the 'best examples' or prototypes of what Western esotericism is all about. Earlier periods may be of interest for providing some historical background, but are not crucial or central to understanding the occult; and any formal criteria for defining and demarcating the field must be derived from its *post*-Enlightenment manifestations. Programmatic statements of this position are far more difficult to find than in the case of the first model, because its main representatives tend to come from the social sciences and are seldom very interested in broader historical contextualizations. Their main focus is on what exists here and now, and much less on where it may have come from. In other words, we are not dealing here with any explicit (or even implicit) theory or conviction about the nature and historical development of esotericism before and after the Enlightenment, but simply with an interest in studying the occult as a phenomenon in modern or contemporary popular culture.[9]

In this second model, 'esotericism' or the occult does not function as an object of nostalgia for a lost or forgotten enchanted worldview, but as a dimension of the here and now, with implications for the future. When sociologists first began studying the occult during the 1960s and 1970s, they saw it as a surprising and somehow disconcerting phenomenon of social 'deviance' concerned with 'anomalous' claims of knowledge that seemed to reflect a movement of youthful rebellion against science and established religion.[10] They had trouble seeing anything else in it than a heartfelt but obviously futile reaction against rationalization and the forward march of modernity. In more recent years, however, sociologists and historians of religion have begun to see the occult as a significant manifestation *of* modernity.[11] Predictions about the imminent demise of religion have turned out to be premature, to say the least; and it has become ever more evident that esoteric or occult currents are a permanent feature of modern culture. They have been around since the birth of modernity, and whether we like it or not, it seems that they are here to stay. In current scholarship, the occult is therefore no longer perceived as a marginal and irritating anomaly – something that 'should not be there' – but, on the contrary, as a highly important manifestation of how religion is continuously being reinvented under new historical and social conditions. For example, the rapid expansion of new information and communication technologies since the 1990s, and the spectacular development of new media during the same period, now seems to result in a *post*modern occult that, among other things, playfully but deliberately blurs the boundaries between fiction and reality. It should be noticed that, in the emerging scholarship about such topics, notions of 'the occult' tend to be used rather vaguely, and mostly as shorthand for anything touching on the psychic or paranormal: for example, scholars of religion are now pointing to the fascination with 'superpowers' in popular comics or role-playing games as a significant example of how 'the sacred' manifests itself in contemporary popular culture.[12]

Far from referring to any specific historical tradition, then, the occult tends to be understood in much of current scholarship as just a convenient modern term for strange phenomena and radical experiences that (presumably) have been reported from all times and places and are obviously still with us in modern and contemporary society. Such research is recognized in the present Introduction as an important part of the study of Western esotericism – but still as one dimension only. The essential weakness of the first model outlined above (that of 'early modern Enchantment') is that it is not capable of taking modern and contemporary forms of esotericism completely seriously on their own terms: it perceives them only in relation to their pre-Enlightenment forebears, who must necessarily be superior by comparison. But the weakness of the second model lies in its lack of historical depth. It does take the modern and contemporary occult seriously on its own terms, but fails to recognize that the roots and origins of any phenomenon are an inextricable part of that phenomenon itself. Studying the occult without placing it in historical perspective is a bit like reducing 9/11 to 'a terrorist act', period, while dismissing the history of Islamic radicalism or Western colonialist politics as irrelevant to understanding what it was and why it happened. Likewise (against the anti-historical drift of the second model) we will fail to understand the occult unless we integrate its study in a wider historical context; but in doing so (against the anti-modern drift of the first model) we should take it as seriously as its pre-Enlightenment forebears.

Model 3: Inner traditions

According to a third influential model of Western esotericism, the term stands for 'inner' traditions concerned with a universal spiritual dimension of reality, as opposed to the merely external ('exoteric') religious institutions and dogmatic systems of established religions. This model stays closest to the original meaning of the adjective 'esoteric' in late antiquity, when it referred to secret teachings reserved for a spiritual elite, such as the Pythagorean brotherhoods or some mystery cults. Exoteric teachings, according to this model, are meant for the uneducated masses that can be kept satisfied with mere ritual observance and dogmatic belief systems. Underneath the surface of conventional religion, however, there are deeper truths that are known only to initiates into the true mysteries of religion and philosophy.

According to this model, the true esoteric spirituality must ultimately be one, independent of social, historical or cultural circumstances. Regardless of the tradition in which one has been raised, those who refuse to be satisfied with outward appearances and limited dogmatic systems will always be able to find access to the universal truth about the nature of the world, of divinity and of human destiny to which all the great mystics and spiritual teachers have been referring. Therefore 'Western' esotericism is only one part of a much larger domain: the esoteric teachings of all non-Western religions and cultures, such as Hinduism, Buddhism, Shamanism and so on, must ultimately point towards the same esoteric reality underneath surface appearances.

In the modern science of religion, the study of historical currents in search of such an 'inner' universal dimension is technically known as 'religionism'.[13] With various degrees of emphasis, and sometimes with considerable subtlety and sophistication, this agenda has strongly influenced the way in which religion has been studied after World War II, especially in the United States under the influence of Mircea Eliade and his school; and some of the most influential scholars of Western esotericism – from Henry Corbin and Antoine Faivre in his earlier work, to contemporary authors such as Arthur Versluis and even Nicholas Goodrick-Clarke – have been inspired clearly by religionist agendas. But while the study of Western esotericism owes much to the work of these pioneers, the mainstream of scholarship has begun to move away from religionist approaches since the 1990s and increasingly since the beginning of the twenty-first century. The reason is that the 'inner dimensions' model, which in one way or another underlies all forms of religionism, has some highly problematic implications.

Most importantly (and most obviously), it rests upon the conviction that a universal, hidden, esoteric dimension of reality really does exist. Scholarly methods, however, are 'exoteric' by definition and can only study what is empirically available to observers regardless of their personal convictions: the academy has no instruments for gaining direct access to the true and absolute nature of reality that is claimed to exist according to this model, and it has no methodologies for either verifying or falsifying the claim that such a reality exists in the first place. The Absolute or the Divine is simply not a possible object of research: all that scholars can do is study the beliefs, convictions or theories that have been formulated *about* it, but as scholars they are not qualified to assess their truth or falsity. Initially, many students of esotericism find this disappointing and frustrating, but it is a simple matter of recognizing the limitations of what scholarly research can and cannot do. Some academics claim that since science and scholarship cannot discover the divine or the absolute, it therefore does not exist. However, it is logically more consistent to admit that we simply do not know – and cannot know. This position, which neither affirms nor denies that it might be possible to discover the true nature of reality by *other* means than science and scholarship (such as spiritual techniques or mystical contemplation), is technically known as 'methodological agnosticism'.

The model of esotericism as the 'inner dimension' of reality is also problematic from the perspective of strictly historical research. If all that really matters about esotericism is the one universal truth, this leaves little or no room for recognizing or giving attention to historical specificity, individual creativity, novelty, change and development. But historians are bound to emphasize that, claims to unity and universality notwithstanding, there are in fact enormous differences between various 'esoteric' currents and ideas in different historical periods and social contexts. Hermetic texts from antiquity, theosophical visionaries like Jacob Böhme or Emanuel Swedenborg, occultist magicians like Aleister Crowley, contemporary New Agers, and so on, have extremely different and often mutually exclusive worldviews and agendas that are typical of their specific historical and social context. Religionists tend to play down the importance of such contextual factors because they see them as merely 'external' and ultimately irrelevant with respect to the all-important 'inner' dimension. As a result, the study of esotericism, for them, amounts to providing illustrative examples of thinkers and practitioners who best exemplify what they themselves see as true and eternally valid – with reference to criteria, as we have just seen, that remain inaccessible for normal scholars.

In this Introduction, none of these three models will be the normative basis of discussion. We will be looking at Western esotericism as a radically pluralistic field of currents, ideas and practices that can be studied from late antiquity to the present day, *without* seeking to privilege any historical period or any particular worldview as 'more truly esoteric' (i.e. closer to some preferred model) than any other. From that perspective, there is no such thing as a 'best example' of esotericism, and there are no prototypical 'esotericists'. But obviously, such an approach begs the question of definition and demarcation, for it still assumes that the field *as a whole* can be set apart as somehow different from other fields of inquiry.

On what basis, then, can we do so? Very briefly, and with reference to the opening paragraph of this chapter: the field that we now call Western esotericism may be described as the chief casualty of academic specialization after the eighteenth century. What initially sets it apart is its modern status as 'rejected knowledge': it contains precisely everything that has been consigned to the dustbin of history by Enlightenment ideologues and their intellectual heirs up to the present, because it is considered incompatible with normative concepts of religion, rationality and science. Imagined as the radical counterpart of everything that educated people are expected to take seriously, the consensus among mainstream intellectuals after the eighteenth century was that this domain should better be avoided and ignored in academic discourse rather than being dignified by detailed study and analysis of its ideas and their development. We will see that this process of exclusion and neglect did not just happen overnight: on the contrary, it was the final outcome of a long history of apologetic and polemical battles and negotiations, beginning in late antiquity, about the question of which worldviews and approaches to knowledge should be considered acceptable and which ones should be rejected. It is through these debates that the emerging religious and intellectual elites have been defining their own identity.

That Western esotericism is the academy's dustbin of rejected knowledge does not imply that it is just a random collection of discarded materials without any further connection. On the contrary, a broad consensus had emerged around the eighteenth century about the chief characteristics of the rejected domain. Although one can never take polemical narratives at face value – almost by definition, they exaggerate and simplify for maximum effect – those characteristics do in fact correspond to recognizable worldviews and approaches to knowledge that have played an important although always controversial role in the history of Western culture. In sum: in the rest of this book we will be studying a large and complicated field of research that (1) has been set apart by mainstream religious

. culture as the 'other' by which it defines its own
.) is characterized by a strong emphasis on specific
id epistemologies that are at odds with normative
p.. ᴀment intellectual culture. This is the closest we will
get to a deɴɪɴtion of Western esotericism.[14] The first element is discussed in Chapter Three, the second in Chapters Four and Five.

The rest of the west: Judaism, Christianity, Islam

What do we mean, exactly, when we refer to this field as *Western*
esotericism? There are several ways of answering that question,
and we will see that they carry important implications with respect
to the nature of this field of research and its essential agendas.
Since there is much confusion about these issues, it is important to
address them explicity.

An initial point of concern is that the terminology might easily
suggest some fundamental East-West distinction *within* the field
of esotericism as a whole, implying that there must be an 'Oriental
Esotericism' next to the Occidental variety. We have seen that the
religionist perspective based on the prototype of 'inner dimensions' makes precisely that assumption. Since it holds that personal
inner access to universal spiritual truths is available to all human
beings in principle, Western esotericism must have its parallels in
the East. The logical result of such a perspective is that the study
of 'esotericism' turns into a form of comparative religious studies that seeks to discover the universalia of 'inner' religion world-
wide. But whatever one might think of such a project in itself, it is
certainly not representative of the study of Western esotericism as
understood here. Even apart from the problematic nature of religionism as such (see above), comparative studies of religious experience on religionist foundations have no need for the 'esotericism'
label. Such lines of research have developed and organized themselves independently, ever since the nineteenth century, and now
have well-developed agendas, networks and bodies of literature all
of their own. For sure there is much in Western esotericism that
is bound to interest students in this field, and it is certainly true
that much can be learned from systematic comparisons between

Western and Eastern forms of experiential religion, but the two programmes simply do not coincide. To avoid any confusion, then, it should be clear that the adjective 'Western' is not understood here as a qualifier within a larger field, demarcating the occidental section of some general world-wide 'esotericism'. On the contrary, it is meant to highlight the *specificity* of esotericism understood as an inherently Western domain of research, in contrast to globalizing or universalizing understandings of the term.

But making any such claim brings up another important issue regarding the notion of 'Western' esotericism. The category of 'rejected knowledge' that emerged during the Enlightenment, and that we have inherited, is the final outcome of complicated apologetic and polemical debates dominated by *Christian* intellectuals from antiquity to the eighteenth century. It has sometimes been argued that referring to such a category as 'Western esotericism' is inappropriate because that label implicitly marginalizes the important role of Jewish and Islamic esoteric currents in the history of religion in Europe. This argument carries considerable weight, for it is true that traditional grand narratives of the 'Christian occident' (essentially based on models adopted from Church History) used to highlight the role of establishment Christianity in Europe at the expense of almost everything else. Such approaches are rightly criticized by modern scholars who emphasize that, to the contrary, religion in Europe has always been marked by religious diversity and pluralistic competition.[15] Next to Christianity and its various denominations, Judaism and Islam should be seen as integral parts of the story of religion in Europe, and the same goes for the various 'pagan' traditions from antiquity and indigenous European cultures that continued to exert an important influence in learned discourse and popular practice. From such a perspective, it may seem natural to conclude that any field that calls itself 'Western esotericism' must cover occidental culture in all its complexity and diversity, and should therefore give equal attention to esoteric traditions in Judaism, Christianity and Islam.

Although strong arguments can be adduced in favour of such an approach, at least in theory, for a combination of reasons we will not adopt it in this Guide. An initial and rather pragmatic reason is that both Jewish and Islamic 'mysticism' (another problematic term, that still tends to be preferred over 'esotericism' by most scholars in these fields) have already developed as relatively autonomous and independent fields of research, and there is no particular need to duplicate those bodies of scholarship here under another label. Additionally, there are limits to the possibilities for interdisciplinary research across the borders of these different fields, mainly for linguistic reasons: one will not make much headway in the study of kabbalah without being fluent in Hebrew and Aramaic, or in Sufism without deep knowledge of Arabic or Persian, and much of the relevant modern scholarship is simply not available in English or other modern Western languages. All this puts serious practical constraints on the attractive ideal of a comparative esotericism of the three Abrahamic religions. It is probably for this reason that even the most vocal defenders of such an inclusive programme of Western esotericism have not been able to put it into practice.

A second argument has to do with the internal histories of the relevant traditions in Jewish, Christian and Islamic cultures. Scholars have become much more attentive in recent years to the importance of interconfessional exchange and 'discursive transfer' across the boundaries of established religions, and this is an important corrective to the idea that the monotheistic or scriptural religions developed each in some kind of splendid isolation. But the point should not be exaggerated. It still remains the case that Jewish and Islamic forms of 'esotericism' have emerged and developed as largely self-contained and relatively autonomous traditions, accessible during most of their histories only to pious Jews and Muslims within their own respective communities. The simple reason is, again, that they required fluency in the relevant languages and deep familiarity with their respective holy scriptures: one cannot study classical Jewish kabbalah without intimate knowledge of the Hebrew bible and its commentaries, or understand Islamic 'mysticism' without access to the poetic language of the Quran in Arabic. Unless one adopts an extreme religionist perspective, by which anything 'external' derives from some universal 'inner' source, this in itself makes it quite implausible a priori that more or less the same kind of 'esotericism' would have developed independently in Jewish, Christian and Islamic contexts. There is much more reason to emphasize the specificity and relative uniqueness of each. This point can be illustrated by the example of the very term 'esotericism'. In the Jewish context, it has to do with complex procedures for disclosing hidden or secret levels of meaning of the Torah. In Christian contexts, much of the concern with 'secrecy' or 'hidden knowledge' is indebted, rather, to the concept of 'occult' (hidden) qualities in nature. And in Islamic cultures – not just in their mystical or esoteric forms of expression, but even in the very text of the Quran itself (Sura 57.3) – we find a fundamental distinction between the apparent or outward dimension of reality (*zâhir*) and its hidden or inward dimension (*bâtin*). The list could be extended. Although they all have to do something with secrecy or concealment, these are very different concepts with different historical and conceptual backgrounds, which cannot be reduced to one another without simplification and distortion. In short, it is by no means so easy as it might seem to demonstrate some basic underlying structure that allows us to see Jewish, Christian and Islamic forms of 'esotericism' as variants of essentially one and the same field. In all likelihood, the very idea of such a transconfessional esotericism common to the monotheistic or scriptural religions has emerged as a preoccupation of post-Enlightenment scholars.

In this Guide we will therefore concentrate on the lineage that runs from late antiquity through predominantly Western Christian culture up to the Enlightenment, and the subsequent development of modern and secular culture up to the present. Obviously we will give due attention to interactions and exchanges with Jewish, Byzantine and Islamic culture wherever that is relevant; but the dialectics with *pagan* traditions inherited from late antiquity will prove to be more important in explaining why the field assumed a status of relative autonomy. It remains true that the very term 'Western esotericism' could be seen as reflecting an unfortunate hegemonizing perspective, which, against the evidence that religious pluralism has been the rule in Western culture, marginalizes Judaism and Islam in Europe in order to promote an ideological 'Christendom narrative'. But alternatively, it could be argued that this is precisely the point. As will be seen in Chapter Three, the very perception of 'Western esotericism' as a domain of its own *did* in fact emerge as a singularizing and hegemonizing construct – directed, however, against 'paganism' rather than against Judaism or Islam – in the context of specifically Christian apologetic and polemical debates. Whether we like it or not, this is the legacy that we have inherited, and that we should try to understand.

CHAPTER TWO

A very short history

There have been several attempts at writing a 'history of Western esotericism', and reliable historical introductions are available for each of its most important components (see Chapter Nine). Since this Guide for the Perplexed takes a thematic and problem-oriented approach, we will restrict ourselves in this chapter to just a short overview of the basic historical currents and traditions that are indispensable for understanding the field, without any attempt at going into details. The goal is simply to provide a basic 'map' of the terrain, as an initial means of orientation in what could otherwise be an extremely confusing field of exploration.

Gnōsis in Hellenistic culture

The origins of Western esotericism are in the Hellenistic culture of late antiquity, marked by complicated mixtures between Greek philosophy and indigenous religious traditions, especially those of the Egyptians. In the writings of many authors during the late Hellenistic period, *Platonism* was transformed into a religious worldview with its own mythologies and ritual practices, focused on the attainment of a salvational gnōsis ('knowledge') by which the human soul could be liberated from its material entanglement and regain its unity with the divine Mind. Among thinkers of such a persuasion, it was widely assumed that Plato's philosophy was not an original product of Greek rational thinking but was grounded in the much more ancient religious wisdom traditions of the Oriental peoples, notably the Persians, the Egyptians or the Hebrews. This widespread understanding of Platonism as 'religious wisdom from the East' may be referred to as *Platonic Orientalism*, in contrast to Platonism understood as a tradition of Greek philosophical rationalism grounded in Socratic dialogue.

The concern for a salvational gnōsis in a broadly platonic framework was widespread among thinkers whom we would now classify as Middle Platonists. Among its most important manifestations in view of the later history of Western esotericism is the Egyptian Hellenistic tradition known as *Hermetism*.[1] The name refers to a legendary and more or less divinized wisdom teacher, Hermes Trismegistus (originally a syncretic mixture of the Greek Hermes and the Egyptian Thoth), who was believed to have flourished in Egypt in very ancient times. The surviving texts attributed to Hermes, or in which he plays a central role, can in fact be dated to the second and third centuries CE. As far as the religious teachings of Hermetism are concerned, the most important of these texts are the so-called *Corpus Hermeticum* (17 separate treatises collated together in medieval Byzantium); a larger work that has survived only in Latin, under the title *Asclepius*; and an initiatic text known as the *Treatise of the Eight and the Ninth*, discovered only as recently as 1945. These texts contain technical discussions about the true nature of God, the world and man, but point out that philosophical discourse is just a preparation for religious salvation. The Hermetic devotee must transcend mere rational understanding and worldly attachments, to find salvation and ultimate release through being reborn – quite literally – in a spiritual body of immaterial light. This process of liberation and transformation culminates in spiritual ascent and, finally, blissful unity with the supreme powers of divine Light. The material body and the sexual urges are obstacles that must be overcome to achieve this goal; but once the hermetist has been reborn and his 'spiritual eyes are opened', he discovers that the divine is invisibly present throughout the whole of creation. Whether the Hermetic writings were a purely literary textual phenomenon or were used in actual communities, with a distinctive ritual practice, remains controversial among scholars.

Whereas Hermetism was a product of pagan Egyptian Hellenism, the search for gnōsis was widespread among Christians as well. The term was used in a positive sense by a few Church fathers, notably Clement of Alexandria, but is mostly associated with the phenomenon known as *Gnosticism*. Under the influence of polemics by church fathers such as Irenaeus, Hippolytus or Ephiphanius, who presented it as the heresy of heresies, gnosticism has traditionally been perceived as a dualistic religion which taught that sparks of the divine light had become imprisoned in the world of matter and must escape from it, in order to find their way back to their divine source. According to basic gnostic mythology, those human beings who carried the spark in themselves were rebelling against the demiurge, an ignorant or evil deity (often associated with the God of the Old Testament) who had created this lower world of darkness and ignorance as a prison for the soul, and therefore sought to prevent human beings from waking up to their true divine identity. By attaining gnōsis (knowledge) of their divine origin, gnostics were set on their way to escape from the world of the demiurge and his demonic helpers, the archons, who would try to prevent them from rising up through the heavenly spheres after death and finding their way back to their divine home of Light. After the sensational discovery of the so-called Nag Hammadi library in Egypt in 1945, which contained a whole range of previously unknown manuscripts, our picture of these gnostic currents and their relation to Christianity has become much more complex than before. In contrast to the simple antithesis between theological orthodoxy and gnostic dualistic heresy ('the gnostic religion' against the religion of the church), scholars are now emphasizing that Christianity as such existed in many shades and varieties, including more or less 'gnostic' ones. Following that logic, some scholars are now arguing that the very term 'gnosticism' should better be discarded.[2]

A third important trend in Hellenistic late antiquity is a ritual practice known as *Theurgy*. Its earliest testimonies are the so-called *Chaldaean Oracles*, attributed to Julian the Theurgist (second century CE), and it flourished in the philosophical milieu nowadays known as Neoplatonism. Theurgy remains rather mysterious in many respects, because the surviving sources do not tell us enough about how it worked exactly, but it clearly involved a ritual practice in which the gods were believed to manifest themselves and get in connection with the Neoplatonic practioners. Iamblichus, the most central authority when it comes to theurgy, was at pains to emphasize that it involved neither a 'magical' practice in which the gods are invoked or compelled to appear, nor a philosophical procedure based on the finite capacities of the human intellect. Instead, the theurgist performed 'unspeakable acts' and worked with 'ineffable symbols' that were understood by the gods alone, who then, by their own power, lifted the theurgist's mind up to the reality of the divine.[3] Like many other manifestations of the search for gnōsis in late antiquity, notably Hermetism, theurgical union seems to have required the induction of unusual, ecstatic or trance-like states of consciousness through which the divine realities were believed to be experienced directly.

The secrets of nature: Magic, astrology, alchemy

Next to the search for spiritual salvation and knowledge of divine realities, Western esotericism involves the study of nature and its hidden or secret laws and dynamics. In modern secular culture we are used to delegating these concerns to the separate spheres of 'religion' and 'science', but in pre-Enlightenment contexts the boundaries were much more ambiguous and permeable: if nature has been created by God, or, more radically, has emanated from God's own being, then its secrets must somehow participate in the sphere of divinity as well, or at least mirror the mysteries of the divine economy. In Chapter Three we will see how complex and controversial such notions could be. Often referred to by the problematic label 'occult sciences', which we will be avoiding here,[4] the three most relevant domains in the study of nature are those of magic, astrology and alchemy.

Of these three, *magic* is the most difficult to grasp. The main reason is that in post-Enlightenment scholarship, countless authors have used it as a universal category pitted against 'religion' and 'science'. But from a historical point of view this will not do: the famous magic–religion–science triad (pioneered by Edward Burnett Tylor and James Frazer) leads to gross simplification and anachronistic distortions if projected back onto the past,[5] and in the history of Western culture 'magic' has in fact a range of different and much more specific meanings. One of them is a direct legacy of Jewish and Christian polemics against pagan idolatry, in the wake of the First and Second Commandment. According to this understanding, all forms of 'magic' are based upon contact with evil demons, who are none else than the old pagan deities that are still trying to deceive human beings, for example by posing as angels of light and promising them power in return for obedience and worship. The great wave of Witchcraft persecutions in early modern Europe was grounded in such an understanding of 'demonic magic'. More relevant to our present concerns, however, is the alternative concept of *magia naturalis* (natural magic). It emerged during the later Middle Ages in an attempt to demonstrate that many wondrous and miraculous phenomena attributed to demons by the common people could in fact be explained in purely natural terms. In other words, the concept of natural magic was an attempt to withdraw the study of nature from theological control by arguing that it had nothing to do with demonic intervention. Such a notion had become all but necessary because of the large-scale rediscovery, since around the eleventh century, of the extensive literature on natural science from late antiquity. This intellectual tradition had been suppressed and neglected in Christian culture after the decline of the Roman Empire, but preserved by Islamic scholars, who had kept studying the sources while translating many of them from Greek into Arabic. A rich and vibrant intellectual culture had developed on the Spanish peninsula during the Middle Ages; and after the fall of Toledo in 1085, Christians gained access to the wealth of learning and scholarship preserved in the superior Muslim libraries. Great numbers of manuscripts concerned with the ancient sciences were now translated from Arabic into Latin, and the result was a medieval 'scientific revolution' with enormous consequences for the subsequent development of Western culture. One important part of *magia naturalis* was the study of so-called occult (lit. hidden) qualities, that is to say, of mysterious forces in nature such as magnetism or the influence of the moon on the tides, which could not be accounted for in terms of medieval science. Eventually the notion came to include 'invisible forces' of all kinds, such as the influences radiating from the stars, the (de)formative powers attributed to the human imagination, or the evil eye. In principle, *magia naturalis* attempted to explain such phenomena in natural scientific terms; but in their very attempts to do so, scholars were giving credence to the reality of 'occult forces' that were seen by others as supernatural and most likely demonic. From the latter perspective, the sciences of the Hellenistic world were a Trojan horse through which the demonic influence of paganism was once again allowed entrance into Christian culture. Hence, magic has always remained a deeply ambiguous category hovering between demonism and natural science.

In sharp contrast to its post-Enlightenment reputation as an 'occult science' or epitome of superstition, classical *astrology* was grounded in a concept of universal, immutable natural law. In Egypt, around the second century BC, it had been developed into a rigorous causal model of cosmology that sought to explain all changes and effects in the sublunar world with reference to the eternally repeating rotations of the celestial bodies. It has therefore been described as 'the most comprehensive scientific theory of antiquity', which could use mathematical models in order to predict all possible changes in the world of cause and effect.[6] On the basis of Aristotelian natural philosophy, the assumption was that the sublunar world constituted of the four elements (earth, water, air, fire) was inert and incapable of moving by itself: the *primae causae* (first causes) of motion were the stars, which were endowed with life and intelligence and influenced the sublunar world through a subtle invisible medium known as the fifth element (*quinta essentia*). Alternatively, in terms of the ruling notion of 'as above, so below', the sublunar and supralunar worlds could be seen as corresponding with one another in terms of a pre-established harmony inherent in creation itself. Astrology was still widespread in pagan, Jewish and Christian milieus before Constantine; but as a divinatory art that suggested divinization of the heavenly bodies and a universal determinism that was seen as threatening the notion of free will, it was broadly dismissed and suppressed as pagan superstition until the later middle ages. From around the eleventh century, the rediscovery of the ancient natural sciences preserved in Islamic culture (see above) led to a widespread Christian revival of astrology as indispensable to the new framework of *magia naturalis*. Particularly important, in that respect, is the notion of *astral magic*: the belief that powers and virtues from the stars can be 'channelled' or drawn down by means of images or ritual techniques – for purposes of medical or psychological healing, but perhaps also to harmful ends. Astrology flourished during the Renaissance and remained an important dimension of natural science even during the period of the scientific revolution. But it was also part and parcel of the 'occult philosophy' of the Renaissance (see below), with its many religious connotations and implications. As this occult philosophy lost the battle with Protestant and Enlightenment opponents during the seventeenth and eighteenth centuries, astrology entered a second period of decline during the nineteenth and the first half of the twentieth. Astrology re-emerged after World War II in new and heavily psychologized forms, largely under the influence of Carl Gustav Jung and his theory of 'synchronicity'.

Western *alchemy*, finally, emerged during the late Hellenistic era as a laboratory practice concerned with the transmutation of material substances. On the basis of the four-elements theory of Aristotelian natural philosophy, it should be possible in principle to change any substance into any other (including gold), and alchemists tried to discover the secrets of transmutation by experimental means. Already at an early stage, in the writings of Zosimos of Panopolis, technical descriptions of laboratory procedures were combined with vivid accounts of visions or dreams about initiatory processes of death-and-rebirth grounded in alchemical symbolism, suggesting that human beings could escape from gross materiality by being transmuted into spiritual beings. Like the other forms of Hellenistic science, alchemy was essentially forgotten during the early medieval period but rediscovered from Islamic sources during the later Middle Ages. Medieval and early modern alchemy is grounded in laboratory procedures pertaining to the domain of science or natural philosophy; but it so happened that its language of transmutation was a natural match for religious narratives about 'spiritual' transformation and rebirth, suggesting that human beings can move beyond their material and sinful condition and attain a superior state of salvation and grace. From such perspectives, for example, Christ could be described metaphorically as the 'philosophers' stone' through whose action human beings were transmuted from gross materiality into spiritual 'gold'. Such religious interpretations and adaptations grew in popularity after the Renaissance and flourished from the end of the sixteenth through the seventeenth century, whether in close connection with laboratory practice or entirely separate from it. As far as the history of science is concerned, it is practically impossible in this period to separate alchemy from what we would now see as chemistry, and hence the contemporary term 'chymistry' has been proposed as a general label (next to 'chrysopoeia' for alchemical attempts at making gold).[7] Like astrology, alchemy was expelled from official science during the eighteenth century and came to be perceived, very misleadingly, as mere pseudo-science or superstition during the nineteenth and much of the twentieth century. After World War II, Jungian and Traditionalist authors (see below) have sought to rehabilitate alchemy by downplaying its 'scientific' nature in favour of its 'spiritual' aspects, but such interpretations are esoteric rather than scholarly in nature. From the perspective of the study of Western esotericism, alchemy is best understood as a complex historical and cultural phenomenon that cannot be contained within any single discipline but is characterized by basic procedures of transmutation that may be pursued as science in laboratory settings *and* function as narratives in religious, philosophical or even psychological discourse.

The Renaissance

During the period of the Renaissance, a range of creative and influential thinkers took up the task of synthesizing ancient 'pagan' learning and religious speculation with Christian thought, along with the newly discovered Jewish kabbalah. In so doing, they created what has been called the 'basic referential corpus' of Western esotericism. This phenomenon of intellectual innovation was essentially a side effect of military conquests and geopolitical changes involving the three 'religions of the book' and, particularly, the shifting balance of power between Christianity and Islam. We have seen that the Christian conquest of the Spanish peninsula, with the fall of Toledo in 1085 as a pivotal event, led to a flood of translations from arabic sources that revolutionized the natural sciences in the Latin west. Five centuries later, the armies of the Ottoman Empire were advancing from the east, culminating in the conquest of Constantinople in 1453. In response to the political expansion of Islam, great numbers of ancient Greek manuscripts were brought from Byzantium to Italy. And on the Spanish peninsula the Catholic monarchs Isabella I of Castile and Ferdinand II of Aragon pursued a virulent anti-Jewish policy culminating in the expulsion of the Jews from Spain in 1492. As a result of this pressure, many Spanish kabbalists arrived in Italy during the later decades of the fifteenth century. In a nutshell, the phenomenon of Renaissance esotericism resulted from the willingness of Christian intellectuals to learn from all these newly available bodies of pagan and Jewish learning, and integrate their contents in what was and remained essentially a Roman Catholic theological and philosophical framework.

The history of Renaissance esotericism is dominated by a core group of influential intellectuals, surrounded by much larger networks of lesser thinkers who adopted their ideas and developed them further. Among the indispensable names, the earliest one is the Byzantine philosopher George Gemistos (1355/60–1452?), who came to call himself *Plethon*. He arrived in Florence in 1437, at the occasion of the Council of Ferrara and Florence, where the Eastern and Western churches were trying (unsuccesfully) to overcome their differences and unite against the threat of Islam. Plethon, who was already around 80 years old, was a living embodiment of what we have referred to as Platonic Orientalism, and impressed the Florentine humanists with his first-hand knowledge of Plato and Aristotle. He highlighted the code of theurgy, the *Chaldaean Oracles*, as a supreme example of the superior religion of the ancients that he believed had been inherited by the Platonists, and he claimed (incorrectly, of course) that they were written in very ancient times by none other that Zoroaster, the chief of the Persian *Magi*. This was the opening shot in a long history of Western fascination with Zoroaster, who came to be imagined as a supreme authority of ancient wisdom.[8]

The second crucial figure is *Marsilio Ficino* (1433–99), whose talents were discovered around 1460 by the ruler of Florence, Cosimo de' Medici. Cosimo had met Plethon during the time of the Council, and had been impressed by his advocacy of Plato. A manuscript with Plato's complete dialogues had arrived from Byzantium in the meantime, and Ficino was ordered to translate them into Latin. The task was finished in 1468, and Ficino went on to summarize the essence of Plato's philosophy in a commentary on the *Symposium* titled *De amore*, presenting it as eminently compatible with Christian truth. With these and other seminal works, Ficino laid the groundwork for a large-scale Renaissance revival of Platonism – or more precisely, Platonic Orientalism. During the rest of his career he translated a whole range of later Platonic authors as well, and published profound studies in which Platonism was presented as the key to Christian revival and renewal. Early on, during the early stages of his Plato translation, he also translated the *Corpus Hermeticum*, from an incomplete manuscript that contained its first 14 treatises. It was published in 1471, so that contemporaries now had direct access to what was believed to be the work of the most ancient Egyptian teacher of wisdom, Hermes Trismegistus. Ficino himself believed that the Persian Zoroaster, with his *Chaldaean Oracles*, was even older and hence more authoritative; but in his later work, notably his influential *De Vita Coelitus Comparanda*, he highlighted Hermes as a teacher of astral magic that could be used for the benificent goals of medical and psychological healing.

The remaining treatises of the *Corpus Hermeticum* were translated from another manuscript by Ficino's younger contemporary *Lodovico Lazzarelli* (1447–1500), a minor but fascinating figure who also wrote a small masterpiece of Christian hermetism that would become a major influence on the much more famous Cornelius Agrippa (see below).[9] But neither of these works became available during Lazzarelli's lifetime, and they were printed only during the first decade of the sixteenth century. In the wake of Ficino's pioneering work, countless authors began to pick up the notion of a profound inner unity between the ancient wisdom from the Orient, Platonic philosophy and Christian theology. Prominent examples are the Vatican librarian *Agostino Steuco* (1497/98–1548), who published the fundamental Renaissance treatise on 'perennial philosophy' in 1540, and *Francesco Patrizi* (1529–97), whose grand synthesis on Platonic Orientalist foundations *Nova de Universis Philosophia* (New Philosophy of Everything, 1591) was condemned by the Vatican in 1594.

The third crucial innovator next to Plethon and Ficino was *Giovanni Pico della Mirandola* (1463–94). An intellectual prodigy, he created sensation in 1486 by inviting intellectuals from all over Europe to engage with him in public debate, presided over by the pope, about no less than 900 theses written by him. The theses reflected Pico's wide-ranging familiarity with all the major traditions of learned speculation in philosophy, theology and science, including the 'ancient wisdom' and, most innovatingly, the Jewish kabbalah. But nothing ever came of the project. To Pico's alarm and disappointment, Pope Innocent VIII responded by censoring 13 theses and eventually condemning all of them, with special emphasis on those 'renovating the errors of pagan philosophers' and those 'cherishing the deceits of the Jews'. Pico's ambition had been to demonstrate that all the conflicts between the different philosophical and theological schools, including the systems of Platonism and Aristotelianism, could be resolved in a grand harmony of universal wisdom and truth. His project culminated in the sensational claim that all the fundamental truths of Christianity were already contained not only in the various traditions of the pagan nations but, most surprisingly and controversially, in the secret tradition of kabbalah that God had revealed to Moses at Mount Sinai. As a result, the true Christian tradition would rule supreme: not only would the pagan sages be seen as bowing down symbolically before the truth of the gospel, but the Jews would have to convert quite literally, as it dawned on them that Jesus had been the true secret of their own ancient traditions all along. Pico's grand debate never took place, and even his famous opening speech, later known as the 'Oratio on the dignity of man', was never published during his lifetime. With prominent references to the Hermetic literature and emphasizing man's unique freedom to choose his own destiny, it has been hailed as an ultimate statement of the Renaissance mentality.

Pico stands at the origin of at least two new, distinct but intimately related developments in Renaissance esotericism. One of them is the complex speculative tradition of *number symbolism* (not to be confused with numerology), much indebted to Pythagoreanism, which assigns qualitative meanings or virtues to the first ten decimals and interprets them as constitutive of reality in all its dimensions. The other is the *Christian kabbalah*. In their efforts to understand the hidden dimensions of Creation and Scripture, Jewish kabbalists had developed a range of specific and unique concepts and approaches, such as the system of ten *sefirot* or divine manifestations, and exegetic techniques such as *gematria*, based on the assignment of numerical values to the Hebrew letters. Having adopted these elements into the framework of their own religion, Christian intellectuals now began to discover unexpected, sensational mysteries and hidden structures in their own scriptures (both the Old Testament and the New) as well as in the natural world around them. The chief pioneer of Christian kabbalah after Pico was the German *Johannes Reuchlin* (1455–1522), the most prominent Christian Hebraist of his day, whose *De arte cabalistica* (1517) has been called 'the bible of the Christian kabbalists'. Among many later intellectuals involved in Christian kabbalistic speculation, we might highlight the Frenchman *Guillaume Postel* (1510–81), a linguistic virtuoso and messianic prophet who believed to have found the messiah incarnated as a woman.

The most impressive and influential attempt at integrating both the philosophical *and* the scientific traditions of antiquity within a comprehensive Christian kabbalistic framework was published by the German Heinrich Cornelius Agrippa (1486–1535/36) under the title *De occulta philosophia libri tres* (1533). This work has long been seen as no more than a compendium or *summa* of all the available traditions of ancient learning, and has been plundered for information ever since, but it was much more than that. Agrippa's three books were dealing with the three 'worlds' or domains of reality according to the prevailing Aristotelian and Ptolemaic system, which described the cosmos as a gigantic sphere: our world was located in its centre with the moon and the other planets circling around it, and the stars (including, of course, the astrological constellations) were fixed on the interior surface of the sphere. Agrippa's first book dealt with everything pertaining to our sublunar world constituted of the four elements; the second book was about the more abstract realities pertaining to the 'middle realm' of the planetary spheres, between the moon and the fixed stars; and finally, the third book discussed the angelic and divine realities outside the cosmic globe. This last book was dominated entirely by Christian kabbalah. Although posterity came to imagine Agrippa as a black magician in league with the devil (a model for Goethe's Faust), he was in fact an extremely pious Christian. Strongly influenced by Lazzarelli's Hermetism, his intention was to show a way of mystical ascent leading from the world of matter all the way up to unification with the divine intellect.[10] In his youth, Agrippa was strongly influenced by the Abbot *Johannes Trithemius* (1462–1516), a Renaissance pioneer of cryptography, demonology and angelic magic; and although Agrippa's own work was a theoretical treatise rather than a practical manual, it became an inspiration to occult practitioners working along similar lines. A notable example from a later generation is the Elizabethan magus *John Dee* (1527–1609). He combined a strong focus on the natural sciences with an obsession for magical evocations by means of mediumistic trance, in which angelic beings were consulted about religious and philosophical as well as scientific matters. The 'Enochian' language that he learned from the angelic sessions has fascinated occultists to the present day.

Agrippa's great synthesis was still based upon the traditional geocentric cosmos; but due to the work of Copernicus, this closed world was beginning to give way, by the end of the sixteenth century, to the new vision of an infinite universe with an infinite number of solar systems. Since all the ancient sciences had been based upon the pre-Copernican model, this revolution was bound to have a major impact on Renaissance concerns with the traditions of antiquity. One can see this in exemplary fashion in the work of *Giordano Bruno* (1548–1600), perhaps the most brilliant thinker among all the Renaissance figures discussed in this section. Bruno realized that if the universe is infinite, this must have enormous implications for God and his relation to man and the cosmos. Formulated simply: if someone had asked Agrippa where God is to be found, he would have pointed up to the sky, for just by moving upwards beyond the fixed stars one was bound to reach the metaphysical world of angelic and divine realities. In Bruno's post-Copernican universe, however, one could keep travelling through space for all eternity without ever meeting God or the angels: all one could expect to find was a never-ending series of further solar systems. Bruno's multifaceted oeuvre reflects a persistent and systematic attempt to rethink all the ancient philosophical and scientific traditions from the bottom up (next to other ones such as, notably, the so-called *art of memory*, particularly the system of the Catalan thinker *Ramon Llull* [1232/33–1316]), and he did not stop at the sacred truths of Christian orthodoxy. Arrested by the Venetian Inquisition in 1592, then transferred to Rome, Bruno spent eight years in prison and was finally burnt at the stake for heresy at the Campo de' Fiori in 1600.

Naturphilosophie and Christian theosophy

The Renaissance thinkers discussed in the previous section were all highly erudite intellectuals (most of them Roman Catholics) engaged in the bookish project of synthesizing pagan and Jewish traditions with Christian theology and contemporary philosophy or science. Essentially we are dealing with a tradition of learned commentaries on the writings of ancient and authoritative thinkers.

Figures as independent as Bruno or, to a lesser extent, John Dee, are already less typical of this phenomenon, and could be seen as boundary cases in relation to the category we are now about to discuss. Whereas the former movement had its intellectual and geographical centre in Italy, this one is very much dominated by German thinkers. The emphasis shifts from learned commentaries on ancient and venerable authorities to original speculations legitimated by references to the authors' own, direct individual experience. Although speculative traditions derived from late antiquity and medieval kabbalah continue to be important in this new genre, it refers much more explicitly to only two basic sources of authority: the 'two books' of Nature and Holy Scripture. As could be expected, given this emphasis on the bible and the centrality of German culture, the emphasis in this lineage shifts from Roman Catholics to Protestant (mostly Lutheran) authors.

The German term *Naturphilosophie* is usually preferred over its literal equivalent in English, because the latter ('philosophy of nature') could as well refer to all kinds of other approaches that have little to do with the specific tradition under discussion here. Without any doubt, its foundational author is the German physician Theophrastus Bombastus von Hohenheim (1493/94–1541), who called himself *Paracelsus*. Taking inspiration from alchemical literature as well as close personal acquaintance with traditional 'folk' healing methods, he attacked the contemporary medical establishment and its blind reliance of the theories of Galen (second century). Instead, physicians should learn directly from Nature herself, by means of personal experiment. Paracelsus introduced a whole new medical terminology, complementing the four elements with a new triad of mercury, sulphur and salt. Paracelsus' later works were increasingly concerned with religious questions. Writing in German instead of the Latin of the intellectual elites, he has been called the 'Luther of medicine', and it is true that he instigated a Reformation all of his own. With countless adherents during the sixteenth and seventeenth centuries, the Paracelsian tradition, also known as the 'Chemical Philosophy', spread beyond Germany to France and England, and became a major force of innovation in medicine and alchemy/'chymistry' (see above). The development of Western esotericism in the early modern period is unthinkable without it.

Apart from science and medicine, Paracelsian thought became essential in more strictly religious contexts as well. From around 1600 it developed into an alternative religious current in conflict with the established churches, sometimes known as *Theophrastia Sancta* but eventually known as Weigelianism (with reference to the dissenter *Valentin Weigel* [1533–88]).[11] Paracelsus himself was cast in the role of a divinely inspired Seer who had revived a kind of perennial tradition that had been practiced by the apostles. It is from a rather similar perspective that in the first decades of the seventeenth century, the German cobbler *Jacob Böhme* (1575–1624) wrote an oeuvre of impressive depth and originality that has become foundational for one of the major currents in the history of Western esotericism: *Christian theosophy*. In a heartfelt attempt to understand how a good God could have created a world so full of evil and suffering, Böhme developed a dramatic visionary cosmogony filled with alchemical and Paracelsian references, that described the 'birth of God' himself out of the unfathomable mystery of the *Ungrund*. Referred to as 'Eternal Nature', God's body was imagined as a luminous substance, constituted of a dark and wrathful core (associated with God the Father) redeemed and rendered harmless by the complementary forces of light and love (associated with God the Son). Lucifer, the greatest of the angels, was born as a perfect creature of light in the body of Eternal Nature; but in an attempt to rise even higher by achieving his own 'rebirth', he turned into a creature of darkness and destroyed the integrity and harmony of the world of light. As the result of Lucifer's Fall our own world came into being: no longer Eternal Nature, but a fallen Nature subjected to time and change, in which the dark Wrath of the Godhead is unleashed as a separate force in mortal combat with the power of Light. Our spiritual calling as sinful human beings born in this dark and threatening world is to achieve an inner transformation, which reverses the process of the Fall and mirrors the primordial birth of God himself. By doing so we are literally reborn as the 'son of God' in a subtle body of light, and contribute to the reintegration of fallen Nature: God's own body that is yearning to return to its original state of harmony and bliss.

Written in a strange German full of flashes of poetic vision, Böhme's works were widely disseminated already during his lifetime, and caused him much trouble with the Lutheran authorities. Later during the seventeenth century, many authors took inspiration from Böhme's work and developed it into new directions. Some of them formed small spiritual communities: the first clear examples of what might be called esoteric organizations, with devotional practices of their own. Thus the German theosopher *Johann Georg Gichtel* (1638–1710) formed a group called the 'Angelic Brethren' in Amsterdam, and in England a 'Philadelphian Society' formed around *John Pordage* (1607/08–81) and *Jane Leade* (1623–1704, perhaps the earliest example in Western esotericism of a woman playing a central role). Ecstatic and visionary experiences played an important part in these communities; and based upon discussions in Böhme, their members developed a strong fascination with the figure of Sophia (Wisdom) as an explicitly feminine manifestation of divinity. After a transitional period during the eighteenth century, with *Friedrich Christoph Oetinger* (1702–82) as the most important figure, Christian theosophy entered its 'second golden age' from the final decades of the eighteenth century through the Romantic era. The Frenchman *Louis-Claude de Saint-Martin* (1743–1803, the 'unknown philosopher') and the German *Franz von Baader* (1765–1841) were perhaps the most important thinkers in an emerging network of Christian theosophers who rediscovered Böhme and interpreted him in new ways, partly under the influence of contemporary developments such as German Idealist philosophy and the vogue of Mesmerism (see below).

Initiatic societies

The belief that ancient wisdom or the secrets of nature had been transmitted and kept alive by wise men through the ages belongs to the central tenets of Western esotericism. Remarkably, however, that such a transmission might require some kind of formal organization does not seem to have occurred to anyone before the seventeenth century. The idea emerges in the first of the three so-called *Rosicrucian Manifestoes*, published in 1614. This text, known as the *Fama Fraternitatis*, describes a mysterious brotherhood founded by an equally elusive adept called 'C.R.', later identified as Christian Rosenkreutz. After travels through the Middle East and profound studies of the 'occult' sciences, the *Fama* tells us, he had returned to Germany where he founded a secret organization that would ensure that his supreme wisdom would not get lost. At one point the members decided to spread 'through all countries' while keeping their brother-hood a secret, but each of them promised to find a suitable successor who would carry their wisdom on to the next generation, and so on. After a 100 years had passed, a member of the brotherhood is said to have discovered a secret crypt in Christian Rosenkreutz's house, containing his perfectly preserved body and secret information of all kinds. The Brotherhood now announced its existence to the general public by means of the *Fama Fraternitatis*, followed by a *Confessio Fraternitatis* in 1615, predicting a new Reformation that would transform European culture along the lines of the ancient Hermetic and related sciences. A third manifesto, published in 1616, was quite different in nature: called the *Chemical Wedding of Christian Rosenkreutz*, it was a complex allegorical account of Christian trans-formation based upon alchemical symbolism. Its protagonist was Christian Rosenkreutz, but the brotherhood played no role in it.

There is no evidence that any Rosicrucian brotherhood really existed at this time or before, let alone that Christian Rosenkreutz was a historical personality. The Manifestoes are now generally seen as a literary invention, attributed to the Lutheran theologian *Johann Valentin Andreae* (1586–1654) and his circle of friends in Tübingen. But they made a great impression on many readers, resulting in a stunning amount of public responses, whether from critics who denounced the brotherhood as a hoax or defenders and true believers who would like to contact its members. As one effect of this furore, important authors in the field of ancient wisdom and the 'occult' sciences, such as *Robert Fludd* (1574–1637) or *Michael Maier* (1569–1622), began to identify themselves as 'Rosicrucians', and authors claiming special esoteric knowledge have kept doing so ever since. Some marginal groups concerned with alchemy or other 'occult' practices may have begun calling themselves 'Rosicrucian' during the later seventeenth century or the first half of the eighteenth, but the evidence is vague and ambiguous. The first irrefutable case of a Rosicrucian organization is the Order of the *Gold- und Rosenkreuzer*, which flourished in Germany in the second half of the eighteenth century. After that period, as the increasing separation of church and state now made it possible to create religious or initiatic organizations next to the established churches, many initiatic organizations have come into existence that think of themselves as Rosicrucian and usually claim to pre-serve the true secrets of the ancient wisdom.

The ritual and organizational frameworks of such initiatic Orders have been inspired, in most cases, by models derived from *Freemasonry*. In Scotland by the end of the sixteenth century, the medieval guilds of stonemasons were transformed into a new kind of organization that began to accept 'Gentlemen Masons' (individuals who were not masonic craftsmen) during the seventeenth century. Up to the first decades of the eighteenth century, Freemasons were widely perceived as Rosicrucians and practitioners of alchemy; and the brotherhood attracted much curiosity because of suspicions that it might have preserved the mysterious secrets of antiquity, including that of the philosophers' stone. In England, Freemasonry distanced itself from such esoteric pursuits as it developed into an essentially rationalist and humanitarian movement after the foundation of the Premier Grand Lodge of England in 1717. But in other countries, notably France, the concern with alchemical and other 'hermetic' ideas and practices flourished as never before: after having been initiated into the three basic Masonic grades of 'Apprentice', 'Fellowcraft' and 'Master Mason', Masons could progress deeper into the masonic mysteries through elaborate systems of higher grades. As many different higher-degree systems were developed during the later eighteenth century, joining Freemasonry became the logical thing to do for anybody fascinated by hidden mysteries and the secrets of the ancients. The flowering of Christian theosophy in high-degree masonic systems during the Age of Reason – see especially Jean-Baptiste Willermoz's 'Rectified Scottish Rite' and its backgrounds in Martinez de Pasqually's 'Elus Coëns' – is known as *Illuminism*. Since the prevailing class system was suspended within the lodge – a member of the upper nobility might well receive his initiation from a Master belonging to the working class – Freemasonry was also highly attractive as a context where one could experiment with socially egalitarian ideas; and finally, it functioned as an effective international network which assured that travellers far from home could always find a place where they would be welcomed by their fellow brethren. Since all this made Freemasonry into something like a society within public society, protected from outside scrutiny by its cultivation of secrecy, it was bound to evoke suspicions from the political rulers; and in a few cases, notably Adam Weishaupt's Order of *Illuminates*, a vehicle for radical revolutionary politics, such concerns were indeed justified. Particularly after the French Revolution, Freemasonry has become a favourite target of conspiracy theorists who attributed the breakdown of traditional religious and political authority to the subversive machinations of Masons and 'Illuminati'.

From the beginning, Freemasons were concerned with creating a historical pedigree for their organization. Sometimes the institution of Freemasonry was traced as far back as Noah and his sons after the Flood, but Masons developed a particular fascination with speculative historical lineages that connected the ancient sects of the Essenes and Therapeutae to the medieval Knights Templar. Masonic ritual is grounded in architectural symbolism, with a central role for Solomon's Temple in Jerusalem as the image of the perfect building, so it was natural for Freemasons to develop a special interest in the chivalric order that had been charged with its defence. The idea was that during the times of the crusades, Templar Knights in the Holy Land had established contact with surviving branches of the Essenes/Therapeutae, who had preserved the ancient secrets from the Orient, including the supreme pythagorean art of geometry. After the dissolution of the Order in 1307, surviving Templars were believed to have brought it secrets to Scotland, often considered the homeland of Freemasonry. This is the origin of the influential Templar legend, which has led not only to special Templar degrees within Freemasonry, but eventually also to non-masonic neo-Templar organizations up to the present day – not to mention a burgeoning Templar mythology in popular literature from Umberto Eco to Dan Brown.

The modernist occult

With the 'media revolution' of the eighteenth century and the dwindling ability of church and state to censor or prohibit dissenting voices, all the bodies of traditional literature discussed above became available to larger and larger audiences. Next to a stream of sceptical literature that dismissed 'the occult' as ridiculous superstition, publishing entrepreneurs catered to the public's curiosity about ancient secrets and mysteries. The 'modernist occult' is marked by complex and multifaceted attempts at coming to terms with modern science and Enlightenment rationality, combining a deeply felt resistance against the 'disenchantment of the world' with an equally strong attraction to modern scientific models. As

Europeans and Americans entered the nineteenth century, nobody could deny that society was moving with accelerating speed into new directions, and thus the question became relevant of whether 'progress' meant a radical break with 'tradition' or, rather, entailed a transformation that allowed ancient truths to be perceived in a new light.

It is no coincidence, then, that the two most influential forces of innovation in Western esotericism during the nineteenth century had their origins in the work of Enlightenment scientists. The Swedish naturalist *Emanuel Swedenborg* (1688–1772) studied philosophy, mathematics, physics and applied mechanics and went on to produce an impressive oeuvre in the physical and organic sciences. Trained in the Cartesian philosophy of his day, with its strict separation between matter and spirit, he experienced a deep religious crisis in 1744: forced to admit to himself that his scientific explorations led him to the 'abyss' of pure materialism, he prayed to God for help and was granted a vision of Christ. After this pivotal event, he spent the rest of his life writing visionary works, in Latin, on the true meaning of the bible and the spiritual realities of heaven and hell. Deeply influenced by Pietist concepts of 'internal' versus 'external' levels of reality, his theory of correspondences claimed that the visible world mirrors the invisible one without any need for causal relations between the two; and his works were filled with matter-of-fact descriptions of his visionary travels to heaven and hell and his conversations with spirits and angels. While followers created a Swedenborgian 'New Church' after his death, the influence of Swedenborg's writings is by no means limited to that community: they have inspired a wide range of major writers, poets, painters and even composers, and its basic ideas were picked up and developed in new directions, as will be seen, by spiritualist, occultist and metaphysical authors and practitioners during the nineteenth and twentieth centuries.

The second major innovation came from a German physician, *Franz Anton Mesmer* (1734–1815), who invented a theory and practice of healing known as *Animal Magnetism*, later also known as *Mesmerism*. Mesmer claimed that an invisible 'fluid' permeated all organic bodies, and all illnesses were caused by disturbances or blockages in the flow of this universal life force. By making 'passes' over the patient's body, the normal circulation of energy could be restored, and the resulting transition to health and normality was typically marked by a short but violent 'crisis' in which the patient made uncontrollable movements and sounds. One of Mesmer's many followers, a Marquis de Puységur, discovered that mesmeric treatment could induce a strange condition of sleeplike trance, in which many patients displayed remarkable 'paranormal' abilities and entered visionary states in which they claimed to communicate with spiritual beings on other levels of reality. This phenomenon, known as artificial *somnambulism*, has exerted an incalculable influence on the history of Western esotericism during the nineteenth century.

No less than three major new developments have their origin in Mesmerism. First, somnambulist trance became central to the vogue of *Spiritualism*. In the wake of a media hype in 1848, around the Fox sisters in Hydesville who claimed to be in contact with a poltergeist, spiritualist séances became a popular pastime in America and Europe. The technique of somnambulic trance induction now made it possible for any citizen to satisfy his or her curiosity about the 'invisible world' and survival after death without any need for mediation by the church. Much of spiritualism was a practical affair with little theoretical depth, but influential authors such as *Andrew Jackson Davis* (1826–1910), who was strongly influenced by Swedenborg's writings, or the French spiritualist *Allan Kardec* (ps. of Hippolyte Rivail, 1804–69), whose work has become a major religious tradition in Brazil, developed full-blown theologies and cosmologies on spiritualist foundations. Scientific curiosity about the phenomena and spectacular claims of spiritualism, finally, led to the development of *psychical research* or what would now be referred to as parapsychology.

Secondly, artificial somnambulism is at the origin of the new disciplines of *psychology and psychiatry*, as physicians were quick to realize that it opened up unheard-of possibilities for studying the human soul and its mysterious powers on an empirical and experimental basis. The concept that we now refer to as the 'unconscious' emerged in the literature of German Romantic mesmerism during the first half of the nineteenth century, originally under the label of the 'nightside of nature'; and the development of psychological investigation based on somnambulism can be traced in straight lines from there to the experimental psychology of Charcot, Flournoy and others, and finally to Carl Gustav Jung and his school. In all these developments, psychology was inextricably entwined with study of 'the occult': it is only during the twentieth century, with the rise of psychoanalysis and behaviourism, that academic psychology distanced itself from its deep historical involvement with Western esotericism.

Thirdly and finally, the American career of artificial somnambulism led to a widespread milieu of religious innovation known as *New Thought*, based upon a radical doctrine of 'mind over matter'. This development had its origin in the work of a Mesmerist called *Phineas P. Quimby* (1802–66), who abandoned Mesmer's 'fluidic' theory as the explanation for somnambulic healing in favour of a radical emphasis on the universal and omnipotent power of belief. Eventually it was claimed that not only all forms of illness could be cured by means of changing one's beliefs, but other negative conditions, such as poverty, as well. Also known as *Mind Cure*, the basic doctrines of New Thought have been institutionalized in new religions such as Christian Science and a series of similar churches, and they have become deeply ingrained in American popular culture. In contemporary 'New Age' contexts, this development is basic not only to an endless series of 'self-help' books but also to the widespread claim that we literally 'create our own reality' by means of our beliefs.

During the second half of the nineteenth century, all the ancient, medieval and Renaissance traditions discussed above were rediscovered and reconceptualized by groups and individuals who had been influenced by spiritualist and somnambulist practice and tried to find a 'third way' between traditional Christianity and positivist science. This phenomenon is usually referred to as *occultism*, and it comes in different forms. The 'occultism of the right'[12] that was dominant in France was very strongly influenced by Roman Catholicism: it was frequented by countless *abbés*, pretended or real, who were trying to come to terms with the legacy of the Revolution and its sensationally successful assault on the traditional authority of 'altar and throne'. Politically, their approaches varied from deeply conservative to progressive, but they all shared an obsessive nostalgia for the lost unity of a universal 'Tradition' that had expressed itself by means of spiritual symbolism. Among the most important figures, representing successive generations in French occultism, are *Eliphas Lévi* (ps. of Alphonse-Louis Constant, 1810–75), whose works on magic and kabbalah were highly influential within the occultist revival, and *Papus* (ps. of

Gérard Encausse, 1865–1916), the 'pope of occultism', who played a central role in a whole range of occultist organizations and networks that flourished during the *fin de siècle* and left important traces in the art, literature and music of that period.

This concern of French occultists with 'Tradition' found its most extreme expression in the work of *René Guénon* (1886–1951). During his younger years he was deeply involved in a range of occultist organizations, but he finally rejected all of them as misguided products of compromise with modernity. Guénon claimed the existence of one single, universal Tradition, based on metaphysical 'first principles' that were beyond any critical debate or refutation. He rejected the modern world and all its values as the absolute antithesis of Tradition, and spent the last decades of his life as a Sufi recluse in Egypt. Guénon's many writings are at the origin of an independent esoteric tradition known as *Traditionalism* (sometimes *Perennialism*). In its very rejection of modernity in all its aspects it is, ironically, a typical product of the modern world. In cases such as the major Traditionalist author *Julius Evola* (1898–1974), contempt for modern democracy and social egalitarianism led to open sympathy for Fascist and National Socialist politics; in other cases, such as that of *Frithjof Schuon* (1907–98), perhaps the most influential Traditionalist after World War II, it inspired the creation of new organizations and communities that allowed its participants to follow 'traditionalist' lifestyles in relative seclusion. Yet other post-war Traditionalists, such as notably *Seyyed Hossein Nasr* (b. 1933) and *Huston Smith* (b. 1919) have been vocal defenders of Traditionalism in academic settings.

In contrast to nineteenth-century France, the anglophone world was characterized rather by an 'occultism of the left', strongly indebted to anti-Christian mythographical traditions grounded in the work of Enlightenment libertines who had argued that religion had its origin not in divine revelation but in a 'natural religion' of solar worship and phallicism.[13] The 'occult tradition' came to be perceived as an ancient and superior wisdom grounded in pagan traditions opposed to the exclusivism and dogmatism of established Christianity. Erstwhile spiritualist mediums such as *Emma Hardinge Britten* (1823–99) and *Helena P. Blavatsky* (1831–91) had become disillusioned with what they saw as the superficiality of spiritualism, and found inspiration in all the major 'hermetic', 'occult' and related traditions prior to Swedenborg. In their view, the universal 'occult science' of the ancients, both east and west, should be revived against the narrow materialism of positivist science. The major classic of this new approach was Blavatsky's *Isis Unveiled* (1877), later followed by *The Secret Doctrine* (1888), in which the sources of occult wisdom were moved from Egypt to the Far East. Blavatsky presented 'occult science' as the central, ancient and universal tradition of superior knowledge and wisdom that should be revived, in the modern world, as an alternative to traditional Christianity and positivist science. In 1875 she co-founded the *Theosophical Society*, which became the most influential occultist organization at least up to the 1930s. Under the leadership of *Annie Besant* (1847–1933) and *Charles Webster Leadbeater* (1854–1934), modern theosophy was reinterpreted increasingly in terms of an ecumenical esoteric Christianity, culminating in a long phase of messianic fervour around the Indian *Jiddu Krishnamurti* (1895–1986), who was raised as the coming 'World Teacher' but finally rejected that role in 1929. Largely in response to the Krishnamurti cult, most of the German theosophists under the leadership of *Rudolf Steiner* (1861–1925) broke away from theosophy in the 1910s. The resulting *Anthroposophical Society* was based upon a Christian interpretation of theosophy bolstered by Steiner's claims of superior clairvoyant access to the spiritual world, against a background of philosophy in the German Idealist tradition.

Magical traditions had been reduced to mere objects of antiquarian curiosity by the mid-nineteenth century, but occultists began to cultivate magical practice in the decades thereafter. The result was an entirely new understanding of 'magic', claiming ancient roots but in fact based on highly innovative concepts and interpretations. An important pioneer was the American *Paschal Beverly Randolph* (1825–75), who was the first to argue that sexual energy and psychoactive drugs could be harnessed to magical ends. In England by the end of the nineteenth century, an initiatic Order called the *Hermetic Order of the Golden Dawn* cultivated an elaborate and sophisticated system of symbolism and ritual practice, based upon the kabbalistic system of the *sefirot*, that has become a major source of inspiration for many magical groups up to the present. The most notorious occultist magician of the twentieth century, *Aleister Crowley* (1875–1947), broke away from the Golden Dawn and went on to join Theodor Reuss's *Ordo Templi Orientis*, which eventually developed under his leadership into an order with a strong emphasis on sexual magic. His self-stylization as the 'Great Beast' of the Apocalypse, whose new religion, Thelema, was destined to supplant Christianity, and his systematic experimentation with every conceivable form of transgression, has made Crowley controversial even among occultists, but the impact of his writings has been enormous. In many respects, these organizations and many similar ones that flourished before World War II can be seen as attempts to compensate for the prosaic world of disenchanted society by cultivating the powers of the imagination as a means of experiential access to parallel realities of magical enchantment. Ultimately, the focus in these contexts is more on individual 'inner development' of the magician than on influencing events in the outside world. This means that the very concept of magic acquires new shades of meaning particularly under the impact of popular psychology. With regard to the focus on 'inner development' in an esoteric context, but now without overt reference to magic, mention must finally be made of the enigmatic Greco-Armenian teacher *George Ivanovitch Gurdjieff* (1866–1949) and his Russian pupil *Piotr Dem'ianovich Ouspensky* (1878–1947). Gurdjieff developed an independent and original esoteric system that includes a neo-gnostic cosmology and a complicated training system for liberating the mind from social control and attaining spiritual freedom. Gurdjieffian techniques were adopted by various esoteric teachers and movements after World War II, and have become an important dimension of the post-1960s concern with 'self-realization'.

Esotericism after World War II

Most of the esoteric activities mentioned in the previous section are aspects of what has been called the *cultic milieu*[14] or, more recently, *occulture*.[15] These terms refer to what appears to have become a constant phenomenon in modern and contemporary society: the existence of interlocking, continually fluctuating and evolving networks of groups and individuals who share a dissatisfaction with the approaches to reality, knowledge and lifestyle that are promoted by mainstream educational institutions and channels of information. The search for 'alternatives' results not only in widespread fascination with non-Western (particularly Oriental) cultures and their spiritual traditions but also in a continuous process of recycling, repackaging and creative reinterpretation of more or less all the esoteric and occultist materials that have implicitly been categorized as 'rejected knowledge' by the dominant culture. The post-war cultic milieu developed during the 1950s and became impossible to deny with the emergence of the so-called *counterculture* of the 1960s and 1970s. As esoteric ideas and practices became more and more fashionable in wider society, its adherents came to see themselves as participating in a spiritual revolution that was transforming the dominant culture and would lead humanity into a new spiritual era, the 'Age of Aquarius'. This millenarian idea of an imminent spiritual revolution had emerged in specific theosophical circles in England, associated with the writings of *Alice Bailey* (1880–1949); but by the 1980s, the term *New Age* was picked up by the mainstream media as a convenient label for the full spread of 'alternative' ideas and practices ingrained in the cultic milieu, whether or not they included a millenarian component. Next to Western esoteric/occultist currents and Oriental spiritualities, popular fascination with the *New Physics* was an important part of the mix as well, as the radical paradoxes of quantum mechanics and relativity theory seemed to confirm that the old scientific ideologies were in the process of breaking down together with the established religions, thus making way for a new spiritual and holistic worldview in harmony with the ancient wisdom of the East and West. As business entrepreneurs discovered the market for spiritual products during the same period, the New Age became a major growth industry; and as an inevitable result of commercial succes, its ideas have gradually become more acceptable in mainstream society than they were in the 1960s. Nevertheless, the original countercultural critique of mainstream culture, including strong belief in an imminent transformation of society, remains very much alive in the more radical branches of the cultic milieu. One sees this especially in the *techno-shamanism* since the 1990s, which has its origins in the psychedelic shamanism promoted in the wake of Carlos Castaneda, but without the anti-technological bias of the 1960s.[16] The pioneer of this radical countercultural form of 'entheogenic esotericism' was Terence McKenna (1946–2000); and with new generation prophets such as Daniel Pinchbeck (b. 1966), it has developed into a vibrant esoteric milieu full of millenarian hopes for an imminent transformation of society.

A special and relatively separate outcome of the 1960s counterculture is the movement known as *neopaganism*. It originated in England, with a new religion created in the 1950s by *Gerald Gardner* (1864–1964), but presented by him as the revival of an underground cult of pagan nature-worship. Referred to as *Wicca*, or the 'Old Religion' of Witchcraft, it combined occultism in the tradition of Aleister Crowley with a fascination for ancient fertility cults. Wicca spread to the United States during the 1960s, where it took on new forms in the countercultural milieu. Radical feminist activists such as *Starhawk* (ps. of Miriam Simos, b. 1951) and others interpreted Wicca as *Goddess Religion*, emphasizing the female principle in nature as an alternative to the male deity of monotheism. From this period on, neopaganism has developed into a whole series of new directions based upon attempts to revive specific regional pagan traditions, such as *Druidry* and similar forms of Celtic revivalism, or neopagan movements such as *Asatru* that take inspiration from the ancient Germanic and Scandinavian pantheons. Today, neopaganism exists in many countries as a vital subculture that celebrates diversity and emphasizes natural and ecological lifestyles.

Finally, contemporary esotericism is very much alive in popular culture and on the Internet. Its basic concepts, ideas or terminologies are now no longer tied to any specific religious or intellectual tradition but can be freely recycled and reinterpreted by anybody, without regard for their original meaning or context. No matter how bizarre and mistaken such adaptations may be from the perspective of the historian, they can be fascinating if seen as products of creative syncretism. The overwhelming presence of esoteric motifs in popular novels, comics, music, film, art, or videogaming has hardly yet been researched at all, nor do we have any idea of what this wealth of references could teach us about the 'subzeitgeist'[17] of contemporary culture and society. It is in this domain that esotericism ceases to be an object of historical research altogether, and becomes a vital dimension of the very present.

CHAPTER THREE

Apologetics and polemics

Ideas do not exist in a social vacuum, as topics of polite and disinterested conversation among disembodied intellects. On the contrary: in intellectual or religious history we are dealing with flesh-and-blood people who care deeply, often passionately, about defending their own convictions and criticizing or attacking those of others. These two basic activities – *apologetics* on behalf of one's own ideas and *polemics* against those with which one disagrees – mutually imply one another: by denouncing the doctrines of others as false, one simultaneously asserts one's own claims to orthodoxy and orthopraxy, and conversely, defending one's own position means questioning that of others.[1] Ideas, moreover, do not just exist in people's heads or in the pages of books. They become embodied in social institutions with a lifespan of many generations (churches, universities, political parties, etc.), which have a deep investment in consolidating and maintaining their own identity by any means available to them. Whether by tradition and socialization or by deliberate choice or conversion, individuals may either commit themselves to what such institutions stand for, or criticize and reject them, perhaps giving their allegiance to alternative and competing ones. Whatever side one is on, a particularly effective strategy for establishing and cementing one's own identity is to simultaneously create the image of an 'Other': in order to make clear what *we* are all about, *they* (whoever they are) must be depicted as our perfect antithesis.

What is really at stake in such rhetorics is *power*, that is to say, the ability to dominate an existing discourse to such an extent that one can decide what will and will not be accepted as valid and true.

Once a certain measure of such discursive power has been attained, it can easily be translated into real political power: the ability to put one's own agendas into action, and silence, suppress or discredit dissenting voices. Such measures can be highly effective over long periods of time, particularly because those who dominate the discourse have the power to educate new generations in conformity with their own beliefs – but they are never final and secure. Any dominant party may use the rhetorical weapon of 'othering' to dismiss its opponents as despicable heretics, dangerous subversives or ridiculous fools (thereby implicitly confirming its own identity as orthodox, reliable or reasonable). But those at the receiving end of such polemics will try to use the same weapon against their opponents, for example by depicting them as arrogant and blind oppressors or mindless bureaucrats who rely on power because they lack the arguments to convince (thereby promoting their own identity as champions of freedom, tolerance and reason). If they manage to muster enough support for their narrative, this may affect the balance of power and lead to larger or smaller intellectual, social and even political revolutions.

The category that we now refer to as 'Western esotericism' (but which, it must be repeated, has been known by a variety of other names as well) is the outcome of such discursive processes, involving polemical/apologetic debates that go back to the period of Late Antiquity. To a much larger extent than is usually realized, it stands for the sum total of 'rejected knowledge' against which both mainstream Christian culture and modern or secular society have established their own identity. Even today, it remains their principal 'Other', whether or not we are consciously aware of it. This is a reason to be extremely cautious about trusting the dominant narratives that circulate about its ideas, its practices or its history: there is an enormous difference between how everything that pertains to the field of 'Western esotericism' is depicted in common discourse or imagined in the polemical (and apologetic) imagination, and what we find if we study the historical sources. To give a small and obvious example, Cornelius Agrippa has been remembered through the centuries as a black magician and a model of the Faust figure who sells his soul to the devil; but if one studies his writings, one discovers an extremely pious Christian for whom unquestioning faith in Jesus Christ was the exclusive foundation of any reliable knowledge.

To get a handle on such discrepancies between reality and imagination, it is useful to draw a distinction between *history* and *mnemohistory*.[2] In simple terms, the former refers to what has happened in the past, the latter to how we remember it. Accordingly, the attempt to describe what has actually happened may be referred to as *historiography*, whereas *mnemohistoriography* is the attempt to describe the genesis and development of what a given culture *imagines* has happened. If we stick to our example: a historian will want to know who Agrippa really was and what he really believed, whereas a mnemohistorian is interested in analyzing how Agrippa has been remembered by later generations. His focus is on tracing the chain of reinterpretations, distortions, misunderstanding and creative inventions that have come to be attached to Agrippa's name – and which, it should be emphasized, are mainly responsible for his continuing fame and notoriety. For there should be no mistake about it: in the real world, history is no match for mnemohistory. Mnemohistorical narratives have an enormous power to influence real historical events, regardless of whether they have any basis in demonstrable fact. Even wild historical fantasies may have a greater impact than the carefully documented reconstructions of historians: worrying though the fact may be, what appears to count most is not whether the stories are true, but whether they are believed.

The focus in the rest of this chapter will be on the mnemohistory of Western esotericism: how has this field been constructed in the polemical and apologetic imagination of mainstream culture, and why? To find out, we will focus on the three central contexts in which this process of construction has taken place: Pre-Reformation Christianity, Protestantism and Modernity.

Early Christianity and the Church of Rome

Early Christianity had to establish its identity against both Judaism and the religions of 'Others', referred to by various names such as gentiles, heathens, nations or, eventually, pagans. The apostle Paul inherited from his Jewish upbringing an abhorrence of any worship directed away from the one invisible God towards 'images resembling mortal man or birds or animals or reptiles' (Rom. 1.23), and 'idolatry' became ingrained in Christianity as a sin *par excellence*.

But whereas the cultic practices of pagan religion could be rejected clearly and unequivocally, as worship of demons, the *philosophical* systems of the gentiles were a different matter. It is true that some early fathers of the Church found them incompatible by definition with both Jewish and Christian religion, as shown by a famous statement of Tertullian: 'What indeed has Athens to do with Jerusalem, the Academy with the Church, heretics with Christians?'[3] But many others were willing to engage in some kind of constructive dialogue, particularly with the Platonic traditions that were widespread among intellectuals in the Hellenistic culture of the Roman Empire. The consequences have been enormous, both for the later history of Christianity and for what we now refer to as Western esotericism.

The apologetic fathers

In their attempts to convince gentile intellectuals about the superiority of their new faith, apologists for Christianity were faced with a serious problem. It was a general conviction of the age that any religion worth its salt had to be rooted in ancient and venerable traditions: everybody, including the Jews, agreed that nothing could be both new *and* true.[4] By claiming that their faith had originated very recently, with Jesus Christ, Christians were therefore inviting ridicule. For example, a second-century pagan philosopher called Celsus was making fun of them as a people without roots, who 'wall themselves off and break away from the rest of mankind': 'I will ask them where they come from, or who is the author of their traditional laws. Nobody, they will say'.[5] And a century later, the Neoplatonist Porphyry was equally puzzled by a community of believers who thought that they could just 'cut out for themselves a new kind of track in a pathless desert'.[6] Christian apologists took such accusations seriously, and felt they needed to have an answer. They found it in what we have referred to as *Platonic Orientalism*: the widespread belief that Plato had taught not just philosophy but an ancient religious wisdom, rooted not in his own Greek culture but ultimately derived from the most ancient and venerable traditions of the Orient. Egyptians pointed to Hermes Trismegistus as the original fountain of such 'ancient theology', Persians to Zoroaster, Greeks to Orpheus or Pythagoras; but Christian apologists such as

Justin Martyr, Tatian, Clement of Alexandria, Origen or Eusebius of Caesarea argued that all those gentile philosophers had ultimately depended on the ancient wisdom of the Hebrews, codified by Moses at Mount Sinai, which had now attained its final and full splendour in the teachings of Jesus Christ.

This argument implied that Christianity was *not* radically new. It was a revival – after a long period of decline due to the influence of demons, whom the pagan nations kept worshipping as their gods – of the true ancient religion rooted in Mosaic wisdom. That religion had been inspired by the eternal *Logos*, the divine Word, from the very beginning, even long before it was finally 'made flesh, and dwelt among us' in the person of Jesus Christ (Jn 1.1–14). A particularly eloquent statement of this position comes from one no less than St Augustine:

> The very thing which is now called the Christian religion was with the ancients, and it was with the human race from its beginning to the time when Christ appeared in the flesh: from when on the true religion, which already existed, began to be called the Christian.[7]

The implication, for Christians, was that one could expect to find nuggets of true wisdom not only in the Jewish and Christian scriptures, but even in the writings of pagan sages. Venerable authorities such as the Egyptian Hermes Trismegistus or Plato himself could have drunk from the wells of the Mosaic revelation, or could have been directly inspired by the divine *Logos* even without knowing it. As such, they could be seen as 'unconscious Christians' through whom God had been gently preparing humanity for the advent of the gospel. This notion opened up all the philosophical writings of antiquity as potential sources of study and inspiration for Christians. It could be powerfully supported with reference to Paul's mission to the Greeks. Referring to their altar devoted to 'the unknown God', the apostle had famously told the Athenians that 'whom you ignorantly worship, him I declare unto you' (Acts 17.23).

The importance of this apologetic tradition, for Western esotericism and for Christianity as a whole, can hardly be overstated. Rather than following in Tertullian's footsteps by rejecting any pagan philosophy as incompatible with Christianity, countless theologians came to adopt Platonic and other Greek philosophical frameworks and concepts in their efforts to make sense of the Christian message. A typical and extremely authoritative case is Augustine himself, who stated that 'no one has come closer to us [that is, the Christians] than the Platonists', and affirmed that true doctrines might also be held by wise men or philosophers of other nations, 'be they Atlantic Libyans, Egyptians, Indians, Persians, Chaldaeans, Scythians, Gauls, or Spaniards'.[8] A particularly impressive example, among many others, of how intimately platonic philosophy could become integrated with Christian theology is the anonymous fifth/sixth-century author known as Dionysius the Areopagite (because he was incorrectly identified as a Greek intellectual converted by St Paul at the occasion of his Areopagus speech to the Athenians, mentioned above [Acts 17.34]). The extremely influential writings of this Pseudo-Dionysius were permeated by neoplatonic metaphysics and lent further plausibility to the alliance between Platonic philosophy and Christian theology.

Prisca Theologia and Philosophia Perennis

The Platonism ingrained in Patristic apologetics lost much of its authority during the later Middle Ages, when Plato was largely eclipsed by Aristotle in the philosophical theology known as scholasticism. But it made a strong comeback during the Renaissance, for the simple reason that almost all the relevant original sources (Plato's complete dialogues, the *Corpus Hermeticum*, the *Chaldaean Oracles* and a range of texts by neoplatonic authors such as Plotinus, Iamblichus or Proclus) now became available in Latin translation *and* could be diffused on an unprecedented scale thanks to the invention of printing. This Renaissance revival of Platonic Orientalism became known as *prisca theologia* ('the ancient theology') or *philosophia perennis* ('the perennial philosophy'): two terms that have often been conflated but should be clearly distinguished.

The programme of *prisca theologia*, spearheaded by Marsilio Ficino, carried revolutionary implications of reform and renewal. The second half of the fifteenth century was a period rife with millennial and apocalyptic expectations, and the fact that all the ancient sources of religion and philosophy were now suddenly

becoming available was not seen as mere coincidence. On the contrary, it had to be the hand of Providence at work: God himself was
telling the Christians how they could find their way back to the
original fountains of divine revelation. Much of the excitement generated by the new Platonic philosophy has to do with this hopeful
perspective of imminent renewal. There was, however, one peculiar aspect to Ficino's programme. Although his Christian motivations were undoubtedly sincere, he was following in the footsteps
of Gemistos Plethon by highlighting not Moses but Zoroaster as
the earliest authority of ancient wisdom. This meant that even the
religion of the Hebrews might ultimately be derived from, and
hence dependent on, the teachings of a pagan sage (and even worse,
one who was credited with having invented magic). Giovanni Pico
della Mirandola's programme of Christian kabbalah looks like a
deliberate attempt to correct that perspective and lead it back to a
more orthodox direction.

Like the patristic apologists, and unlike Ficino, Pico pointed to
Moses as the earliest authority of ancient wisdom on whom all the
pagan sages were dependent. But that was not all. Pico claimed to
have made a sensational discovery that provided new and even more
convincing arguments for the truth of the patristic point of view.
At Mount Sinai Moses had received not just the tablets of the Law,
intended for the multitude, but also a secret teaching reserved for
the few, known as the Kabbalah. It was from *this* supreme wisdom
that all the pagan sages had derived anything of enduring value
in their teachings. The kabbalah had been jealously preserved by
the Jews and remained unknown to the Christians. But as the first
Christian to study the Hebrew sources in their original language,
Pico claimed, he had discovered a secret to which the Jews themselves were blind: that all the essential Christian doctrines were
already contained in the kabbalistic scriptures, including even the
name of Jesus! By making this argument (which, needless to say,
finds absolutely no support in modern research of Jewish kabbalah), Pico opened up the gates for the subsequent development of
Christian kabbalah as a specific form of *prisca theologia*. His programme was even more revolutionary than Ficino's, for it implied
not only a concordance between pagan wisdom and Christian doctrine, but would even force the Jews to accept the Messiah and
convert to Christianity: an event that was widely expected to be
the prelude for Christ's return.

Of course, none of these high expectations were to be fulfilled. A few decades after the deaths of Pico and Ficino, a very different kind of Reformation succeeded where theirs had failed: Martin Luther was calling for a 'return to the sources' as well, but Protestantism would turn out to be more hostile to 'pagan wisdom' than Catholicism had ever been. The notion of *philosophia perennis*, highlighted by Agostino Steuco in 1540, must be seen against this background. In contrast to the revolutionary implications of *prisca theologia*, Steuco's understanding of ancient wisdom was deeply conservative. Far from suggesting any need for 'return' or 'reform', he simply stated that the universal and eternal truth had always been available to mankind and would always remain so. Steuco was on a first-name basis with the Pope, and his book appeared on the eve of the Council of Trent, where Roman Catholic theologians tried to find answers to Luther's Reformation. By emphasizing the universal concordance of all ancient wisdom with Roman Catholic doctrine, Steuco was making a final attempt to preserve the unity of the One Church as the divinely instituted repository of everything that had ever been true in religion and philosophy. No reform was necessary or even possible, in his view, for the truth had never been lost: Roman Catholicism had preserved the ancient wisdom intact and inviolate, and kept offering it to all Christians for the salvation of their souls. Thus one sees that the revival of Platonic Orientalism could have either revolutionary or conservative implications in a Roman Catholic context.

The anti-heretical position

If we remember that apologetics are inseparable from polemics, it will come as no surprise that these agendas of integrating 'good' paganism into Christianity are the reverse mirror image of equally powerful agendas of exclusion. First of all, one would obviously be mistaken in assuming that Catholics were uniformly positive about 'pagan wisdom' (no matter how hard Protestant polemicists tried to suggest such a thing). Even the patristic apologists accepted it only in so far as they thought it coincided with Christian doctrine and depended on Mosaic revelation; and other Fathers of the Church were far more sceptical, preferring to emphasize rather than minimize the differences between gentiles and Christians. Tertullian has already been mentioned as an example, and as far as cultic practices were concerned, no compromise could ever be possible with pagan idolatry, which was so clearly condemned by the first two Commandments. Once Christianity became dominant after Constantine, the whole range of divinatory and related practices flourishing in the Roman Empire (such as the reading of signs and omens, visions, dreams, oracles, astrology, necromancy and the various mantic arts) were prohibited under the headings of *magia* and *superstitio*; and it was generally assumed that all of them were ultimately forms of idolatry involving contact with evil demons. This only began to change during the later Middle Ages, as we have seen, with the emergence of the concept of *magia naturalis*.

The most potent legacy that the early Christian polemicists bequeathed to the later Roman Catholic tradition was their conceptualization of *heresy*. As has been convincingly argued by Karen L. King, in line with the mainstream of modern research, anti-heretical strategies 'were devised not in the face of a clear external enemy, but to deal with an internal crisis of differentiation. . . . The polemicists needed to create sharp lines of differentiation because in practice the boundaries were not so neat'.[9] Modern scholarship has come to recognize that early Christianity was indeed a highly diverse phenomenon, with doctrinal interpretations running along a wide spectrum from 'gnostic' to what we would now see as 'orthodox'. In their attempts to create doctrinal unity according to what they saw as the true faith, Church fathers like Irenaeus, Hippolytus and Epiphanius created the idea that it was threatened by a kind of counter-Church of heretics, known as the gnostics. This anti-gnostic polemic is a classic example of establishing identity by means of creating an 'Other', and it is remarkable how uncritically even modern scholars have accepted it (mostly because of a deeply ingrained Protestant bias) until far into the twentieth century.[10]

A particularly effective strategy of polemical discourse is the creation of historical genealogies according to which all forms of heresy can be imagined as having sprung from a single origin. Irenaeus described Simon Magus (Acts 8.9–24) as the original arch-heretic and instrument of the devil, and this narrative was adopted during the sixteenth century by many anti-witchcraft authors and critics of heresy, beginning with Johann Weyer: 'From Simon, as though from a seed pod, there sprouted forth in long succession the monstrous Ophites, the shameless gnostics . . ., the impious Valentinians, Cardonians, Marcionists, Montanists, and many other heretics'.[11] But Simon himself, in Weyer's imagination, was heir to an even older genealogy of pagan idolatry that had its origin in Noah's son Ham and his son Misraim, believed to be identical to Zoroaster, the inventor of magic.[12] Such alarmist 'genealogies of darkness' became a staple of later anti-witchcraft literature, and show how paganism and gnostic heresy could be conflated to a point of virtual identity in the context of a Platonic Orientalism-in-reverse: instead of a narrative of divine wisdom originating with Moses, we now get narratives of demonic infiltration originating with Zoroaster, and in both cases Plato and later platonists are seen as the main channels through which heresy reached Christianity. In reality the relation between 'pagan' hellenistic influences and the religious perspectives associated with 'gnosticism' is extremely complicated, but, as noted above, the simplications of mnemohistorical narrative tend to be much more effective than the careful reconstructions of historians: simply because pagan idolatry and heresy were both wholly negative terms that stood for Christianity's radical 'Other', they were bound to be perceived, in the polemical imagination, as ultimately one and the same phenomenon of demonic error and spiritual darkness.

On the eve of the Reformation, then, two different perspectives on 'paganism', both pioneered by the Fathers of the Church, were present in the Roman Catholic tradition: an inclusive one that accepted ancient pagan wisdom as potentially participating in Christian truth, and an exclusive one that rejected any pagan influence as demonic infiltration leading to heresy. With this paradoxical situation, the stage was set for the second act in the drama from which our concepts of 'Western esotericism' have emerged.

Protestantism

From its inception, the Renaissance revival of Platonic Orientalism in the wake of Plethon, Ficino and Pico della Mirandola provoked a strong anti-Platonic reaction. Already in 1458, reacting to Gemistos Plethon, the Aristotelian George of Trebizond described Plato as the source of every imaginable depravity and the fountainhead of all heresies. The idea of a 'genealogy of darkness', leading from the pagan Orient through Platonism to Christian heresies such as those of the gnostics, was developed especially in anti-witchcraft literature. The anti-Platonic critique culminated by the end of the sixteenth century in a large work by Giovanni Battista Crispo, *De Platone caute legendo* (On the Need to Read Plato with Caution, 1594), who highlighted Plato as the chief agent of corruption in the Church. A crucial point about Crispo's book was that he asked the question of how it was possible that the Church had allowed the dangerous virus of Platonic paganism to enter and spread. His answer was clear: it had all begun with the so-called apologetic Fathers, who, through an excess of kindness, had naïvely accepted Plato's teachings to play a role in theology. The irony is that Crispo, a counter-Reformation theologian who moved in the highest circles of the Catholic hierarchy, does not seem to have realized that this argument was a perfect weapon for Protestants to use in their battle against the Church of Rome.

Of course, Protestant polemicists were already arguing that the Church had badly gone astray between the apostolic period and the present time. A classic example is the large multi-volume church history known as the 'Magdeburg Centuries', published between 1559 and 1574 by Mathias Flacius Illyricus and a team of collaborators. As has been elegantly formulated,

> In this protestant delineation, the church starts in the apostolic age in perfect purity, and is perverted by a process of slow canker, till it has become changed into its opposite, and is now the church not of Christ, but of anti-Christ, an instrument not for saving men but for destroying them.[13]

The Magdeburg Centuries still saw the institution of the Papacy as the main agent of corruption; but from the end of the sixteenth century, more and more authors began to argue that the 'hellenization of Christianity' – that is to say, the influence of pagan philosophy, particularly in the form of Platonism – was the true origin of evil. The patristic apologists, beginning with Justin Martyr, had made a fatal mistake by opening up a dialogue with paganism instead of rejecting it radically, and heresy had been the result. Obviously, the contemporary revival of Platonic Orientalism was seen as particularly dangerous from such a perspective. As everybody could see, it led to a positive appreciation of pagan teachers like the Persian

Zoroaster and the Egyptian Hermes, along with pagan practices such as astrology and magic, as well as the abstruse kabbalistic speculations of the Jews – the traditional enemies of Christ. None of this, Protestant hardliners were arguing, had anything to do with the gospel. That Catholic intellectuals could seriously defend such teachings showed more clearly than anything else how badly they had lost touch with what the Christian faith should be all about.

Anti-apologeticism

In Germany during the second half of the seventeenth century, this line of argumentation led to a school of thought that has been referred to as *Anti-Apologeticism*.[14] This modern label emphasizes the ambition of its representatives to give a radical Protestant answer to the patristic apologetic tradition through which paganism had come to infect the Church. The story of anti-apologeticism is closely linked to the emergence of history of philosophy as an academic discipline, and can be traced to the work of Jacob Thomasius (1622–84). As will be seen, Thomasius started a new line of argument that developed through several stages in the work of his successors. It finally resulted in a conceptual framework that was inherited on a large scale by Enlightenment thinkers and has had a decisive influence on how 'Western esotericism' has been conceptualized as a separate field of research.

Thomasius took the first step in this development, by coming up with a novel way of distinguishing between biblical religion and pagan philosophy. In typical Protestant fashion, he claimed that the former had been revealed straight by God and carried absolute authority. Because the biblical revelation is absolutely true, it does not develop and therefore does not have a history; and because God's Word is wholly superior to human reason, it cannot be subjected to philosophical analysis either. One must simply believe it. The philosophical systems of the pagans, in sharp contrast, rely upon the weak and fallible instrument of human reason, and they all share one central assumption: that the world is eternal, and therefore has not been created by God out of nothing. The doctrine of *creatio ex nihilo* is in fact not biblical (it was introduced by Theophilus of Antioch and Tatian in the second century[15]), but Thomasius did not know that. Against the sharp 'biblical' distinction between God and the world, or Creator and creation, paganism made the world eternal like God himself. All heretical beliefs came from that core error: the doctrine of emanation (souls or intelligences are not newly created by God out of nothing but pour forth from his eternal essence), dualism (form and matter, or God and matter, are equally eternal), pantheism (the world is God) and materialism (God is the world). In their different ways, they all amounted to deification of the creation at the expense of its Creator.

Through the devil's machinations, these doctrines had infiltrated Christianity, particularly in the form of Platonism. Thomasius rejected any such continuation of pagan philosophy in the context of Christianity as a case of *syncretism*, and thus of heresy, whether it occurred in the Fathers and Roman Catholic doctrine or in the various forms of Gnosticism and other sectarian movements that had sprouted from the 'arch-heretic' Simon Magus. It is important to understand that, following the logic of Thomasius' argument, the *entire* history of the Church prior to the Reformation had now become synonymous with the history of heresy. In fact, history *as such* was equivalent to the development of error: in contrast to the absolute truth of God's Word in the bible, which was beyond time and development by definition, Church history as a whole could be described as a continuous emergence of false doctrines followed by successive attempts at pious reconstitution. And this process had not even ended with the Reformation: in spite of Luther's revolution – the most serious attempt, so far, to lead Christianity back to the gospel – the pagan heresies of Platonism were now emerging as heterodox spiritualities even in Protestant contexts. These were the many 'spiritualist' and theosophical sects that flourished during the seventeenth century. What they all had in common, Thomasius pointed out, was their extreme emphasis on personal religious experience at the expense of doctrinal belief. The common term for this phenomenon was *Enthusiasm (Schwärmerei)*, and again it was based on the core error of the eternity of the world – in this case in the form of the Platonic doctrine of emanation and restitution, which claimed that the soul has its origin in an eternal, divine substance (the divine light-world) and will return to it again. Emanationism implied that human beings could return to God by attaining direct experiential knowledge of their own divine essence, by means of 'ecstatic' states of mind, and this was clearly equivalent to the quintessential gnostic doctrine of auto-salvation and deification by means of a salvational *gnōsis*.

As an effective polemical strategy Thomasius' argument was a stroke of genius. It created a razor-sharp distinction between true Christianity and its pagan or heretical 'Other', and showed how the enormous variety of the latter – from the Patristics to their gnostic opponents, and from Roman Catholicism to every form of Protestant heterodoxy – had emanated from one single principle. This principle, the eternity of the world, seemed equally relevant on the levels of ontology and epistemology: it pertained to the general philosophical worldviews of the pagans and heretics (from dualism to pantheism, and everything in between) as well as to their opinions about how to find true knowledge (the primacy of gnōsis based on the eternity of the soul). In short, Thomasius had found a way to kill not just two birds, but the whole family of heretical birds with one single stone!

Thomasius' approach was picked up by a belligerent Lutheran minister, Ehregott Daniel Colberg (1659–98), who used it as the conceptual basis for a radical attack on heresy in two volumes: *Das Platonisch-Hermetisches Christenthum* ('Platonic-Hermetic Christianity', 1690–1). For the first time in history, everything nowadays studied under the rubric of Western esotericism was presented here as belonging to one single 'family tree' of heresy, on the basis of an analysis of what its adherents had believed and proclaimed. The core error was the attempt to apply philosophical reasoning to divine matters, which are simply beyond the scope of the weak human intellect. When human beings are so presumptuous as to 'fathom the nature of the revealed mysteries about which God's Word keeps silent',[16] the result is syncretism. In Colberg's heresiological imagination, the many 'sects' of Platonic-Hermetic Christianity were like a filthy breed of vermin that had come crawling from the 'Platonic egg': yet another example (like the 'seed pod' of Simon Magus, see above) of how vivid images of horror can be combined with historical genealogies that dehumanize the enemy while tracing all forms of otherness back to one single demonic origin. By and large, Colberg saw heresies concerned with the nature of the soul as 'Platonic', and those concerned with the study of nature (especially alchemy and Paracelsianism) as 'Hermetic', but both were conceptually grounded in Thomasius' understanding of paganism as a unified tradition that rejected the doctrine of creation out of nothing.

We will see anti-apologeticism return to the stage in the guise of Enlightenment historiography, in the third and final act of the historical drama from which our concepts of 'Western esotericism' have emerged. But first we need to give some attention to the other side of the story: just as the apologetic tradition in Roman Catholicism stood against a polemical rejection of anything pagan, Protestant polemics against paganism and heresy were accompanied by their apologetic counterpart.

The Pietist reaction

As the Reformation split off from Roman Catholicism, its representatives began to quarrel among themselves about the correct interpretation of the Christian faith. The result was an increasing fragmentation of Protestantism into larger and smaller 'sects' and spiritual communities, including many believers who were appalled by the dogmatic intolerance of 'orthodox' hardliners and heresy-hunters. They felt that true Christians should try to emulate the original apostolic community: instead of fighting like cats and dogs over doctrinal matters, they should concentrate on cultivating an exemplary life of pious virtue in harmony with one another and the moral teachings of Jesus. Such circles were more receptive than their 'orthodox' Protestant counterparts to Platonizing tendencies or alchemical and Paracelsian speculation, leading eventually to Christian theosophy and a fascination with Rosicrucian ideals. Precisely such tendencies were, of course, rejected as 'Platonic-Hermetic Christianity' by Colberg; and towards the end of the seventeenth century, similar accusations began to be levelled at the Pietists. But the latter had ideas all of their own about the true nature of faith and hence about the history of Christianity, and this led towards a perspective that would become extremely influential in the study of Western esotericism.

The central figure here is the radical Pietist Gottfried Arnold (1666–1714), the author of the famous *Unparteyische Kirchen- und Ketzer-Historie* ('Impartial History of Churches and Heretics', 1699–1700). Pietists like Balthasar Köpke or Johann Wilhelm Zierold, whose works are largely forgotten today, had reacted to

anti-apologetic critics by somewhat ambiguous attempts at defending the Patristic apologetic perspective; but very interestingly, Arnold
found a way of using not apologeticism, but *anti*-apologeticism
itself as a weapon to defend the 'heretics'. He agreed with authors
like Tertullian or Thomasius that there could be no concord of any
kind between pagan philosophy and Christian faith, and thus he
gave not the slightest attention to Platonism or other gentile philosophies in his history of Christianity. But at the same time, he
seems to have understood the vulnerable point in the arguments
of the anti-apologists. As Protestant historians became ever more
adept at recognizing traces of pagan philosophy in Christian doctrine, it was becoming evident how little of it was free from such
influence, and how difficult – or rather, impossible – it was to do
without it. It was simply not possible to build a theological system
on the bible alone. The profound irony is that in their obsession
with pagan contamination, the anti-apologists therefore ended up
undermining the very orthodoxy they were trying to defend, while
giving food to the Pietist argument that the bible was all about
practical piety and not about theological doctrine at all.

On that basis, Gottfried Arnold changed the rules of the game:
he built his history of Christianity on the opposition, not between
biblical Christianity and pagan heresy, but between true Christian
piety and doctrinal theology. The question of pagan philosophies
and their historical influence ceased to be of any relevance. The
only valid criterion was whether an author's works exemplified the
spirit of humble faith, love, unity, peace and practical piety that
Arnold believed had been practiced by the original apostolic community. All who did so were true Christians, whether or not they
might be seen as 'heretics' by the official church. The true heretics
were the dogmatic theologians with their endless disputes about
doctrinal details: they were responsible for turning the Church of
Christ into a filthy 'cesspool' of quarrelling, slandering, violence
and vain ambition (another potent image of polemical otherness).
Against the depressing spectacle of historical Christianity, with its
endless doctrinal disputes, Arnold posited a supra-historical principle of immediate religious experience grounded in God's Wisdom
(Sophia). Such an experience of inner illumination, he insisted, is
the work of God in the human soul, and its contents cannot be
expressed in words: it is a hidden and secret mystery that reveals
itself only in the intimacy of the humble and pious heart. Against

the visible church with its endless doctrinal quarrels, bigotry, intolerance and violence, then, such divine illumination gives access to the 'invisible church' in which all true Christians are united. The former is an 'external' phenomenon of history, the latter is an 'inner' phenomenon of the spirit.

If Thomasius and Colberg were pioneers in conceptualizing 'Western esotericism' as a historical phenomenon grounded in the 'hellenization of Christianity', Arnold is the chief pioneer of what we have identified[17] as the 'third model' of Western esotericism, known as *religionism* and grounded in the concept of a universal 'inner' dimension of gnōsis accessible through individual religious experience. As explained in Chapter One, historical research concerned with such questions as how pagan philosophies have influenced the development of Christianity as a religion becomes meaningless in such a context. From a religionist perspective, such investigations make the mistake of reducing religion (or, in this case, esotericism) to a product of external historical factors, whereas its true reference is an independent spiritual reality *sui generis*. But from a historical perspective, religionism makes the mistake of ignoring religious diversity, historical change and any question of 'external' influences because all it cares about is an experiential dimension that transcends history and will always remain inaccessible to scholarly research by definition.

Modernity

We have now reached the third act of our drama of conflicts over identity. First Roman Catholicism had established itself against Judaism and paganism; then Protestantism positioned itself against Roman Catholicism, paganism and heresy; and finally, Enlightenment thinkers took up Protestant arguments, as we will see, in a direction that eventually led them to break loose from Christianity altogether. Of course such a one-line summary of events that took place over eighteen centuries can only be an extreme simplification; but it allows us to perceive at least the central pattern of how, and why, a specific domain of thought and practice has come to be excluded and widely perceived as 'Other' in the dominant narratives of Western discourse.

The history of philosophy

German intellectual culture plays a central role in this third act. Christian Thomasius (1655–1728), the much more famous son of Jacob Thomasius, used the critical tools of his father to liberate the history of philosophy from its theological dependencies and turn it into an autonomous discipline. Instead of rejecting the systems of pagan thinkers, one simply had to recognize them for what they were: attempts to understand the world by purely human means, without the aid of Revelation. Christian Thomasius, traditionally seen as the 'Father of the German *Aufklärung* (Enlightenment)', disliked syncretism as much as his father did; but he argued that one could purify philosophy from pagan prejudices and superstitions, so as to end up with a practical and useful philosophy free of metaphysics. The method for doing so became known as *eclecticism*. Instead of just describing the claims of the various philosophical schools, without distinguishing between true and false, the historian of philosophy should use his own faculties of rational judgement to separate the wheat from the chaff, accepting reasonable ideas wherever he found them while rejecting unreasonable ones.

Eclecticism is a key factor in German intellectual life during the early and later Enlightenment.[18] Not only did it become the central tool of Enlightenment thinkers for distinguishing between reason and superstition, but even authors attracted to 'Platonic/ Hermetic' thinking were using it to highlight what *they* considered reasonable. For our present concerns, the radical Enlightenment wing is most relevant. Christoph August Heumann (1681–1764), dubbed 'the Thomasius of Göttingen' and often seen as the founder of history of philosophy as a modern discipline, wielded the eclectic method to get rid of pagan superstitions once and for all. In his journal *Acta Philosophorum*, in 1715, he presented a set of criteria for recognizing 'pseudo-philosophy', and made clear that he meant the entire lineage of 'ancient wisdom' on Platonic-Orientalist foundations. In his eyes it was nothing but 'foolishness', and so he was cheerfully laughing at its representatives while waving them goodbye forever:

So adieu, dear *Philosophia Chaldaeorum, Persarum, Egyptiorum*, &c, that one usually makes such a fuss about, out

of blind veneration for Antiquity. . . . [N]obody should hold
it against me if I have not the slightest respect for all those
Collegia philosophica secreta, but judge that the passing of time
has quite rightly made a secret of these mysteries, by dumping
them into the sea of oblivion; and that even if the writings of
these *philosophorum barbarorum* were preserved by posterity,
they would deserve to be sent *ad loca secretiora* right away, for
superstitious idiocies belong in no better library.[19]

Heumann was announcing the final disappearance of what we now
call 'Western esotericism' from official philosophical discourse and
from academic discussion generally. In the eyes of authors such
as Jacob Thomasius or Ehregott Daniel Colberg, these pagans
and heretics had still been serious and dangerous opponents, but
Heumann dismissed them simply as fools and idiots who had no
right to be taken seriously and whose writings deserved no place in
scholarly or any other libraries. Academic research after the eighteenth century has essentially followed his advice.

By far the most influential representative of Enlightenment
eclecticism was Johann Jacob Brucker (1696–1770), the author of
a monumental six-volume *Historia critica philosophiae* (Critical
History of Philosophy, 1742–4, revised and expanded edition
1766–7). Brucker's name should be much better known than it is
today: his work was *the* standard reference on history of philosophy from the age of Enlightenment to at least the time of Hegel,
and most of the entries on philosophical subjects in Diderot's
famous *Encyclopédie* (as well as many other, less famous reference
works) were paraphrased or plagiarized from the *Historia critica*.
Based upon the anti-apologetic principles of Jacob Thomasius
and the eclectic method of Christian Thomasius and Christoph
August Heumann, Brucker presented a complete survey of the
entire history of human thought, with the aim of separating the
philosophical 'wheat' from the pseudo-philosophical 'chaff'. As
a result, his *magnum opus* consisted of two interwoven strands:
true philosophy (*philosophia eclectica*) and false philosophy
(*philosophia sectaria*). We have seen that Colberg published the
first 'history of Western esotericism' in 1690–1. Brucker's discussion of *philosophia sectaria* must be recognized as the second one, and, in fact, as perhaps the most extensive and detailed

single survey ever published. Brucker distinguished between three general periods:

(1) the Chaldaean/Zoroastrian/Egyptian philosophies from before the Birth of Christ,

(2) the two great systems of 'Neoplatonism' and 'Kabbalah' during the Catholic era and

(3) the system of 'Theosophy' that had emerged after the Reformation.

The *historia critica* was obviously written from an extremely critical and hostile perspective on all these currents, for Brucker combined Heumann's rationalism with a staunch profession of Protestant orthodoxy; but his work is marked by an acute sense of historical criticism, and rather than just dismissing 'sectarian philosophy' out of hand, he rejected each and every thinker or system only after having studied them thoroughly and seriously, with an impressive command of the primary sources.

In Brucker's synthesis, the domain that we would now refer to as 'Western esotericism' is characterized as *the continuation of pagan religion concealed as Christianity*. With philosophy it shares its pagan foundations, but it differs from philosophy in the fact that it is not based on reason. With Christianity it shares its religious nature, but it differs from Christianity in that it is a false religion, not based on Revelation. Brucker's work is of pivotal importance because it was written at a time when the memory of all these currents and ideas was still intact among intellectuals, while at the same time, it provided compelling reasons for dumping all of them into Heumann's 'sea of oblivion'. Historians after Brucker got the point: if all of this was no more than pseudo-philosophy and pseudo-Christianity, there was no longer any need to dignify it with much attention in the history of either philosophy or church history. From now on, these intellectual and religious currents began to vanish from academic textbooks, where they still have the status of mere footnotes today. No other discipline took them up, and as a result, they became 'academically homeless'. During the nineteenth and much of the twentieth century, scholars and intellectuals prided themselves on not knowing anything about such matters, so that deliberate ignorance about the traditions in question became deeply ingrained in academic life. With only very few exceptions, only amateur scholars kept writing about them, resulting in a hybrid literature full of historical errors and misconceptions. The doubtful quality of such writings further enhanced common perceptions of 'the occult' as a domain below the dignity of serious intellectuals. This downward spiral was continued far into the twentieth century, and only in recent decades does one see a serious effort on the part of scholars to educate themselves about this domain of 'rejected knowledge'.

If Protestantism established its identity against the 'pagan' heresies that had crept into Roman Catholicism, the Enlightenment built further upon Protestant polemics to establish its own identity against 'superstition' and 'prejudice'. There is a popular assumption that the rational Enlightenment was attacking the irrationality of Christian belief and practice, but this is only half the truth. It is more correct to say that the true target was the paganism that had become ingrained in Christianity. One can see this clearly, for example, in a case like Voltaire's. In a well-known witticism, he wrote that superstition was born from religion, 'as the very foolish daughter of a wise and intelligent mother'. Religion as such, reduced to 'the worship of a supreme Being and the submission of the heart to his eternal orders', was therefore wise and reasonable enough for Voltaire. The problem was elsewhere: 'Born in paganism, adopted by Judaism, superstition infected the Christian church from the very beginning',[20] and it was against that infection with 'occult' prejudice that the Enlightenment was defining its own identity. Peter Gay's famous characteristic of the Enlightenment as 'The Rise of Modern Paganism'[21] is therefore spectacularly off the mark, but illustrates how thoroughly the modern academy has forgotten its own origins.

The Romantic reaction

We are confronted with a similar case of mnemohistorical amnesia in the case of German Romanticism and Idealism. Their importance as cultural and philosophical phenomena is well-known, but the general trend of eclectic historiography (see above) has resulted in selective pictures of what Romanticism was all about. Most relevant for our concerns is the impact of Mesmerism and somnambulism during the first decades of the nineteenth century. The remarkable powers of vision and cognition that were displayed by somnambules in a state of trance, and widely discussed in contemporary society, were understood by Romantics in terms of a full-blown counter-metaphysics directed against Enlightenment rationalism. The shallow 'daylight' world of the rationalist, who reduces everything to cold logic and discursive prose, was placed in polemical constrast with the profoundly meaningful 'noctural' world of the somnambules, which expressed itself through symbols and poetic language. When the bodily senses shut down and we descend into dream or somnambulic trance, so the argument went, our soul wakes up to the larger spiritual world that is its true home. In other words, it is in fact the rationalist who is asleep and unconscious of the deeper levels of reality, and it is out of sheer ignorance that he dismisses the 'higher' human faculties of supranormal cognition and occult power as superstition.

Insisting that somnambulism revealed empirical facts about nature and the soul that were ignored by Enlightenment ideologues, Romantics were defending the scientific superiority of an 'enchanted' worldview on Paracelsian and Christian-theosophical foundations. And this perspective had far-reaching implications for the history of human thought: Romantics could now argue that all the marvellous phenomena consigned to the wastebasket of history by the Enlightenment – magic, divination, clairvoyance, symbolism, the occult – were in fact natural manifestations of the soul and its hidden powers, and *central* to the development of human culture. Combining Idealist narratives of how the Spirit comes to self-realization through history with a Pietist emphasis on interiority, authors such as Joseph Ennemoser published large histories of 'magic' in which external events were only the reflections of deeper 'inner' events of the soul and its mysterious powers. In such narratives, the ancient world was idealized as a 'golden age' in which humanity had still understood the mysterious language of nature, and the Orient was the original home of the 'ancient wisdom'.

We have seen that mesmerism and somnambulism developed in straight lines towards experimental psychology and psychiatry as practiced in the decades around 1900. The psychology of Carl Gustav Jung was grounded in German Romantic mesmerism to a much larger extent than is usually appreciated, and he adopted an approach to history on Romantic and Idealist foundations. According to Jung's account, which has exerted an enormous influence on popular notions of 'esotericism' after World War II, a continuous spiritual tradition could be traced from Gnosis and Neoplatonism in late antiquity, via medieval alchemy to Renaissance traditions such as Paracelsianism, and from there to German Romantic mesmerism and, finally, modern Jungian psychology. Jung formed the centre of what has become a highly influential tradition of modern thought in which psychology is combined with a fascination for myth and symbolism, in deliberate reaction against the dominant trend of rationalization and disenchantment of the world. Intellectuals and scholars who sympathized with such an agenda met at annual conferences at Ascona in Switzerland, known as the Eranos meetings.[22] What they had in common was a conviction that man is not capable of living by reason alone, as naïvely assumed by Enlightenment and positivist thinkers: if the non-rational, 'savage' or 'primitive' energies of the psyche are not allowed to express themselves and are suppressed into the unconscious, they will sooner or later break through the surface, with destructive results. This was held to be true not only for individuals, but for the collective as well, and hence catastrophes like World War I and II would be interpreted as examples of what happens if the non-rational is repressed by the official discourse instead of integrated in the general culture.

After World War II, Eranos became the annual meeting place of an impressive series of high-level scholars and intellectuals, including the historian of Jewish kabbalah Gershom Scholem, the scholar of Islamic mysticism Henry Corbin and the religious comparativist Mircea Eliade. In different ways, they shared a deep concern with emphasizing the vital importance of myth, symbolism and gnosis, and in crucial respects their work is a continuation of German Romantic and Idealist approaches combined in specific cases with elements of esoteric currents such as, notably, French Illuminism and Traditionalism. Most important for us, Eranos became by far the most influential twentieth-century representative of religionism, combining the widespread nostalgia for an enchanted worldview with strong emphasis on an 'inner' spiritual dimension as a means of escape from (in Eliade's words) 'the terror of history'. During the 1960s, this European intellectual tradition spread to the United States, and its main representatives attained an almost iconic status as modernist critics of the positivist mainstream: Jung, Eliade, Scholem and Corbin became famous in this period, along with American representatives of the same Eranos tradition, such as Joseph Campbell, James Hillman and many others. Eliade's so-called Chicago School even came to dominate the study of religion in the United States for several decades. Eranos scholarship appealed not just to a new generation of academics but to a very wide audience of readers, and many of the books by its main authors have become classics that remain easily available as paperbacks in general bookshops.

The general approach and underlying assumptions of the Eranos school were adopted as a matter of course by most scholars who, since the 1960s and 1970s, began to get interested in 'hermetic' or 'occult' traditions as objects of study. The most prominent example of all is Antoine Faivre, who was closely associated with Eliade and Corbin and participated in several Eranos conferences in the first part of the 1970s. We have seen that his famous definition of Western esotericism is a prototypical example of the 'enchantment model', and we can now see that his understanding of Western esotericism comes out of the religionist stream mediated primarily by German Romanticism. Faivre distanced himself from religionism during the 1990s, but his definition has exerted a very strong influence on the historically oriented scholarship that has emerged during the last two decades.

Having traced a series of polemical and apologetic conflicts from antiquity to the present, we may conclude that the conflict between biblical Christianity and paganism dominated the first and second act of the drama, in the contexts of Roman Catholicism and Protestantism. The situation changed in modernity. The anti-pagan Protestant argument was transformed in Enlightenment contexts into a blanket dismissal of 'magic', 'the occult' or 'superstition' as a wastebasket of irrational nonsense below the dignity of serious scholarship; but a Romantic reaction to this Enlightenment approach, grounded in German culture, developed during the twentieth century into a highly influential religionist perspective that came to dominate popular perceptions of Western esotericism. Both approaches were based on ultimately anti-historical foundations: the former chose to ignore any historical currents and ideas that were not considered reasonable and scientific enough, whereas the latter claimed that esotericism was really about a supra-historical 'inner' or spiritual dimension, not about any 'external' influences or developments. This is why neither of these approaches, nor the mnemohistorical narratives that are based upon them, will be followed in the rest of this book.

CHAPTER FOUR

Worldviews

In one way or another, all historical currents that fall within the purview of Western esotericism are concerned with asking and answering questions about the nature of the world, its relation to the divine and the role of humanity in between. Strict philosophical argumentation can be part of such discussions; but the underlying motivation is primarily religious, in the sense of a deep concern with the true meaning of life and the ultimate spiritual destiny of human beings in the universe. When the church father Clement of Alexandria noted down the kinds of questions that heretics were concerned with, he was referring to the Valentinians in his own time, but his description is quite applicable to other forms of esotericism as well.[1] Who are we? Where have we come from (where were we before we were born)? What is this world in which we find ourselves? How did we end up here, and why? And where will we ultimately go after we die? Obviously, the answers given to such questions are of an enormous variety – there is no such thing as 'the' esoteric worldview – but they fall within a limited number of main approaches or perspectives. In this chapter we will make a general distinction between two ways of thinking about the relation between divinity and the world, or spiritual and bodily realities, and the place of human beings within that duality. On the one hand, we come across 'metaphysical radicals' who think in terms of sharp either/or choices. On the other hand – and much more frequently, in the context of Western esotericism – we find 'metaphysical mediators' who think, rather, in terms of both/and.

Metaphysical radicalism

The American writer J. D. Salinger has left us a famous description about what could be called the radical monistic or pantheistic option in thinking about the relation between God and the world:

> 'I was six when I saw that everything was God, and my hair stood up, and all that', Teddy said. 'It was on a Sunday, I remember. My sister was only a tiny child then, and she was drinking her milk, and all of a sudden I saw that *she* was God and the *milk* was God. I mean, all she was doing was pouring God into God, if you know what I mean'.[2]

Salinger's pantheism was not based upon originally Western esoteric traditions, but reflected the Hindu philosophy of Advaita Vedanta as expounded by Sri Ramakrishna. Its unavoidable implication is that the 'world of division' in which we live our lives is ultimately an illusion of the mind, and by dispelling that illusion we discover that we have never been separated from the divine. From such a perspective, we have not 'come' from anywhere at all and do not need to 'go' anywhere either: we are already one with God, and all we need to do is recognize the fact. This radical doctrine became quite popular in New Age circles after the 1970s, particularly in the form of a 'channelled' text known as *A Course in Miracles*, but also in the message of influential spiritual teachers such as Jiddu Krishnamurti or Deepak Chopra. Moreover, it lies at the bottom of the so-called quantum mysticism of Fritjof Capra and a whole range of similar authors.[3] However, if we search for evidence of such radical pantheism in the Western esoteric corpus before the twentieth century, the results are scanty and ambiguous at best. Pantheism exists as a technical philosophical doctrine, notably in Spinoza, but we hardly encounter it as an explicit religious doctrine of salvation that tells us to dispel the illusion of the world as a separate reality. At most, we find traces of what might be called an *implicit* religious pantheism. For example, the visionary in the Hermetic *Poimandres* (C.H. I.3–8) is told that his own mind is identical with God, that both are ultimately nothing but divine Light, and the whole universe exists as thoughts within it.[4] But although the pantheistic implications are certainly there, they are not highlighted or emphasized with any radical intent: in the end, the Hermetica come down on the side of a pan*ent*heist perspective (see below) rather than a radical doctrine similar to that of Advaita Vedanta.

Radical metaphysical *dualism* is more prominent in Western esotericism than its monistic or pantheistic counterpart. One particularly clear example is taken here from the work of the twentieth-century Rosicrucians Jan van Rijckenborg (ps. of Jan Leene, 1896–1968) and Catharose de Petri (ps. of Henriette Stok-Huyser, 1902–90):

> We are pursuing a pilgrimage, deliberately and methodically. We do not want to die anymore and we do not want to live, we no longer want to be found anywhere. That is to say, we do not want to go to the mirror-sphere, nor to the sphere of matter: we want to go into "the Eternal Nothing", as the dialectical world and all her aeons and entities call it. . . . We have . . . investigated dialectical nature. We could do so because we are of this nature. With our ego-essence we were able to profoundly grasp and taste all that this world has to offer. And see, it was all trouble and misery. We have found this nature to be a nature of death, and we did not desire to sing with the blessed in front of the throne, or put any effort in trying to make this cursed order acceptable in any way. After years of experimentation, we concluded that this could not be the meaning of the true life, and that it was not good to collaborate any longer in deluding humanity in this nature of death.[5]

Such an attitude of radical world-rejection is usually described as gnostic or Manichaean dualism. The gnostic experiences himself as a 'stranger' thrown in an alien and hostile world that is based on rules and values he refuses to accept. His overwhelming feeling is that he does not belong in this world, and so he seeks to escape from it: his true 'home' is elsewhere, in some spiritual reality that is entirely different from this world of matter, darkness, suffering and ignorance. Such painful existential anguish about being a stranger or exile in a threatening or absurd world, and a deeply felt nostalgia for 'home', may be part of the human condition as such; but these feelings and experiences become relevant to the history of Western esotericism to the extent that people start developing religious theories and mythologies to account for them and explain 'what went wrong'.

Again, the answers have been widely divergent. Some have imagined two eternal worlds, one of darkness and one of light, which should have remained separate: our world is an unfortunate mixture of the two, where the sparks of spiritual light that are trapped within ourselves are longing forever to return to their original state of purity and bliss. Others have claimed that, originally, there was only one divine world of unbroken harmony, light and bliss: our world of darkness and division is an accident or mistake, resulting from some kind of primordial Fall or cosmic disaster – like a cancerous growth that has developed in an otherwise healthy tissue as the result of some infection or genetic defect. This error or illness must be cured in order to restore the whole of Being to its original state of health and wholeness. Some have claimed that this world was deliberately created as a prison for the soul, by an evil or ignorant deity (the 'demiurge') who tries to make us believe that he is the true God, and whose demonic helpers (the 'archons') try to prevent us from 'waking up' to who we really are, and from finding our way back to the world of divine light out of which we have come and where we really belong. It is easy and natural for such mythologies to take the form of dramatic narratives: the universe then comes to be imagined as a battlefield where the divine forces of light are struggling with the demonic powers of darkness over the liberty or captivity of human souls.[6]

Whether pantheistic or dualistic, all forms of metaphysical radicalism have one thing in common: *the World* as it appears to us in our daily life constitutes a problem that must somehow be resolved or overcome, because it falls short of the divine ideal of spiritual perfection. Divinity means bliss; the World is full of suffering. Divinity is pure light; the World is darkness. Divinity is whole; the World is divided. Divinity means eternal life; the World is the domain of time and transitoriness, death and dissolution. Divinity is good; the World is flawed, imperfect or downright evil. Divinity is truth; the World is full of falsity and error. Divinity is beauty; the World is full of ugliness. In sum: the World is the problem. Whether they are pantheists or dualists, metaphysical radicals refuse to settle for compromise when it comes to solving this problem. The pantheist solution consists of realizing that all this lack and imperfection is in fact just an illusion, like a dream or nightmare: once we have woken up to the truth, none of it can touch us anymore, because none of it is real. We are not really in trouble: we just think we are. For dualists, in contrast, the World is definitely real, at least as long as we are still trapped in it: we are in trouble indeed, and must do something about it. The only solution is to fight against the world and its powers of domination, in a struggle for liberation.

It is hardly an accident that the stronger the element of radical dualism, and the more seriously it is translated into a comprehensive worldview or metaphysical doctrine, the greater the chance that it may lead to militant activism and result in violent conflicts between 'sectarian' movements and the 'powers of this world'. One may think here of the Bogomil and Cathar heresies in the Middle Ages, and their violent suppression by the authorities, but also of extremist groups such as the Order of the Solar Temple and Heaven's Gate, whose members decided to escape from this world by committing collective suicide/murder in 1994 and 1997.[7] In the field of Western esotericism as a whole, such cases of 'spiritual extremism' are fortunately rare exceptions. Certainly the potential for radicalization is always there, at least in theory; but much more frequently than an extreme and uncompromising 'either/or' stance, we find a more inclusivist 'both/and' attitude towards the relation between divinity and the world, or spirit and matter, and the role of human beings within that polarity. More typical than the demand of a radical choice for the divine or the spiritual against the world of matter (whether by unmasking it as an illusion or trying to escape from it) is the attempt to find ways of mediation in which both are recognized and accorded a legitimate role, although the spiritual pole is always seen as superior. In this regard, we propose to distinguish between two dominant models or paradigms of mediation in the history of Western esotericism: we will refer to the first one as 'Platonic', and to the second as 'Alchemical'.

Platonic mediation

In a notable passage, the great American historian of ideas Arthur O. Lovejoy has called attention to the fact that, as a result of the persistent influence of Platonism, the more philosophically inclined forms of religion in Western culture have always been torn between two different and logically antithetical understandings of God:

> The one was the Absolute of otherworldliness – self-sufficient, out of time, alien to the categories of ordinary human thought and experience, needing no world of lesser beings to supplement or enhance his own eternal self-contained perfection. The other was a God who emphatically was not self-sufficient nor, in any philosophical sense, 'absolute': one whose essential nature required the existence of other beings, and not of one kind of these only, but of all kinds which could find a place in the descending scale of the possibilities of reality – a God whose prime attribute was generativeness, whose manifestation was to be found in the diversity of creatures and therefore in the temporal order and the manifold spectacle of nature's processes.[8]

The former understanding is more naturally suited to dualist perspectives: it suggests that from this world of division and multiplicity we must find the way back to the pure and otherworldly unity of the 'self-sufficient absolute'. But the latter understanding suggests exactly the opposite: it implies a movement not from the world back to God, but from God down to the world. God is conceived as the 'generative source' of all being, and since this makes the whole world into an admirable manifestation of divine power and creative abundance, it suggests a positive this-worldly attitude on the part of human beings. This second aspect of Platonism leads to what is known as the 'great chain of being:' the boundless creativity of the divine source was believed to have resulted in the enormous diversity of the universe, from the most exalted angelic intelligences to the lowest animal creatures, all of which had their divinely appointed place in an ordered hierarchy that stretched out between the ultimate poles of spirit and matter.

The paradoxical combination of two antithetical understandings of God, both of them implied by the same Platonic tradition in Christian culture, had the effect of casting human beings in a unique although highly ambiguous role: that of 'mediating' between the opposed forces of attraction towards the divine, on the one hand, and towards the world, on the other. In a famous passage, Giovanni Pico della Mirandola describes how God 'took man as a creature of indeterminate nature', assigning him 'a place in the middle of the world', and addressing him as follows:

We have set thee at the world's center that thou mayest from thence more easily observe whatever is in the world. We have made thee neither of heaven nor of earth, neither mortal nor immortal, so that with freedom of choice and with honor, as though the maker and molder of thyself, thou mayest fashion thyself in whatever shape thou shalt prefer. Thou shalt have the power to degenerate into the lower forms of life, which are brutish. Thou shalt have the power, out of thy soul's judgment, to be reborn into the higher forms, which are divine.[9]

This passage has deep resonances in Platonic literature, notably with the image of the human soul as a 'charioteer' whose carriage is drawn by two horses: a good one that tries to lead him upward towards the purity of the divine ideas, and an unruly one that drags him down towards the things of the body.[10] That human beings have the power to rise upward to heaven and even be reborn as divine beings, but are continuously tempted by bodily desires that draw them down to the world of matter, is a recurring motif in Platonic and Hermetic literature, and one of the most fundamental 'deep structures' of Western esoteric speculation from antiquity to the present. It could inspire passages of heroic exaltation about 'human dignity', as in Pico, but could also be cast in a more ironic register, as seen in Alexander Pope's *Essay on Man* (1734):

Placed on this isthmus of a middle state,
A being darkly wise and rudely great:
With too much knowledge for the Sceptic side,
With too much weakness for the Stoic's pride,
He hangs between, in doubt to act or rest;
In doubt to deem himself a God or Beast;
In doubt his mind or body to prefer;
Born but to die, and reas'ning but to err;
Alike in ignorance, his reason such,
Whether he thinks too little or too much;
Chaos of thought and passion, all confused;

Still by himself abused or disabused;
Created half to rise, and half to fall:
Great lord of all things, yet a prey to all;
Sole judge of truth, in endless error hurl'd;
The glory, jest, and riddle of the world![11]

In very broad terms, and allowing for quite some exceptions and qualifications, it may be said that the world-denying and ascetic implications of the divine as 'self-sufficient absolute' have been more prominent in the earlier phases of Christian Platonism, while the world-affirming emphasis on the divine as 'generative source' has gradually become more prominent in later periods. This is part of the general drift, in Western culture, from a primary concern with religious salvation in the afterlife towards an increasing focus on 'conquering the world' by means of reason and scientific progress. As a result, the ascetic implications of Platonic otherworldliness have gradually become alien to the modern and contemporary mind: contemporary esotericists, too, may be inheritors of Platonic frameworks but are rarely interested in mortifying the body or renouncing sexuality in order to gain unity with the divine.

But the 'middle place' of human beings did not just imply that they could choose to steer their chariot either upwards or downwards, away from the world towards unity with God or away from God towards immersion in worldly pleasure. It also meant that, while pursuing an ideal of spiritual purification, they could simultaneously try to profit from the multiple virtues or 'gifts' that were believed to be emanating from the inexhaustible source of divine power. In other words, 'mediation' can mean the attempt to find some kind of balance between the upward movement of souls towards the divine *and* the downward movement of divine powers towards the world. One sees this clearly in the work of Marsilio Ficino on 'how to bring one's life in harmony with the heavenly bodies'.[12] Human beings are subject, each second of their lives, to influences that are coming down from the stars according to the constantly changing astrological constellations. We can use these 'gifts' for our own benefit if we know how to channel them. But critics were quick to point out the other side of the coin: by the same procedures one might attract evil or demonic influences as well, and was it really possible to distinguish between the two?

If the attempt to transcend the world and unify with the Absolute is conventionally referred to as 'mysticism', this complementary attempt to draw down powers from above tends to be described as astral 'magic'. A classic reference is the Hermetic *Asclepius*, where we find descriptions of how the ancient Egyptians learned to attract the powers of angels and demons down into their temple statues, which thereby gained the power to do good or evil.[13] St Augustine had rejected such practices as pagan idolatry, but Renaissance authors who admired Hermes as an ancient sage were not so sure. Great authorities like the theologian Thomas Aquinas had made a sophisticated distinction between 'talismans' and 'amulets' (material objects, like the Hermetic statues, which could function as the receptacles of spiritual powers channelled from above): the former were inscribed with linguistic signs, which could only be interpreted as attempts to communicate with demons, but the latter were acceptable because they worked by virtue of purely natural causes.[14] By convincing himself, and trying to convince his readers, that the powers from the stars belonged to the latter category, Ficino could legitimate astral magic for beneficent ends such as physical and psychological healing.

The Platonic worldview of mediation – a holistic framework premised on both the 'magical' downward movement of higher powers or virtues and the 'mystical' upward movement of the soul to God – found perhaps its most complete expression in Heinrich Cornelius Agrippa's classic *De occulta philosophia libri tres* (1533). Starting at the bottom and moving from there to the top of the universal hierarchy, it discussed the entire range of traditional (classic and medieval) information about the powers of the elementary, celestial and super-celestial spheres of reality, while suggesting at the same time that by moving towards unification with the divine mind one might ultimately come to participate in the unlimited creative powers of God himself. The idea, therefore, was not some kind of absorption or annihilation of the finite human intellect in the infinite light of the godhead, but rather, a state of deification by which human beings regained the godlike powers that Adam was believed to have enjoyed before the Fall.[15] The context is resolutely Christian, but the core idea would eventually be popularized and psychologized in modern occultist and 'New Age' formulations such as 'self-realization' or finding one's 'true self': an ideal that does not imply passive submission to God or the annihilation of

individuality, but rather, spiritual empowerment and the unfolding of one's full 'human potential'. The Renaissance 'magus' thus
becomes the 'fully realized human being' placed imaginatively
'at the center of the universe', and capable of 'creating his own
reality'. Even in contemporary popular culture, from novels and
comics to video games, often inspired directly or indirectly by esoteric traditions, this core idea of deification and access to spiritual
'super-powers' has become a major theme.

Agrippa's Platonic worldview was still based on the traditional Ptolemaic cosmos: placed 'in the middle of the universe',
human beings could gaze downwards to matter as well as upwards
to where God could be found. But we have seen (Chapter Two)
that the Copernican revolution made such a 'vertical' perspective
untenable. As seen first in Giordano Bruno, and increasingly in a
range of later thinkers, God could no longer be imagined as resid-
ing somewhere high up 'above the stars'. In an infinite universe, the
infinite God could no longer be found in any spatial location but
had to be present everywhere, as an invisible power that perme-
ates the whole of reality – a bit like the force of life that animates
the body. A convenient term for this perspective is *panentheism*:
God is omnipresent in the world and the world is somehow contained in God. Something very similar had been stated already in
the Hermetic literature of antiquity, suggesting a kind of 'cosmic
religiosity' that resonates strongly with the expansive and optimistic Romanticism of American transcendentalism and its many successor movements:

> Think of God as having everything – the cosmos, himself, the
> universe – like thoughts within himself. Thus, unless you make
> yourself equal to God, you cannot understand God: like is
> understood by like. Make yourself grow to immeasurable size,
> be free from every body, transcend all time, become eternity,
> and you will understand God. Suppose nothing to be impossible
> to you, consider yourself immortal and able to understand
> everything: all arts, all learning, the nature of every living
> thing. Go higher than every height and lower than every depth.
> Collect in yourself all the sensations of what has been made, of
> fire and water, the dry and the moist. Conceive yourself to be in
> all places at the same time: in earth, in the sea, in heaven, not yet

born, in the womb, young, old, dead, beyond death. And when you have understood all these at once – times, places, things, qualities, quantities – then you can understand God. . . . When you take this road, the Good will meet you everywhere and will be experienced everywhere, where and when you least expect it: as you lie awake, as you fall asleep, sailing or walking, by night or by day, as you speak or keep silent. For there is nothing that it is not. Do you say then that God is invisible? Be careful – who is more visible than God? This is why he made all things: so that through them all you might look on him.[16]

Welcomed especially since the 1960s as an alternative to traditional Christian notions of ascetic otherworldliness, depravity and sin, but also of the existentialist despair and pessimism that had dominated intellectual life for decades,[17] such expressions of confidence in the beauty and goodness of the universe and the capacity of human beings to understand it as God's living body were obviously congenial to the emerging environmentalist ethic and a whole range of further spiritualities that emphasized the unlimited possibilities of 'human potential'. For example, one may think here of the movement of that name that is linked to the famous Esalen centre in California,[18] but also of an author such as Jane Roberts and her extremely influential 'Seth Books'.[19] In such contexts, human consciousness came to be seen as the vanguard of spiritual evolution, and we will now see that this notion has deep historical backgrounds in Western esoteric speculation as well.

Alchemical mediation

The Platonic model conceives of the universe in essentially spatial terms: it is spread out as a 'great chain of being' between the poles of spirit and matter, with human beings located somewhere in between and participating in both. Its premise is the idea of universal harmony and hierarchical order, in which all power and authority resides forever in the divine principle of unity up above, from where it is channelled downwards step by step through all the lower degrees of being. During the Renaissance, this powerful paradigm had its centre in Italian culture, and it was obviously

congenial to the concept of one universal 'Catholic' religion represented by the Church of Rome, with its hierarchical organization
under the divinely instituted leadership of the Pope. But this image
of unbroken unity, wholeness and harmony was shattered forever
by the events of the Reformation, and Protestant revolutionaries
needed different models to make sense of their own experience. The
new sensitivity was very clearly formulated by the great church historian Ferdinand Christian Baur in the mid-nineteenth century:

> If for the Catholic there is no such thing as a historical movement
> through which the Church has become essentially different
> from what it was at its origin, if in the entire development of
> the Church he merely sees its immanent truth coming to ever
> greater realization and ever more general recognition, from the
> perspective of the Protestant, in contrast, the Church as it exists
> in the immediate present is separate from what it originally was
> by an abyss that is so wide, that between these two points in
> time there must have been an immeasurable series of changes.[20]

In other words, the Protestant revolution implied a new kind of
historical consciousness. Rather than a spatial model of unchanging harmony and beauty – congenial to the idea of a *philosophia
perennis* – it required a *linear* perspective based on temporality and
irreversible change that could account for the unprecedented struggle in which the reformers found themselves. Many Lutherans and
spiritualist sectarians appear to have discovered such a model in
alchemical narratives of transmutation, leading to a new and very
different paradigm that had its geographical centre in the German-
speaking heartland of the Reformation. The relation between the
two paradigms may be summarized approximately as follows:

'Platonic' paradigm	'Alchemical' paradigm
Spatial	Linear
Static (harmony)	Dynamic (process)
From metaphysics to nature	From nature to metaphysics
Fall: from light to darkness	Birth: from darkness to light
Traditional authority	Individual experience

In terms of an alchemical model interpreted from Protestant perspectives, God has not placed man 'at the world's center' from where he is at liberty to choose between spirit and matter, or God and the world, but at the beginning of a linear process or quest with an uncertain outcome. His situation is precarious: as a fallen creature born in a fallen world, everything begins for him in a dark place of insufficiency and sin. In alchemical terms, this is the *nigredo*, the first phase of darkness in which the Great Work begins. Contrary to the logic that governs the Platonic paradigm, salvation from this state cannot be a matter of 'remembering' one's divine origin and escaping from the body to find the way back to one's spiritual home: in sharp contrast to such cyclical narratives of the soul's alienation and return, it is the body itself that must be transmuted and reborn together with the soul.

Man therefore does not begin as a 'great miracle',[21] that is to say, as an already semi-divine being standing halfway between matter and spirit. He begins as a merely natural creature that is wholly dependent on God's grace, and must somehow turn *himself* into the medium for attaining a higher state. To clarify the difference by means of an image, according to the Platonic model we might picture him as standing on the middle of a bridge, where he just has to make a choice of whether to turn left towards the body or right towards the spirit. But in the alchemical model, more congenial to Protestant spiritualities, there is no bridge to begin with, and even the state of salvation does not yet exist for man but must still be achieved in and through his own body. He stands in front of a dark chasm and can only move forward. He must try, somehow, to build a bridge that reaches out to the other side, step by step, always at risk of crashing down into the abyss halfway during the attempt. One sees that this model of spiritual attainment has a potential for high existential drama that is absent from the far more static, harmonious and reassuring model of the Platonic universe. Unregenerated man can hardly hope to succeed without divine assistance: he can only pray that, by the grace of God, his bridge will be prevented from collapsing, and that Christ himself will make the Great Work succeed by reaching out to him from the other side. He cannot be reborn by any power or wisdom that is already his own, but can only hope that Christ will miraculously be born as divine light in his inner darkness.

The Platonic model is deductive: it begins with the whole and then proceeds to assign to everything its proper place downwards through the great chain of being. The alchemical model is inductive: it begins with the most concrete, tangible realities of nature and the physical body, and works its way upwards from there. This narrative logic is clearly present already in the work of Paracelsus. Instead of relying blindly on the authority of the ancients, he insisted on beginning with the empirical and experimental investigation of nature and our own bodily constitution. Although he never became a Protestant, he was not called 'the Luther of medicine' for nothing: writing in German instead of Latin, and thereby addressing a much larger audience than just the intellectual elites, he emphasized the responsibility of the individual to think for himself and find his way to salvation. Perhaps most important of all, salvation and healing were two sides of the same coin for him. Human beings are vulnerable to illness because they are born in a fallen state, for which Paracelsus had invented the term *cagastrum*, and therefore the attainment of health ultimately implies spiritual as well as bodily regeneration towards a state of purification. Healing means ultimately reversing the Fall.

Under the strong influence of Paracelsian concepts, the alchemical model of salvation came to full development in the system of Jacob Böhme, from where it became central to Christian theosophical traditions far into the nineteenth century. As we have seen in Chapter Two, Böhme describes how God himself is born out of the mysterious *Ungrund*, and how his own body grows and develops from an initial state of wrath and darkness towards a redeemed state of love and light: from a frightening 'hellish' world of suffering and strife (associated with the Father) to a luminous world of harmony and light referred to as Eternal Nature (associated with the Son). Light is born from darkness, love is born from wrath, the Son is born from the Father. All of this was modelled after alchemical narratives of transmutation, including their frequent refences to sexuality and bodily processes ('fertilization', '[re]generation', 'birth', etc.).[22] The redemption of human beings and of the whole world of nature – the fallen body of God – follows the same pattern: Christ was born as the Light of the World for the salvation of humanity, and likewise he must be born in our own inner darkness as well. The hoped-for goal is not an escape *from* the body, but a transmutation *of* the body into a subtle vehicle of superior luminous matter that will survive death: as formulated by Friedrich Christoph Oetinger in the eighteenth century, *Leiblichkeit ist das Ende der Werke Gottes* ('Bodiliness is the end [goal] of God's works').[23]

The above should be sufficient to show that the Platonic and the Alchemical narratives each have their own internal logic, somewhat more congenial to Catholic and Protestant sensititivies respectively, but this does not mean that they were kept strictly separate in practice. On the contrary, the *occulta philosophia* of the sixteenth and seventeenth centuries is full of creative attempts at synthesizing platonic and alchemical theories, or elements of them, within comprehensive frameworks that reject or ignore conventional demarcations of religion, philosophy and science. There has always been a strong tendency in Western esotericism towards formulating 'theories of everything', encompassing the whole of reality from matter to the divine, and nothing could be more tempting for speculative minds than trying to capture both the unity and harmony of Being *and* its processual development through time. Among the most important, most intriguing, but also most elusive chapters in the history of these attempts is German Idealism and its impact on nineteenth-century evolutionist thought. Some scholars have seen the alchemical-theosophical tradition from Böhme to Oetinger, or even the 'Hermetic Tradition' as a whole, as a major key to understanding philosophers like Schelling or Hegel.[24] Others have dismissed the significance of such influences, and the truth is that we are still far from any scholarly consensus in this matter. This reseach deficit illustrates the need for a radical interdisciplinary perspective, which begins by recognizing that neither the proponents of *philosophia occulta*, nor the Romantic and Idealist philosophers, would have accepted the disciplinary straitjackets that the modern academy imposes on them: they all saw their speculative worldviews as *equally* relevant to philosophy, religion, science and the arts, and they felt much more free than their contemporary interpreters to draw upon anything they could use in any of these domains.

To what extent Romantic evolutionism is indebted, from a historical point of view, to the processual dynamics of the alchemical model is a question that has not yet been resolved. There can be no doubt, however, about the subsequent influence of Romantic and Idealist narratives on how esotericism has developed since the

nineteenth century.[25] It is well known that evolutionism emerged
as a dominant new paradigm during this period. It transformed
not only existing disciplines such as biology, geology, the history of
culture or the study of religion, but was also intimately interwoven
with the emergence of a brand-new one: psychology. Romantic and
Idealist narratives were still indebted to Christian theological models – Hegel's Absolute Spirit coming to self-realization through history must somehow be the Spirit of God – but they could easily be
psychologized and thereby transformed into narratives about the
evolution of the human spirit, or human consciousness as such.[26] A
perfect example is the Swiss physician Joseph Ennemoser and his
large *History of Magic* (1844) on Romantic and Idealist foundations, which became a crucial although largely unacknowledged
source for central esoteric authors as different as H. P. Blavatsky
and C. G. Jung.[27] The true impact that Idealist philosophy and its
historical narratives have had on the popular practice and understanding of religion and spirituality in the modern West still tends
to be underestimated by scholars.

For our concerns, in this short overview, the most important
example is Jungian psychology and its historical backgrounds in
German Romantic mesmerism. Jung was partly drawing on gnostic
models to describe the goal of psychological self-knowledge as an
'interior sun' (the inner light of the human psyche through which
man gains access to a numinous, transpersonal spiritual reality).
But his most potent models were derived from alchemy, understood
from a perspective heavily influenced by German Romanticism and
Idealist philosophy, including its backgrounds in Christian theosophy and Pietist culture.[28] The basic alchemical narrative of transmutation – a difficult struggle leading from prime matter to gold,
or from darkness to light, accompanied at all stages by numinous
symbolic imagery – turned out to be a perfect match for describing the psychological process of 'individuation', understood as an
arduous process of self-discovery in which one confronts the symbolic images that emerge from the unconscious. The initial state
of 'darkness' is no longer understood here as a state of sin, as in
the original Protestant model, but as a state of spiritual ignorance
and immaturity. Even in this psychologized version of theosophical salvation, however, the ultimate goal (as we already saw in the
previous section) can still only be described as deification.

It bears repeating that radical pantheism, radical dualism, Platonic mediation and Alchemical mediation are seldom, if ever, encountered in pure or perfect form. They are offered here as structural *models* or ideal types that can be used as hermeneutical tools to bring some degree of order to the complexities of intellectual history, but should not be misunderstood as straightforward descriptions of what we find in specific historical or contemporary sources. In spite of their different and even contradictory internal logics – or better perhaps, because of them – there have been countless attempts at achieving some synthesis, particularly by authors who wish to believe that the various traditions that have come down to us must be ultimately one in essence. Quite predictably, none of these attempts has been wholly successful. Scholars of esotericism should better not waste their time on attempts to lend credibility to such pursuits of an artificial chimera called 'the' esoteric worldview. No such thing exists. Rather, our goal should be to understand how specific authors or historical currents have *attempted* (more convincingly or less so) to formulate comprehensive worldviews that might help them find answers to the basic questions outlined in the opening section of this chapter.

CHAPTER FIVE

Knowledge

How do we find answers about the true nature of the world, spiritual or divine realities, the meaning of our lives or our destiny after death? Should we just believe what traditional authorities – churches, theologians, sacred scriptures – tell us about such matters? Should we not rather try to find out by ourselves, using the evidence of our senses and our rational faculties? Or are such traditional avenues to knowledge insufficient when it comes to answering the deepest and most essential questions about the mystery of existence? If so, are there other ways?

Such a line of questioning is typical for the authors and currents that are discussed in this book, and they usually come up with positive answers. It has sometimes been suggested that 'claims of higher or perfect knowledge' are the central characteristic of esoteric discourse,[1] but it is more correct to say that its representatives *aspire* to such knowledge. They typically believe that it is possible, at least in principle, to gain direct and unmediated, suprarational and salvational access to the supreme spiritual level of reality. Higher or perfect knowledge may sometimes be claimed as a proud possession, but more often it is held out as a promise, and the basic worldviews discussed in the previous chapter serve to lend theoretical legitimacy to such hopes for discovering the ultimate truth about existence. According to the platonic doctrine of emanation and restitution, and its gnostic derivates, the soul has its origin in an eternal, divine reality or substance, and can or will return to it again. This implies that, as human beings, we have an inborn capacity for knowing the divine: we are not dependent on God revealing Himself to us (as in classic accounts of monotheism, where the creature is dependent on the Creator's initiative), nor is our capacity for knowledge limited to the bodily senses and natural reason (as in science and rational philosophy), but, in contrast to both alternatives, the very nature of our souls allows us direct access to the supreme, eternal substance of Being. According to the alternative alchemical model, the attainment of supreme knowledge is not so much a matter or 'remembering' our divine origin (implying a cyclical pattern of fall or decline and restitution) but is conceived of as a latent capacity, or human potentiality, that must be developed in ourselves by our own efforts: it is the *telos*, or final goal, of the human quest.

It would be a mistake, however, to assume that Western esotericism is concerned *solely* with such higher or absolute knowledge of the soul and its spiritual salvation, to the exclusion of more conventional goals or modes of knowledge. The fact is that many of its representatives have been deeply involved in philosophical and scientific pursuits, as well as in traditional forms of biblical or dogmatic theology. The point about esotericism is not that such approaches are necessarily rejected – although they sometimes are – but that they are considered incomplete: there are limits to how far they can lead us, or so it is argued, and they must be complemented by more radical avenues for attaining knowledge. So let us first take a closer look at the complicated interplay, in Western esotericism, between different kinds of questions and different ways of answering them.

Reason, faith and gnosis

In modern and contemporary society we are most intimately familiar with claims of knowledge that focus on scientific or scholarly exploration and rational understanding. To find answers to our questions we are dependent on the evidence of our senses, enormously extended today by the invention of technologies that allow us to investigate the whole of physical reality from the infinitely small to the infinitely large. In the humanities and the social sciences, too, sophisticated instruments have been developed for studying sources and gathering data. For evaluating, interpreting or explaining what we discover, as well as for formulating theories and hypotheses as guides for further investigation, we rely on rational argumentation and informed speculation, often using highly technical languages by which we can discuss the extreme complexity of the data with a high degree of precision; in fact, even the limitations of reason itself can be made into an object of reasoned discourse about how our subjective biases are involved in any attempt at gaining some degree of objective certainty. The ambitious project of trying to understand the reality around us by relying on empirical evidence and rational argument is traditionally known, of course, by terms such as philosophy and science (or scholarly research, in the case of the humanities). If anybody claims to know something and wishes to be taken seriously in these contexts, at least two basic conditions must be fulfilled: he or she must be able to *communicate* what s/he claims to know by means of discursive language, so that others can understand it, and somehow it must be possible for others to *test* or evaluate whether it is true or not, or at least whether the arguments stand up to logical scrutiny. Unless these two conditions are fulfilled, we have no philosophy, no science, no research. In what follows, the term 'reason' will be used as shorthand for this first approach to knowledge.

There are, however, claims of knowledge that can be communicated by discursive language but the truth or falsity of which cannot be tested independently. For example, traditional Christianity claims to know that God is a trinity of Father, Son and Holy Spirit, the second person of which was incarnated as Jesus Christ. Highly erudite and intelligent theologians have formulated these convictions in exact discursive prose that can be readily studied by anybody who takes an interest, and these statements present us with no problems as to understanding what they mean to tell us: the Son of God was born as a man. But how does one determine whether such statements are true or false, convincing or unconvincing? Theologians have come up with sophisticated arguments, but the truth is that we simply have no independent procedures for finding out whether an entity such as God exists or not, let alone whether He might have a triune nature and a son who was born in the flesh. When all is said and done, these are statements of belief that have to be accepted on the basis of authority and tradition, but cannot be tested independently in any way. Therefore they cannot be accepted in the domain of 'reason'. Obviously this example of

Christian theology can be extrapolated to many other contexts: the point is that one chooses to believe in certain claims that have been handed down, and thereby accepts them as valid knowledge without insisting on independent verification (and in this context, it is useful to remember that most of us accept scientific claims not because we have checked them, but because we choose to *believe* that scientists know what they are doing). In what follows, the term 'faith' will be used as shorthand for this second approach to knowledge.

Finally, there are claims of knowledge that go even a step further: like those in the previous category they cannot be tested independently, but remarkably enough, it is claimed that they cannot be communicated by discursive language either! And yet they are held with great conviction, and presented as superior to any other kind of knowledge. This third type, to which we will be referring as 'gnosis', is of fundamental importance in the history of Western esotericism. In sum, then, we end up with something like the following:

	Communicable	Testable
Reason	+	+
Faith	+	−
Gnosis	−	−

How claims of non-communicable and non-testable knowledge are to be understood will be explored at greater length below. But before concentrating on this core element of Western esotericism, let us first take a closer look at the two alternatives.

As already noted in the introduction to this chapter, Western esotericism does not necessarily entail a simple rejection of 'reason' and 'faith', or of their characteristic procedures for finding answers and discovering truth: usually, its representatives state simply that these approaches have their limitations, and only knowledge of the 'gnosis' type leads us as far as the truth itself. A paradigmatic formulation is found in the *Corpus Hermeticum*, where 'mind' (*nous*) is described as the human faculty for attaining gnosis. The passage uses technical language to explain its relation to reasoned discourse (*logos*) and faith (*pistis*):

> If you are mindful [ennoounti], Asclepius, these things will seem true to you, but they will seem incredible [apista] if you are not mindful [agnoounti]. To understand [noesai] is to have faith [pisteusai], and not to have faith [apistesai] is not to understand [me noesai]. Reasoned discourse [logos] does <not> get to the truth, but mind [nous] is powerful, and, when it has been guided by reason [logos] up to a point, it has the means to get <as far as> the truth.[2]

What we read here is that, in order to gain true understanding, one must have faith and make good use of one's rational faculties; but the final step is taken by mind, and leads us to a level beyond reason. The Hermetic writings keep emphasizing that if you want to have a shot at attaining gnosis, you will first have to master the 'general discourses' (*genikoi logoi*) concerned with rational and natural philosophy.

This basic principle is clearly evident throughout the corpus of texts that are seen as pertaining to 'Western esotericism', at least up to the eighteenth century. Foundational Renaissance authors such as Marsilio Ficino, Pico della Mirandola, Heinrich Cornelius Agrippa or Giordano Bruno (but the list can be extended indefinitely) were all highly erudite scholars who had studied and mastered the entire corpus of traditional Western philosophy: not just the Platonists and 'mystical' authors such as Dionysius the Areopagite, but the Aristotelians and scholastics as well, and much else besides. Authors such as John Dee, Robert Fludd, Heinrich Khunrath or Emanuel Swedenborg (again, this is just a random selection) were deeply involved in the natural sciences of their time, such as chymistry, biology or physics, and this scientific involvement is of crucial importance to understanding the more 'esoteric' dimensions of their work: for example, Swedenborg by no means left Cartesian philosophy and natural science behind when he entered his visionary period as a biblical exegete, but, on the contrary, built his religious or spiritual worldview on these highly rationalistic foundations.[3] At the same time, almost all the authors associated with Western esotericism, at least up to the eighteenth century, were Christians who deeply believed in the truth of the biblical revelation. Agrippa even went out of his way to emphasize the absolute superiority of faith in Jesus Christ over any knowledge gained by the human arts and sciences.[4] The suggestion – so natural in the context of contempory popular esotericism – that by attaining ultimate knowledge or gnosis one leaves the Christian faith behind, or renders it irrelevant, would have sounded like dangerous nonsense to them. Likewise, they did not see themselves as opposed to science and rational inquiry, but believed that these important and necessary avenues towards knowledge must be expanded and complemented by approaches that ultimately went beyond human reason alone and were felt to be more congenial to the trancendant realities of the divine.

In this regard, as in so many others, the Enlightenment was a caesura that changed the rules of the game. After the eighteenth century, esoteric authors tend to become much more aggressive in presenting their 'higher knowledge' as a superior *alternative* to the claims of traditional Christianity and mainstream science, and not just as an extra level built on the foundations that they provide. For example, Mme Blavatsky's *Isis Unveiled* (1877) consists of a virulent polemic against established 'science' (vol. I) and 'religion' (vol. II), claiming that her 'occult science' of theosophy has existed since times immemorial as the superior alternative to the positivist worldview and the traditional Christianity of her time. If many other occultists still kept presenting their worldviews as Christian (think, for example, of theosophists from Anna Kingsford, Annie Besant or Charles Webster Leadbeater to Alice Bailey or Rudolf Steiner), they usually meant their own esoteric understanding of Christianity: this was believed to be based on direct spiritual insight or gnosis, and should not be confused, in their opinion, with the merely 'exoteric' beliefs of the churches and theologians. In contemporary 'New Age' contexts one still sees the same pattern, particularly among people who have been raised with Christianity and do not want to leave it behind entirely, but feel that the church has lost touch with the true message. Alternative forms of spirituality are then presented as a better way of understanding the Christian message, for example by referring to the gnostic gospels (while downplaying inconvenient aspects such as radical dualism and ascetic rejection of the body and sexuality). The importance of direct spiritual gnosis is obviously highlighted in this context; but contrary to pre-Enlightenment contexts, very little tends to be left of traditional Christian dogma, resulting in predictably negative responses from the side of professional theologians and church representatives. Esoteric understandings of Christianity are not seen as an extra level built upon the existing theological structure, but as alternatives that should replace it.

As far as science is concerned, the situation is comparable but slightly different. Traditional Christianity may be widely perceived, by contemporary esoteric audiences, as old-fashioned, stuck in the dogmas of the past, and out of touch with contemporary spiritual concerns; but in contrast, it is impossible for anyone living in modern society to doubt that natural science has continued to make spectacular advances, and so its prestige and authority remains very high even among an audience searching for gnosis (in contrast, it might be added, to scholarly research in the humanities, which seems to have no impact whatsoever!). There is a remarkable degree of consensus in modern and contemporary esotericism about the need for science and spirituality – rather than religion, which has mostly negative connotations – to 'come together' in some kind of higher unity. The continuous refrain is that the old positivist worldview based on Cartesian and Newtonian foundations is dead and buried, but radical avant-garde theories such as relativity theory, quantum mechanics or string theory (indeed, if truth be told, any scientific approach that is new and sexy) are not just perfectly compatible with belief in spiritual realities but may even provide a scientific foundation for it. The classic example of such science/spirituality parallellism is Fritjof Capra's *The Tao of Physics* (1975), followed by a continuous stream of popular books on similar themes ever since. All of this has very little to do with the hard sciences as they are actually practiced, but a lot with the widely perceived need for some kind of new *Naturphilosophie* that should close the gap between 'matter and meaning'.[5]

In sum, the general pattern is that pre-Enlightenment esotericism saw gnosis as pertaining to the highest level of truth, while respecting both faith and reason as not just legitimate, but necessary components within the total fabric of knowledge. In post-Enlightenment esotericism, on the other hand, that fabric seems to have broken apart. From being a dimension solidly integrated in the existing religious and scientific culture, esotericism now sets itself up as a *counter*culture, and thus gnosis tends to be presented as a 'spiritual' *alternative* against the misleading claims of faith (seen as mere blind belief in authority and tradition) and reason (seen as closed-minded rationalism and reductionism). This does not mean that representatives of contemporary esotericism see themselves as irrationalists: on the contrary, they usually hold that accepting the evidence for spiritual realities is much more reasonable than denying or ignoring it, and therefore gnosis and reason may well be united in a higher synthesis if only scientists will learn to abandon their bad reductionist habits. When it comes to the relation between gnosis and faith, on the other hand, such a future reunion is neither expected nor desired: unquestioning belief in tradition or authority is simply not appreciated. There is something deeply ironic about this constellation, for in actual fact, contemporary esotericists tend to believe with as much devotion in their *own* traditions and authorities (e.g. inspired scriptures 'channelled' from spiritual entities) as traditional Christians believe in theirs. Faith is by no means absent in the esoteric community today: on the contrary, it reigns almost universal. At the same time, a consistent appeal to reason – in the precise sense defined above! – is in fact quite rare. Critical questions about such matters as the historical or textual foundations of cherished esoteric tenets (where have they come from? can we trust these sources?) are seldom appreciated, and engagement in such lines of questioning tends to be rejected out of hand as a sign of spiritual immaturity or limited consciousness. It must be said that this resistance is based on a correct intuition: similar to the case of other religious contexts such as traditional Christianity, the practice of historical criticism is potentially more damaging to esoteric convictions than anything else, much more so than research from the natural sciences.[6]

Reason, then, may be applauded in theory even if it is rejected or curtailed in practice. Conversely, faith may well be rejected in theory even though it is embraced in practice. But gnosis is certainly central to all forms of esotericism, both on a theoretical and on a practical level, and in both the pre- and the post-Enlightenment phase. What, then, is meant by this mysterious 'third approach' to knowledge?

Alterations of consciousness

The topic of gnosis confronts us with a strange research lacuna: although countless scholars have tried to answer the question 'what is gnosticism?' serious attempts to answer the question 'what is gnosis?' are extremely scarce. One can fill a library with learned studies about the mythology, doctrinal contents, cultural context or historical sources and influence of the gnostic and hermetic currents of late antiquity; but about the nature of the salvational knowledge that was at the heart of these religious milieus, even deep specialists in the field rarely have much to tell us.[7] This silence on the part of scholarship seems to result directly from the claim of incommunicability, which, as argued above, is central to the very concept of gnosis. Gnostics and hermetists declare that they are unable to say in clear and straightforward language what it is that they have seen and discovered, and this seems to have discouraged most historians from trying to say anything more.

This is unfortunate, for in fact there is much that can be said. It is true that, already in the foundational sources of late antiquity, references to gnosis are puzzling to say the least: especially with regard to what is seen as the highest levels of absolute knowledge, we typically encounter stammering expressions of amazement and awe about a range of impressive spiritual experiences that are said to defy verbalization and can only be hinted at by very inadequate analogies. Here are some examples from the dialogue between Hermes and his pupil known as *The Ogdoad and the Ennead*:

> [pupil]: I see, yes, I see unspeakable depths. . . . I also see a Mind that moves the soul. By a holy ecstasy I see him that moves me. You give me power. I see myself! I want to speak! Fear holds me back! I have found the beginning of the Power above all Powers, and who does not himself have a beginning. I see a fountain bubbling with life. . . . I have seen. It is impossible to express this in words.[8]

It is only consistent – and not a sign of deliberate obscurantism – if those who claim to have had such experiences insist that, in order to really understand what they are talking about, one must have such experiences oneself. For example, the Islamic Platonist

Suhrawardī – a direct heir of these traditions from late antiquity[9] – tried to convince the Aristotelian philosophers of his time that since rational knowledge is restricted to the lower and secondary realm of 'darkness' that is our world, it cannot be expected to grasp the superior and primary reality of 'light' from which everything has been born:

> That there are dominating lights, that the Creator of all is a light, that the archetypes are among the dominating lights – the pure souls have often beheld this to be so when they have detached themselves from their bodily temples . . . Whose questions the truth of this – whoever is unconvinced by the proof – let him engage in mystical disciplines and service to those visionaries, that perchance he will, as one dazzled by the thunderbolt, see the light blazing in the Kingdom of Power and will witness the heavenly essences and lights that Hermes and Plato beheld.[10]

So what are those mystical disciplines by which one detaches oneself from one's 'bodily temple'? If one tries to read the hermetic writings with the gaze of an anthropologist or a psychologist, while paying close attention to textual detail, one will notice that they continuously refer to specific bodily conditions combined with unusual states of consciousness. For example, in *Corpus Hermeticum* X we read the following (emphasis added):

> In the moment when you have nothing to say about it, you will see it, for the knowledge [gnōsis] of it is divine silence and *suppression of all the senses.* One who has understood it can understand nothing else, nor can one who has looked on it look on anything else or hear of anything else, *nor can he move his body in any way. He stays still, all bodily senses and motions forgotten.*[11]

Many similar hints and references can be found throughout the Hermetic literature (beginning with the opening line of CH I). The fact is that an extremely rich technical vocabulary existed in antiquity for describing such conditions and distinguishing between their different modalities (e.g. *ekstasis, alloiōsis, kinesis, entheos, enthousiasmos, daimonismos, theiasmos, apoplexia, ekplexis, mania*),[12] and this suggests that the experiences and bodily phenomena that such terms tried to capture must have been common and well-known. In the Hermetic literature we find several idealized narratives of how exemplary seekers (Hermes Trismegistus, or his pupil Tat) are initiated step-by-step into successively more exalted states of consciousness: it all begins with philosophical instruction during a normal state (words), but then they move towards knowledge imparted in a trance-like condition by means of direct vision (images), next the pupil is purified of demonic forces and literally reborn in an invisible body endowed with 'higher senses', which allows him to perceive realities beyond the reach of our normal faculties of perception, and finally he moves towards the eight and the ninth sphere where he is granted the ecstatic vision of ultimate divine reality and participates in ineffable 'hymns sung in silence' (gnōsis).[13]

Unusual states of consciousness and their attending bodily conditions are well documented in anthropology and the history of religions, but there is little agreement about how to study them, or even about basic questions of terminology: for example, some scholars speak of 'trance', others of 'ecstasy', yet others of 'dissociation', or 'altered states of consciousness'. To make matters even more complicated, these terms have routinely been used in the wider context of theoretical frameworks that are riddled with ideological assumptions and moralistic agendas, notably 'mysticism', 'magic' and 'shamanism'.[14] Ever since the eighteenth century, reports of ecstatic experiences – particularly in combination with strange and erratic patterns of behaviour – have mostly been associated with the 'irrationality' of 'primitive savages', or romanticized in terms of a primordial 'archaic' mentality: they seemed to illustrate the threatening or desirable 'otherness' of peoples and cultures far removed from us in space and time. As a logical counterpart to such perspectives, the abundant amounts of textual evidence concerning similar states or conditions in our *own* history were largely overlooked, ignored, marginalized or distorted: they did not fit accepted pictures of what Western religion and intellectual culture was all about, or should be all about. All of this exemplifies the apologetic/polemical dynamics of Western identity politics (see Chapter Three), resulting in a highly confusing discourse that is often more concerned with imaginary theoretical constructs than empirical or historical evidence.

To steer clear of this theoretical and terminological minefield as much as possible, while staying close to up-to-date scholarship in cognitive studies, we will here adopt Imants Barušs's concept 'alterations of consciousness'.[15] The better-known terminology of 'altered states of consciousness' (ASCs) carries problematic implications. It suggests that there must be some kind of baseline state of consciousness, whereas the evidence suggests rather that our consciousness is never entirely stable to begin with, and should be thought of in terms of a continuum rather than sudden shifts from normal to altered states. Another problem is that the terminology was actively promoted by the countercultural generation of the 1960s and remains strongly associated with psychedelic agendas. As a result, psychoactive drugs still tend to dominate the popular perception of what ASCs are all about, whereas in fact they represent only one category within a much wider spectrum of consciousness-altering factors.

By speaking of 'alterations of consciousness' instead, one simply acknowledges the full breadth and diversity of experiences, or modes of experience, that are potentially available to human beings. Quite a lot is known about how the human psychophysiological organism reacts to specific kinds of sensory input, or restriction of input, and how increased or decreased mental focus or alertness, as well as alterations of body chemistry or neurophysiology, affect our modes of experience and perception.[16] In principle, awareness of these mechanisms should serve to 'normalize' the many accounts of extraordinary experiences that can be found in the source materials of Western esotericism. We are not dealing with weird anomalies that conflict with our knowledge of how reality really is, so that scholars should refuse to lend credence to them or dismiss them as irrational or crazy delusions. On the contrary, specific types of unusual experiences and bodily phenomena are simply to be expected if one exposes people to specific psychophysiological conditions, for instance in a ritual context or through applying spiritual techniques. Particularly if this happens in the framework of an esoteric worldview or symbolic system that has the capacity of integrating such experiences in a meaningful context,[17] such as the 'Platonic' or 'Alchemical' ones discussed in the previous chapter, it is not suprising if the experiences will end up confirming the worldview and make a deep impression on the individuals involved.

If we accept alterations of consciousness as normal phenomena that are known to occur under specific conditions, and have a certain degree of regularity and even predictability about them, we can begin to look with new eyes at the sources of Western esotericism. For instance, already in Plato's *Phaedrus* we find an influential description of four types of *mania* ('frenzy', or 'madness') through which the true philosopher gains access to the divine, but that look like madness to the common crowd: 'Standing aside from the busy doings of mankind, and drawing near to the divine, he is rebuked by the multitude as being deranged, for they do not know that he is full of God.'[18] One type of *mania* is believed to bestow the gift of prophecy, and the three others are linked by Plato to specific triggers or conditions: poetry/music, ritual practices of purification and love or erotic desire (*eros*) can affect our state of consciousness in such a manner that they detach our souls from normal consensus reality and bring it closer to the divine. Due to Plato's great authority, his discussion of *mania* (translated as *furor* in Latin) became particularly attractive for Italian Renaissance philosophers – from Marsilio Ficino to Giordano Bruno and many lesser authors – who needed a terminology to speak about 'higher or absolute' knowledge attained or received in a state of divine exaltation.[19] The term 'gnosis' itself was not yet available to them, because it was still linked too strongly with the image of despicable heresies, and even Hermetic enthusiasts still did not recognize the specific connotations of the Greek term *gnōsis*.[20] It is only after the discovery of the Nag Hammadi scriptures in the mid-twentieth century that the term as such has come to play a role in esoteric discourse.[21]

From a platonic perspective, it is natural to interpret alterations of consciousness as experiential symptoms of the soul's temporary liberation from its exile in the body (even modern accounts of 'near-death experiences' still fall within that pattern). From an alchemical perspective, on the other hand, it is more consistent to see them as signs, or anticipations, of interior rebirth. A classic example is Jacob Böhme, who describes how he had been 'wrestling with God' for enlightenment about the cause of evil and suffering in the world, until finally,

. . . my spirit [has] broken through the gates of hell and into the innermost birth of the Godhead, where it was received with love, the way a bridegroom embraces his dear bride. But this triumph in the spirit I cannot express by the written or spoken word; indeed it cannot be compared with anything but the birth of life in the midst of death, and with the resurrection of the dead. In this light, my spirit has right away seen through everything, and in all creatures, even in herbs and grass, it has seen God: who he is, how he is, and what his will is.[22]

This breakthrough experience to direct gnosis must have come after long periods of intense and concentrated prayer: presumably, this emotion-laden practice ended up triggering the enlightenment experience. During the later history of Christian theosophy, in spiritual groups and communities such as the Philadelphian Society or the Angelic Brethren, vivid religious visions under trance-like conditions seem to have become quite common, together with strange behaviour that caused doubts about the sanity of these ecstatics. All this was part of a more general and widespread phenomenon in heterodox spiritualist and Pietist contexts, usually known as 'Enthusiasm' (*Schwärmerei* in German), and notable for extreme forms of bodily expression such as fits, convulsions, trembling, swooning, shrieking or what looked like possession by alien spirits. The history of such 'ecstatic religion' can be traced through the eighteenth and nineteenth centuries and finally led to the phenomena of 'hysteria' studied by early clinical psychology.[23]

Alterations of consciousness thus seem to be an essential key to understanding the frequent claims of 'higher or absolute' knowledge common in Western esotericism. However, in all the representative examples referred to above (ancient Hermetism, the Platonic frenzies, Böhme's enlightenment experience), we are dealing with the typical pre-Enlightenment situation where gnosis is understood as the highest level in a hierarchy of knowledge that includes reason and faith. In the post-Enlightenment situation, where 'gnosis' is set in polemical opposition against its competitors, 'reason' and 'faith' (understood quite negatively as the dogmatic claims of established religion and science), it tends to absorb the claims of the latter as well. Gnosis ceases to be just the ineffable cherry on the cake, so to speak, and becomes the whole cake. Thus it is no longer the case that one believes in spiritual beings such as angels or demons on the basis of faith in traditional religion and authority: it is now because one claims to have seen and encountered them in person – or lends credence to reports from those who claim to have done so (that is to say, claims of gnosis become objects of faith, as discussed above). Personal experience is now presented as empirical proof, not just of the ineffable Absolute, but *even* of spiritual realities that lend themselves to being described and communicated at least to some extent. Spiritual techniques such as meditation, or a variety of other trance-inducing procedures, are now promoted as quasi-scientific tools for testing and verification. In short: alterations of consciousness (under whatever name they may appear) advance to a position where they are claimed to give empirical proof of anything – communicable or not – that exists on the normally invisible plane of spiritual reality.

The paradigmatic example of this new development is Emanuel Swedenborg, with his colourful and meticulously detailed descriptions of the environments and inhabitants of heaven and hell, based upon what he claimed was direct spiritual vision granted by God to him alone. The other main force of innovation in esotericism since the Enlightenment, mesmerism, was likewise grounded in alterations of consciousness – known as artificial somnambulism – but made them accessible to everybody by means of easily applicable techniques. Somnambulic patients gave descriptions of spectacular visionary journeys similar to Swedenborg's: they claimed to have travelled to the realm of spirits and angels, but also to other planets in the universe, as well as to the more 'interior' and increasingly abstract dimensions of reality as such.[24] As demonstrated in an exemplary study by the Austrian scholar Karl Baier,[25] the patterns of experiential religion that were established by somnambulism have become essential to many forms of later esotericism up to the present day. One may think, for example, of 'astral travel', past-life explorations, clairvoyant 'investigations' of the human aura or even such a thing as 'occult chemistry' in theosophical and other occultist contexts; reading the 'akasha chronicles' and other forms of clairvoyant exploration of the 'higher worlds' in the Anthroposophy of Rudolf Steiner; but also the New Age phenomenon known as 'channelling' spiritual entities that are believed to exist in 'other dimensions' of reality. In all these and countless comparable cases, the constant underlying claim is that by means of altering one's consciousness it is possible to gain access to higher, deeper or even absolute knowledge about the otherwise invisible levels of existence. The various forms of 'entheogenic esotericism' since the 1960s, which use psychoactive substances to gain access to invisible levels of reality,[26] are just one specific part of a much broader spectrum.

As already suggested above, the role that alterations of consciousness have played in esoteric contexts (not to mention other ones) has been overlooked to an extent that is truly surprising. This hiatus will not be filled unless scholars in the field are willing to combine expertise in such domains as anthropology, psychology, neurobiology or cognitive studies, with precise textual study of the source materials of Western esotericism. Once again, it is only on a radical interdisciplinary foundation that we can hope to begin understanding crucial aspects of its history within the wider context of Western culture as a whole.

CHAPTER SIX

Practice

Religion is much more than belief. It is not just about holding certain worldviews, asserting to specific doctrinal propositions, or making claims about the true nature of reality. To a very large extent, religion is something that one *does*. People pray, go to church, meditate, take confession, light candles, listen to sermons, sing psalms or hymns, partake of the eucharist, practice penitence, study scripture, fight against unbelievers, celebrate religious holidays, go on pilgrimages, and so on and so forth. Doing certain things, and refusing to do certain other things, belongs to the very essence of what it means to be religious – regardless of whether one is very clear in one's own mind about the exact nature of one's beliefs, or one's reasons for holding them. Since esotericism is an integral part of religion in Western culture – while participating in domains such as philosophy and science as well – no overview can be complete unless it pays attention to its practical dimensions next to its worldviews and ways of gaining knowledge. What do people involved in esotericism actually *do*? Perhaps no other aspect of the field is so difficult to study and understand, for a whole number of reasons.

● First, there is the problem of *sources*. Because beliefs and convictions are usually written down at some point, information about them is transmitted to posterity much more easily and with more precision than information about practices. There is often no great need to describe religious practices in detail: in most cases, religious practitioners learn by oral instruction, daily experience or observation and imitation of 'how things are done', and have little need of written reminders about what everybody already knows. As a result, we are usually better informed about religious or esoteric beliefs than about practices.

● Second, there is the problem of *verbal description*. Practices are inherently more difficult to describe than theories or doctrines. Even a simple ritual act is overdetermined with countless details that impinge on all the senses simultaneously, and hence even simple ceremonial procedures that are easily learned by observation and imitation are very difficult to capture in words. As a result, even if we have sources about esoteric practices, they tend to be incomplete.

● Third, there is the problem of *(crypto)Protestant bias*. Classical approaches to the study of religion have been heavily influenced by Protestant assumptions, including an implicit polemics against Roman Catholicism as crypto-'pagan' practice,[1] resulting in a structural over-emphasis on doctrine and belief and a corresponding lack of attention to ritual and other forms of practice.[2] As a result, most scholars concentrate on the history of esoteric ideas or the study of esoteric discourse, while giving only scant attention to esoteric practice: even when they are studying contemporary currents first-hand, they often still tend to avoid engaging the relevant practices directly.

● Finally, there is the problem of *method*. Even if the importance of practice is acknowledged in principle, it is not easy to decide on appropriate methodologies for studying it. Anthropologists have built up much experience with participant research, and have become increasingly interested in contemporary forms of esotericism, but attempts to apply anthropological approaches to historical materials remain a relative exception.

As a result of all these factors, our knowledge of esoteric practice is considerably less developed than that about the history of esoteric ideas or organizations. There are no general studies covering the domain as a whole, and therefore the present chapter cannot do more than make a first attempt at mapping largely uncharted territory. The wide range of practices in the context of Western esotericism will be discussed here under eight headings, according to their intended goals: (1) Control; (2) Knowledge; (3) Amplification; (4) Healing; (5) Progress; (6) Contact; (7) Unity; (8) Pleasure. While the precise meaning of these eight categories will be further explained below, it should be emphasized from the outset that they are not meant to be mutually exclusive. For example, some kinds of knowledge [2] may be pursued in an effort to gain control over one's environment [1] or heal oneself of illness [4], but they may also be seen as belonging to a certain stage of spiritual progress [5]. Again, by trying to contact spiritual entities such as angels or demons [6], one may hope to gain knowledge [2], control [1] or medical advice [4]. And so on.

Before discussing some examples for each of the eight categories, it is of crucial importance to get rid of one major obstacle in the study of practice: the concept of 'magic' as a universal reified category pitted against 'religion' and 'science'. The idea that some practices are inherently 'magical', as opposed to 'religious' or 'rational/scientific', was created by armchair anthropologists and sociologists during the latter half of the nineteenth and the first half of the twentieth century (notably the schools of Tylor/Frazer and Mauss/Durkheim). They did so against the background of Enlightenment polemics contra 'superstition' that were, in turn, heavily indebted to Protestant polemics contra 'paganism' and 'heresy'. As a result, the famous magic–religion–science triad is riddled with ethnocentric and moralistic prejudice, leading to systematic distortions and misperceptions if applied to the history of religion both in Europe and in other parts of the world. Perhaps no other category has been more harmful to an adequate understanding of esotericism and its role in Western culture, and to the study of religion in general.[3] Due to its enormous influence in popular and academic discourse, most of the practices discussed in this chapter still tend to be perceived almost automatically as somehow 'magical', with the equally automatic implication that they must be somehow different from 'genuine' religion (usually a code for 'Christianity', or even more precisely, 'Protestantism') – not to mention science. We cannot hope to understand the complexity of religion in Western culture unless we take leave of this magic–religion–science triad and its ideological underpinnings.

The term 'magic' has acquired a whole range of specific meanings in the course of European history, and these should obviously be recognized and studied; but the point is that the practices to which they refer all fall easily within the broader categories of 'religion' and 'science'. For example, there is no good reason to refer to the practice of invoking angels or demons otherwise than as a religious activity. Again, if medieval practitioners of *magia naturalis* are studying the hidden (occult) forces in nature, this makes them practitioners of early science or natural philosophy. Separating such practices from religion and science/rationality by placing them in a third category called 'magic' serves no other purpose than that of distinguishing 'true' from 'false': a normative and subjective pursuit that should have no place in historical and scholarly research. Note that this argument applies not just to traditional usage of the term 'magic' as a negative category for excluding the false or evil 'Other'. It applies also to later attempts at turning it into a positive category, for example, when 'the magical worldview' is embraced and promoted as a beautiful and enchanted alternative against religious dogmatism or materialist science.[4]

On the following pages we will discuss eight different categories of practice relevant to Western esotericism. The examples given for each category are meant to be merely illustrative and make no claim to completeness, but will hopefully give a sufficient impression of the complexity of the field.

Control

This first category concerns practices by which one tries to gain some kind of influence or power over reality. Many of them have their origin, quite simply, in the basic fact of human vulnerability: to a greater or lesser extent we are all at the mercy of external circumstances that might harm us in one way or another, and so it is quite natural for human beings to react by trying to find some ways of control in a threatening world. An obvious example is the widespread use of amulets or talismans for purposes such as personal protection against natural dangers like illness or death, but also against the malicious intentions (imagined or real) of other human beings.[5] For not only may people feel the need for protection against harm, they may also take the initiative and actually try to harm their enemies, by means of similar tools and techniques. Of course, inflicting harm or protecting oneself against it is only one possible motivation for engaging in practices of control: for example, throughout history, men and women have used charms or potions to make other men or women fall in love with them or consent to sex, but similar techniques have also been applied to such goals as the pursuit of power or wealth (e.g. finding hidden treasures). Explanations for why they should work range from natural causes, such as hidden or occult powers and cosmic forces of sympathy and antipathy, to assistance from supernatural agents such as demons or angels.

Most of these practices represent a kind of 'self-help religion' without deeper intellectual pretentions. In fact, popular techniques such as charms and incantations or the wearing of amulets and talismans are by no means restricted to pre-modern times but have continued into the very present. Ancient and medieval popular practices for purposes of control have their direct counterparts in a contemporary multi-million dollar industry, with countless how-to manuals (techniques and prescriptions for getting love, happiness, wealth, etc.) to crystals and gems that are for sale in New Age shops. On a higher intellectual level too, the search for control is certainly far from absent in the domains associated with Western esotericism (how could it be otherwise, since desire for power is among the most common human motivations?), but even among self-identified 'magicians' and occultists, it plays a less prominent role than one might perhaps expect. The case of Aleister Crowley may serve here as an example. At first sight, his famous definition of magic – 'the Science and Art of causing Change to occur in conformity with Will' – might seem like a perfect illustration of the occultist's lust for power over the outside world. But in fact, the wide range of 'magickal' practices with which Crowley experimented during his lifetime were not aimed at goals so naïve as the acquisition of Harry Potter-like abilities: rather, they were subservient to a spiritual goal of personal self-realization described as finding one's 'true Will' (more congenial to the category of 'progress', below). On the whole, the sensational topos of untrammelled lust for power and control has more to do with stereotypical imaginations of 'magic and the occult', pertaining to the level of mnemohistory, than with the actual historical sources of Western esotericism.

Knowledge

A second category concerns practices by which one tries to acquire information. For example, an important group of medieval texts known as the *ars notoria* focused on the acquisition of knowledge of the several liberal arts and related gifts, such as rhetorical skill, through artificial means. The texts ascribe their authority to the bible, where God grants king Solomon *sapientia*, *scientia* and *intelligencia* (II Chron. 1.9–12), and claim that such wisdom, knowledge and intelligence can in fact be acquired through complex rites, purifications, taking confession, the drawing of figures (*notae*) and prayers, orations or invocations including strings of obscure names or words (*verba ignota*).[6] Such practices were unsanctioned by the Church, and sometimes prosecuted, but the number of surviving manuscripts shows that they must have been remarkably popular. Their primary audience seems to have consisted of, in Richard Kieckhefer terms, a 'clerical underworld' of monks who had sufficient education to be able to produce, read and copy such texts.[7] The tradition continued right into the seventeenth century, and became of central importance to a major Renaissance figure such as John Dee. Dee's famous practices of angel conjuration served essentially the same goal of knowledge acquisition: the hope was that angelic entities could provide him with information in the domains of natural philosophy and science that could perhaps not be gained by other means. Dee's ritual practice was derived from the Solomonic tradition of *ars notoria*,[8] but also included the use of a 'scryer' (Edward Kelley) who claimed that the angels appeared to him in the surface of a black mirror while he himself was in a state of trance: an example of how alterations of consciousness in a ritual context may sometimes be used for claims of knowledge that belong to the domain of 'reason' rather than of 'gnosis' (see Chapter Five).

Attempts at acquiring knowledge – about the past, the present and particularly the future – are also central to a wide range of practices that are usually referred to as divination or the divinatory arts.[9] The concept is derived from Isidore of Sevilla's extremely influential *Etymologiae* (early seventh century), but is in fact quite vague. First, it includes practices that ascribe meaning to observable patterns or signs that sceptics might regard as meaningless: examples are the casting of lots, reading a person's destiny from his physiological appearance (physiognomy) or from the lines of his hand (chiromancy), interpreting patterns of apparently random figures according to standardized procedures (geomancy), reading tarot cards and even the interpretation of dreams (oniromancy). Then there are techniques that rely essentially on alterations of consciousness induced by gazing at a reflective surface: Edward Kelley's visions in the black mirror of John Dee are an example of mirror-divination (catoptromancy), but there is also the famous practice of gazing at crystal balls, which appears to have been popular even during the heyday of occultism in the nineteenth century.[10] Finally, there is astrology, here specifically as a technique for predicting events or deciding on the best moment for taking a course of action based on the future constellations of the heavenly bodies, but also as a way of acquiring knowledge about a person's psychological make-up by interpreting his birth horoscope. As an additional note, it should not be forgotten that to a large extent, practitioners of *magia naturalis*, alchemy and astrology were engaged in the business of empirical observation and practical experimentation in view of expanding their knowledge of the workings of nature. In such cases, we are dealing simply with early modern science or natural philosophy.

Amplification

This third category concerns practices by which one tries to expand or maximize the range or quality of one's natural powers and abilities. For example, Marsilio Ficino published a famous treatise titled *De vita coelitus comparanda*: 'how to bring one's life in harmony with the heavenly bodies'. Its central practices, usually ranged under the heading of 'astral magic', are concerned with maximizing one's exposure to the beneficial influences from the stars by using the (Plotinian) laws of sympathy and antipathy. Ficino's pupil Diacceto has left us a description of what such a practice would look like:

If for example [the practitioner] wishes to acquire solarian gifts, first he sees that the sun is ascending in Leo or Aries, on the day

and in the hour of the sun. Then, robed in a solarian mantle of
a solarian colour, such as gold, and crowned with a mitre of
laurel, on the altar, itself made of solarian material, he burns
myrrh and frankincense, the sun's own fumigations, having
strewn the ground with heliotrope and suchlike flowers. Also,
he has an image of the sun in gold or chrysolite or carbuncle,
that is, of the kind they think corresponds to each of the sun's
gifts. . . . Then, anointed with unguents made, under the
same celestial aspect, from saffron, balsam, yellow honey and
anything else of that kind . . . he sings the sun's own hymn . . .
He also uses a threefold harmony, of voice, of cithara, and of the
whole body, of the kind he has discovered belongs to the sun. . . .
To all these he adds what he believes to be the most important:
a strongly emotional disposition of the imagination, by which,
as with pregnant women, the spirit is stamped with this kind
of imprint, and flying out through the channels of the body,
especially through the eyes, ferments and solifies, like rennet,
the kindred power of the heavens.[11]

This unique description describes a ritual practice through which
all the bodily senses, as well as the imagination, are deliberately
saturated with the powers of 'sun'. The goal consists in improv-
ing one's spiritual, mental and bodily well-being. In fact, Ficino's
prescriptions can be read as a remarkable prefiguration of contemporary methods of 'holistic health' as practiced by centres such as
Esalen in California.

   While Ficino's astral magic sought to maximize a person's
'human potential' by manipulating environmental conditions in a
controlled ritual setting, on the assumption that all human beings
are continually exposed to astral influences, other practices are
essentially techniques for *training* one's abilities. For example,
Giordano Bruno was a recognized specialist of ancient and medieval mnemonics: a body of techniques for memory improvement
that require systematic training of one's faculty of visualization.[12]
The ability to visualize (which Bruno seems to have developed
to a stunning degree) became extremely important in the context
of occultist ritual magic towards the end of the nineteenth century. In the *Hermetic Order of the Golden Dawn*, visualization
is essential to such central practices as the 'Middle Pillar Ritual'
(where the practitioner aligns himself to the kabbalistic Tree of

Life, and visualizes how the 'universal energy' descends as iridiscent light through all the sefirot that correspond to his own body) or astral travel (where the practitioners must visualize a hexagram that then becomes a 'doorway' through which they enter another world of the reified imagination, where they encounter angels and other entities).[13] In her seminal study of contemporary occultism in London, the anthropologist Tanya Luhrmann shows that systematic training of one's ability to visualize is central to the process of 'interpretive drift' through which one gets initiated into such forms of ritual magic.[14] Visualization practices similar to the Middle Pillar Ritual (visualizing spiritual 'light' for purposes of healing, etc.) are almost omnipresent today in New Age manuals of all kinds.

It must be noted that modern and contemporary esotericists tend to distinguish between mere fantasy and true imagination: the latter is then considered to be a faculty of perception through which one gains access to realities that are ontologically real in some sense. From such a perspective (also implicit in Antoine Faivre's characteristic of 'imagination/mediation', very close to Henry Corbin's concept of *mundus imaginalis*),[15] by learning to expand one's powers of visualization one is in fact training one's ability to receive true visions of other worlds.

Healing

This fourth category concerns practices through which one tries to cure bodily or mental illnesses. Healing is an important dimension of Western esotericism, and obviously overlaps with all the previous categories: illness may be attributed to the malice of others and one may try to cure it by such means as charms or amulets (cat. 1), the search for knowledge is often focused on medical information (cat. 2) and Ficino's astral magic was intended especially for intellectuals whose health was threatened by the influence of Saturn and the occupational hazards of the scholarly life (cat. 3). Quite a number of central figures in the history of Western esotericism have been physicians, psychologists or psychiatrists. Ficino, the son of a physician, liked to see himself as a 'doctor of souls'; and one of the central figures of sixteenth-century esotericism, Paracelsus, was a major innovator in the history of medicine. In spite of the differences between their systems, which are considerable, they both saw physical healing in a larger context: we are subject to illness because we find ourselves in a fallen state (referred to as *cagastric* by Paracelsus), and the only radical and lasting method of healing therefore consists in spiritual regeneration and salvation of the soul. Logically, in a Christian context, this makes Christ the ultimate healer. Through large parts of its history, the practice of alchemy is inseparable from medical experimentation (obviously, the elixir of life would be the ultimate universal medicine); and in the wake of Paracelsus during the seventeenth century, such medical alchemy became known as iatrochemistry. It is not surprising that in the *Fama Fraternitatis* of 1614, the Rosicrucians are described as a brotherhood of healers whose mission is to cure the ill without asking for payment.

Franz Anton Mesmer's innovative practice of animal magnetism was conceived as a universal method of healing, but we have seen that through its later development as a method for inducing 'somnambulic' states, its range of applications was expanded so as to include not only the body but the mind as well. Yet another physician, Justinus Kerner, published a series of books about his somnambulic and/or demonically possessed patients, with detailed information about a whole range of treatment methods (including even such traditional ones as the use of amulets and talismans). This German mesmeric tradition in a Romantic context stands at the origin of what has been called 'the discovery of the unconscious' leading to the development of modern psychology and psychiatry.[16] Carl Gustav Jung's analytic psychology is strongly indebted to that lineage, to such an extent that this therapeutic practice might be seen as a sophisticated form of applied esotericism. Next to Jung, other new therapies, such as New Thought, were developed from mesmeric origins as well. These various traditions of alternative healing have flourished as never before in the various 'holistic health' movements since the 1960s: in this context we find all the traditional methods, from crystals and gems to various kinds of trance induction, from natural or herbal remedies to techniques for influencing the mind through positive 'affirmations' and from neo-mesmeric practices such a Reiki to entheogenic medicine such as ayahuasca.

Progress

This fifth category concerns practices by which one tries to advance or move forward in one's personal spiritual development. The idea of moving towards a spiritual goal is naturally expressed by the imagery of travel, as in John Bunyan's famous *Pilgrim's Progress* (1678) or somewhat earlier, and closer to the domain of esotericism, Jan Amos Comenius' *Labyrinth of the World and Paradise of the Heart* (1623 and several revisions). As for practices intended to accompany and stimulate such progress, one obviously thinks of structured regimes or cycles of prayer and meditation, whether in organizational contexts such as monasteries and spiritual communities or in individual pious lives. In this regard, at least in medieval and early modern Europe, esoteric practice can often hardly be distinguished from Christian practice more generally. For example, Christian theosophical communities such as the English Philadelphians or Johann Georg Gichtel's Angelic Brethren seem to have differed from other Christian groupings not so much in the nature of their devotional practices as in the contents of their beliefs and experiences.

Much more obvious examples of this category are to be found in the ceremonial practices of Freemasonry and many esoteric organizations inspired by masonic ritual. The idea of moving through a series of progressive initiations staged as ceremonial 'dramas' – Apprentice, Fellowcraft, Master, perhaps followed by a series of higher esoteric degrees – is based on the idea that masonic brethren are progressing in orderly fashion from a state of profane ignorance to ever more exalted states of spiritual insight. This is not supposed to be just a matter of acquiring new knowledge, but of polishing oneself as a human being so as to become more useful as a 'stone' in the great building of the world. The idea of initiation was derived, of course, from the model of ancient brotherhoods such as the Pythagoreans, and the notion that higher spiritual truths must be reserved for those who are worthy to receive them and capable of understanding them. All of this resonated with contemporary ideas of human progress by means of education, as in Jean-Jacques Rousseau's *Emile* (1762) or Gotthold Ephraim Lessing's *Education of the Human Race* (1780).

The ideal of 'working on oneself' and making spiritual progress by means of disciplined practice has become part and parcel of occultism since the nineteenth century, in tandem with the emergence of evolutionist thought: if human consciousness is supposed to evolve to ever higher levels, it obviously makes sense to try and evolve on the personal level as well. Such progress may be expressed symbolically through initiatory rituals, as in the masonic context, but may also be a persistent pursuit in one's individual life. It may simply entail the attempt to live 'consciously' and responsibly, by trying to discipline one's daily thoughts and actions in accordance with one's beliefs, but may also take the form of specific practices such as daily meditation or other spiritual techniques. Teachers such as Gurdjieff, Steiner and many others have presented fully developed systems for helping pupils 'advance on the path', and the number of training programmes now available through esoteric entrepreneurs is simply stunning.

Contact

This sixth category concerns practices by which one tries to get in touch with entities that are claimed to exist beyond the normal range of the senses. Throughout the history of Western esotericism, from antiquity to the present, this has been a quite dominant pursuit. It begins with ritual practices such as neoplatonic theurgy, which were directed at 'disposing the human mind to participation in the gods'.[17] During the middle ages, various kinds of 'ceremonial magic' were developed with the aim of contacting angels and demons. The demonic variety was often referred to as necromancy (or, in corrupted form, nigromancy) and entailed very much the kinds of practice that have survived in common horror stereotypes: magic circles, animal sacrifices, strange words and formulas, cryptic signs and characters, suffumigations, etc.[18] The angelic variety contains many elements of the *ars notoria* discussed above, and worked with lengthy prayers to God, Christ, the Holy Spirit and the various orders of angels, combined with fasting, confession and periods of silence and meditation (a particularly clear illustration of why the category 'magic' is problematic for practices that might as well be described as religious).[19] Medieval traditions of demonic and angelic 'magic' continued right into the Renaissance, as is evident from such cases as Johannes Trithemius or John Dee. It bears repeating that these famous 'big names' are merely the tip of an iceberg consisting of many lesser and mostly forgotten figures engaged in similar pursuits.

Although Emanuel Swedenborg claimed to be in daily contact with spirits and angels, he attributed this to divine grace; except for some inconclusive references to 'circular breathing', we know next to nothing about practices or techniques through which his visions may have been induced. Mesmeric techniques of trance induction, on the other hand, appeared to result in routine visions of spirits and other entities, as in the paradigmatic case of Justinus Kerner's *Seeress of Prevorst*; and the same methods were used during the vogue of spiritualism after 1850 to put mediums in a trance. With the spread of theosophy towards the end of the nineteenth century, and partly influenced by independent occultists such as Paschal Beverly Randolph, the possible range of 'entities' expanded far beyond the traditional categories of angels, demons or spirits of the departed. Randolph himself introduced a sevenfold hierarchy of 'Spirits/Angels, Seraphs, Arsaphs, Eons, Arsasaphs, Arch-Eons, and Antarphim',[20] but this was only the beginning: in later forms of occultism and esotericism, the range of possible entities that are there to be contacted seems to have become almost limitless. The countless trance mediums or 'channels' that are currently active in the New Age context assume that we are living in a multidimensional universe with unlimited forms of consciousness. In the words of one of them:

> There are many levels of guides, entities, energies, and beings in every octave of the universe. There are those who are lords, just like there were Grecian lords on one octave of reality, and ascended masters on another octave of reality. There are lords of the universe, the galactic frequencies. They are all there to pick and choose from in relation to your own attraction/repulsion mechanisms.[21]

One channel even claimed to be in contact with 'The Committee': a geometrical consciousness comprised of a line, a spiral and a multidimensional triangle![22] In this bewildering contemporary scene, the boundaries between esotericism and science fiction become blurred to an unprecedented degree: whatever one is able to imagine is not only real, but can be contacted and asked for information. The result is a never-ending flood of messages and spiritual teachings that are received through practices and techniques for altering one's consciousness (from meditation and visualization through breathing techniques to the occasional use of entheogenic substances).

Unity

This seventh category concerns practices by which one tries to overcome separation. In the context of Western esotericism, unification with God himself is perhaps a boundary case, depending on how far one is willing to expand the field so as to include practices commonly referred to as 'mysticism'. The comparison is tricky, first because the 'classical' mystics in fact report a much larger range of experiences than only unity with God, and secondly because the very category of mysticism has been theologized to such an extent that its study keeps being influenced (read: distorted) by the heavy influence of doctrinal ideologies about 'true' or 'false' mysticism.[23] Beyond the domain of the classical mystics, the search for perfect union with God seems to coincide essentially with a minority of metaphysical radicals (see Chapter Four). On the whole, the insistance in Christianity that the Creator is ultimately distinct from his creatures (requiring Christ as mediator) seems to have worked against a very prominent emphasis on unity with God as a goal to be achieved. And in more recent forms of esotericism, modern individualism and its values of autonomy and self-determinacy are hardly congenial to ideas of spiritual self-annihilation which suggest that the soul is like a drop of water that should aspire to be 'swallowed up' in the ocean of the One. On the other hand – and this adds further complications to the issue – the neurobiology of ecstatic states suggests strongly that experiences of union are in fact inherent to the phenomenology of altering consciousness,[24] so that one can expect them to be reported by practitioners regardless of whether their theology allows it.

Metaphysical radicals apart, the predominance of panentheist tendencies in Western esotericism (see Chapter Four) means that

God tends to be seen as invisibly present throughout the physical cosmos, and therefore the overcoming of separation means a sense of unity with that cosmos rather than an acosmic unity with the One. This implies not the annihilation of individuality, but an awareness of one's inseparable connectedness to the whole of reality. A classic exemple is the passage in *Corpus Hermeticum* XI: 20–2 that was already quoted in a previous chapter;[25] and in *Corpus Hermeticum* XIII we read how this very experience is induced, or made possible, by a deliberate practice of initiation that includes the exorcism of demonic entities out of the pupil's body.[26] Such exorcism is presented there, quite literally, as a techique for healing the pupil from the bodily 'tormentors' that are blocking his further spiritual progress (that is to say, it participates in our cat. 4 and cat. 5, and works by means of contact: cat. 6). Experiences very similar to the resulting unity with 'all that is' may be found scattered through the corpus of Western esotericism from antiquity to the present. For example, in 1982 the transpersonal psychologist Jean Houston published a course book of practical exercises for enhancing one's physical, mental and creative abilities (cat. 3), and sketched her own youthful experience of cosmic unity to give an impression of the kind of consciousness that might ultimately be attained:

> . . . suddenly the key turned and the door to the universe opened. I didn't see or hear anything unusual. There were no visions, no bursts of light. The world remained the same. And yet everything around me, including myself, moved into meaning. Everything . . . became part of a single Unity, a glorious symphonic resonance in which every part of the universe was a part of and illuminated every other part . . . Everything mattered. Nothing was alien or irrelevant or distant. The farthest star was right next door and the deepest mystery was clearly seen. It seemed to me as if I knew everything. It seemed to me as if I was everything.[27]

Pleasure

This eighth category concerns practices that are not a means to an end, but an end in themselves. In other words, one does not necessarily engage in them in order to attain something (power, knowledge, amplified abilities, healing, a next step in one's spiritual progress, contact with invisible entities or unification with God or the universe) but simply because one likes practicing. Again, there is of course a degree of overlap with some other categories: for example, increasing one's well-being or noticing that one begins to be capable of things one could not do before (cat. 3) is inherently pleasurable, as is the experience of cosmic unity that may come with successful practice of Jean Houston's techniques. But apart from all this, practice as such may be a pleasure in itself.

The primary example of this category is ritual. It is certainly true that Freemasons are supposed to make 'progress' through their successive initiations, but there can be no doubt that many of them simply take pleasure in the 'serious play' of dressing up in ceremonial costume and performing their well-defined roles in what amounts to a kind of elaborate ritual theatre. The pleasure may be further enhanced by the opportunity of a temporary escape from normal society and its constraints: an individual may well make social (apart from spiritual) progress within the organization of Freemasonry and become an important and generally respected person in the lodge, even if in general society he has a low-status job and lives a mostly boring life. For example, the illuminist Jean-Baptiste Willermoz earned his living as a simple silk merchant, but his talents as an organizer and administrator made him one of the most powerful and influential persons in the parallel universe of contemporary Freemasonry.[28]

What is true for the case of Freemasonry is also true, *mutatis mutandis*, for countless other esoteric organizations and their rituals systems that have emerged in modern and contemporary society. They all result in parallel universes with their own forms of sociability and collective rituals, within a more general context that has been called the 'cultic milieu'. For example, participants in contemporary Wicca or other forms of paganism often emphasize how good it feels to be among likeminded people, as part of a community that shares the same essential worldviews and values, and to perform rituals that express and further enhance that sense of community and common purpose. Singing or dancing together is a pleasure, and many modern witches will confirm that even invoking the gods can be fun.

As emphasized above, this discussion of practice according to eight basic categories is no more than a preliminary attempt at charting the enormous variety of 'things that are done' by people in the context of Western esotericism. The list of examples is far from complete, and more research is definitely needed. From a scholarly perspective, the significance of esoteric practices is that by studying them in more detail, we greatly expand and transform traditional understandings of what 'religion' in Western culture is all about. As emphasized above, many of these practices have been placed in an artificial special category called 'magic', in order to keep them apart from supposedly more serious or respectable forms of religious worship. If we discard that distinction as normative and misleading, we find that most of what used to be seen as magic may as well be described as religion (or, alternatively, as science or natural philosophy), whereas what used to be seen as religion appears to be full of the very same types of practice.

CHAPTER SEVEN

Modernization

In the three previous chapters we have been looking at general features or structural commonalities between the historical currents, ideas and practices that fall within the category of Western esotericism. In this chapter, we will emphasize the other side of the coin, by focusing on discontinuities and differences. Essentially, what this means is calling attention to *historicity*, against the tendency (not just among enthusiasts but also among many scholars) of presenting Western esotericism as some universal worldview or spiritual perspective based on universal 'enduring truths' that are somehow exempt from history and change. The importance of recognizing discontinuities and differences will be illustrated by the most dramatic example of profound and irreversible change and transformation known to us: the process usually referred to as 'modernization' (including closely related ones known by terms such as 'secularization' and 'disenchantment'). But before focusing on the modernization of Western esotericism as a phenomenon that is central to this field of research, we must first take a closer look at the problem of historicity as such. Why would it be seen as a problem at all? Why is it that even many self-described 'historians' of esotericism (and of religion generally) show such strong resistance against it?

History and truth

A first reason is quite straightforward: there is probably no greater threat to religious conviction than the practice of historiography. If we wish to assess the claims of believers, it is not the natural sciences that provide the 'hardest' evidence and the most incisive critical arguments, but the careful study of historical sources as practiced in the supposedly 'softer' disciplines of the humanities. Philosophical rationalists and natural scientists have come up with sophisticated strategies both for refuting *and* for protecting belief in the existence of God, and no end to such debates seems to be in sight. But the results of critical historiography and philological research are often final and conclusive, in the sense that they may render foundational beliefs of specific religious traditions impossible to maintain without sacrificing one's intellect.[1] This is true in such mainstream domains as biblical studies, and it is true for Western esotericism as well. The most famous case concerns the dating of the *Corpus Hermeticum*. Throughout the fifteenth and sixteenth centuries it was believed to be among the most ancient and hence most authoritative sources of ancient Egyptian wisdom, so that it attained a status close to 'holy scripture' among believers in the *prisca theologia* or *philosophia perennis*. But doubts about its antiquity began to be raised in the decades before 1600; and in 1614, the great philologist and textual critic Isaac Casaubon demonstrated conclusively, on the basis of strict linguistic evidence, that it could not have been written earlier than the first centuries of the Christian era.[2] This was a heavy blow to the intellectual credibility of Renaissance Hermetism, from which it never really recovered. It is a perfect example of how a grand mnemohistorical narrative, with all its far-reaching implications concerning universal meaning and enduring truth, can sometimes be destroyed by strict historiographical research concerned with tiny textual details.

A second reason for the resistance against historicity is more general in nature. In the context of Eranos, where the foundations were created for the religionist study of Western esotericism after World War II, the destructive (or, if one prefers, deconstructive) potentials of 'historicism' were recognized as a major issue, and this legacy has kept influencing researchers up to the present day. For scholars such as Eliade or Corbin, the problem was larger than just the fact that cherished esoteric beliefs may sometimes be undermined by historical findings. On a more fundamental level, they were concerned about the necessarily antithetical relation between history and (metaphysical or esoteric) Truth. They understood that the relativism ingrained in strict historical thinking would ultimately undermine *any* belief in a deeper meaning or a more universal dimension of human life.[3] Perhaps no scholar has perceived this as sharply, or experienced it so painfully, as Mircea Eliade. If anything that happens – the worst tragedies of history as well as its most inspiring victories – might as well have happened differently, or not at all, then history ceases to be a 'story' with some kind of plot that lends significance to the human quest. Instead, it seems to be reduced (in a famous formulation of John Masefield quoted by Arnold Toynbee) to ODTAA, 'One Damned Thing After Another': an apparently pointless series of random events without any deeper significance, goal or direction, beginning with nothing and leading nowhere, for no particular reason at all. Eliade referred to this nihilist implication as 'the terror of history', and spent his life fighting against it. After World War II, his anti-historicism made great sense to a generation that grew up in the shadow of such horrors as the holocaust, the nuclear bomb and the Vietnam war: history as such seemed like a nightmare from which they yearned to escape.

The problem that Eliade saw is a real one, and it is certainly not surprising that in the study of Western esotericism as well, one still encounters quite some scholars who would like to find some antidote against historical relativism. Many of them feel that there must be some kind of 'hidden hand', some kind of providential design, some kind of purpose and direction, some kind of higher guidance, some kind of 'plot' that gives meaning to the events of history – or at the very least, they want to believe in some kind of universal or even eternal esoteric truth, some stable and enduring 'Tradition' that has survived the vicissitudes of history and time, remaining as valid today as it was in ancient times. But understandable though such hopes and wishes may be, the sober truth – recognized implicitly by all the Eranos scholars – is that they find very little support (no support, really) in the evidence that historians can produce. Whether we like it or not, no hidden designs or more-than-human influences are required to account for how esoteric currents and ideas have emerged and developed through time: straightforward historical interpretations and explanations are more than sufficient. Moreover, as we will see, everything we know about these currents contradicts the essentially conservative idea of a universal Tradition or an unchanging esoteric worldview – with its hidden implication, which tends to be overlooked by its defenders, that individual creativity is of no real importance and originality should be discouraged. On the contrary, what we see in the history of Western esotericism is what we see elsewhere too: continuous and mostly unpredictable change, transformation, renewal and creative invention, carried by human beings like ourselves, who keep revising and reformulating their ideas in response to the challenges of their respective intellectual, religious, cultural and social environments. If there is any divine or sacred presence at work in this history, then it does an excellent job of hiding itself.

In sum, the relativist and potentially nihilist implications of critical historiography are real enough, and it is easy to understand or sympathize with the emotional resistance against them. But respect for evidence and the force of arguments – in short, for demonstrable truth – is the *sine qua non* of scholarship, and must prevail whether or not one likes the conclusions to which it leads. Moreover, if it is true that historicity comes at a price, its denial comes at a price as well. Critical historiography and philological research are not just instruments of destruction but have been potent forces of emancipation and liberation from established power and blind authority: we owe them much of our freedom from theological dogmatism and ecclesiastical control. Moreover, it is only by being open to the evidence for continuous change and innovation in Western esotericism that we can even begin to appreciate the creativity and originality of its best representatives. Whether we see them as genuinely inspired or deluded (or both), they had at least the courage – sometimes at great personal costs, from public ridicule to death – to think for themselves and follow their own lights.

In the rest of this chapter we will not try to revisit all the historical transformations that Western esotericism has gone through, because most of them should already be evident from the overviews in Chapters Two and Three. We began our story in the 'pagan' Hellenistic culture of late antiquity, but its complicated further development resulted from the successive impacts of a long series of *new* events. A very incomplete list will at least include the emergence of Christianity; the theological campaign against pagan idolatry and other forms of 'superstition'; the flourishing of the natural sciences in medieval Islam; philosophical innovations such as the rise of nominalism; political factors such as Islamic expansion or the expulsion of the Jews from Spain; new cultural and intellectual developments such as Italian humanism; the dawn of printing; the advent of the Reformation and Protestant sectarianism; the exploration of the world and encounter with non-Western cultures; radical new philosophies such as Spinozism, Cartesianism or Kantianism; the so-called Scientific Revolution (or revolutions); the Enlightenment and the French Revolution; the separation of church and state, leading to a 'religious supermarket'; industrialization and the expansion of technology; Romanticism in literature, art, philosophy and religion; colonialism and the discovery of oriental cultures and religions; the rise of historical consciousness and evolutionist philosophies; the emancipation of women; the emergence of academic psychology; the study of 'primitive' cultures by yet another new discipline, anthropology; the horrors of antisemitism and political totalitarianism; the ascendency of neoliberal market capitalism and globalization and most recently, the rise of information technology, virtual realities and the internet. Literally each of these innovations (and it bears repeating that the list is not complete!) has had a radical impact on Western esotericism, causing it to take on new forms and directions that would have been impossible to predict beforehand. This fact alone, even without any additional arguments, should be sufficient to discard any idea of a universal esotericism or an unchanging Tradition.

But even if change and transformation have always been the rule, some revolutions are more radical than others. As we already saw in Chapter One, the complicated process of 'modernization' (which encompasses a whole series of transformations listed above) is generally highlighted, implicitly or explicitly, as the most decisive of all. This is why some scholars have defined 'esotericism' as the prototype of pre-modern enchantment, others see it as an essentially modern phenomenon, while yet others seem to see in it a way to escape from the modern world to a timeless reality of the spirit. In the rest of this chapter, we will take a closer look at the historical processes of transformation by which pre- and early modern forms of esotericism have given way to modern and even postmodern ones.

Correspondences and causality

A first transformation is concerned with ideas about how the world or the universe is functioning. In pre-Enlightenment periods, we can distinguish between three different perspectives. The first one looks at reality as a grand, harmonious and organic whole in which all the parts correspond to one another *without* a need for intermediary links or chains of causality. The classic reference occurs in Plotinus:

> This whole universe is in a state of sympathy, and is like one living creature; and what is far away is yet close – just like, in a living creature, a nail or horn or finger or another limb that does not lie immediately next to it. What is at distance is affected, although nothing is felt by what lies in between; for things that are similar do not lie next to one another but are separated by things that are different, and yet they are subject to the same influences due to their similarity, and therefore something that is done by a part that does not lie next to it must necessarily reach what is distant. For it is all one living thing and part of one unity, and no distance is so great that things would not still be close enough to be in mutual sympathy as part of this one living being.[4]

The notion that even the remotest parts of the universe can correspond to one another through a kind of secret sympathy, based on their inherent similarity or likeness (*similitudo*), is extremely widespread and has been highlighted by Antoine Faivre as the first intrinsic characteristic of Western esotericism. This notion of 'correspondences' is inseparable from similar concepts discussed under rubrics such as 'analogical thinking', 'correlative thinking', '*ressemblance*', 'signatures', 'participation' or 'synchronicity'.[5] It has often been seen as essential to the worldview of the Renaissance,[6] but critics of 'the occult' have highlighted it as the essence of magical superstition.[7]

In many Renaissance authors, beginning with Ficino, a holistic worldview of correspondences stands next to a second perspective. This one assumes that different parts of the universe do in fact influence one another, even at great distances, by what might conveniently be called 'occult causality'.[8] A classic reference in this case is the medieval Islamic philosopher al-Kindi and his doctrine that all things in the universe send out invisible 'rays'.[9] Ficino used al-Kindi's work to explain astral influences, but also postulated the existence of a universal *spiritus*: a kind of subtle substance or invisible fluid that was believed to permeate the whole of the cosmos. Described as 'a very tenuous body, as if now it were soul and not body, and now body and not soul',[10] it was the ideal medium for explaining causal connections of all kinds (whether involving bodies, souls or both) that could not be explained by visible or material chains of causality. Which brings us to the third perspective that will be referred to here as 'instrumental causality'. In its most basic form this is the familiar 'mechanical' or billiard-ball model by which a thing influences another by means of demonstrable and predictable chains of material cause and effect. With the development of science from its original Newtonian foundations to new perspectives such as relativity theory, quantum mechanics or string theory, this model has obviously been developed in extremely sophisticated new directions, but without sacrificing the essential assumption: it must be possible to explain everything that happens in the world as resulting from material causes, in terms of natural laws that function with strict regularity, and in principle it must be possible for the human mind to discover those laws and principles.

Because all three models had deep roots in classical and traditional sources, they were widely referred to by intellectuals before the eighteenth century. Often they were mixed in confusing ways, as the same author tried to explain the world partly in terms of instrumental or occult causality and partly in terms of correspondences. But as the Scientific Revolution was gathering steam, the lines of opposition hardened: correspondences and occult causalities were fighting a losing battle, and scientists with religious commitments began to realize that the disappearance of 'mysterious and incalculable forces' (as formulated in Max Weber's famous thesis of disenchantment[11]) could seriously threaten the belief in any kind of spiritual or divine agency in the world. The exemplary example is Emanuel Swedenborg. His highly influential theory of correspondences is very different from the Plotinian model: it functioned no longer as an alternative to instrumental causality, but, on the contrary, as a way of preserving it without having to pay the price of sacrificing the belief in a spiritual reality. This was accomplished by presenting the spiritual world as wholly separate from, *and yet* in perfect sync with, a material world that answered to the laws of post-Cartesian physics. No occult forces or influences connect this spiritual world with its material counterpart, but everything in the latter reflects or corresponds to the former because that is how God has ordained it. Swedenborg's worldview has often been presented as a continuation of the kabbalah or other forms of pre-modern esotericism, but this is a mistake;[12] on the contrary, it was a creative new departure based upon the best science of his day and age, and an excellent example of esoteric innovation. And it proved highly influential. From the nineteenth century on, the fundamental notion of two 'separate-yet-connected planes' of reality became a bedrock assumption of spiritualism and occultism, because (as was already the case in Swedenborg) it protected spiritual realities from scientific falsification and disenchantment.[13] We are not dealing here with the holistic universe of Plotinian or Renaissance correspondences, but with an essentially dualistic concept (modelled partly on Cartesian dualism but partly also on Kant's distinction between a noumenal and a phenomenal world).

As the model of instrumental causality was widely perceived as superior from the eighteenth century on, culminating in an intellectual climate often referred to as positivism, traditional models of occult causality or correspondences have come to be perceived as unscientific and superstitious. It must be noted, however, that one should be cautious about the nature of this transformation, particularly with respect to occult causality. Contrary to common assumptions, the new science did not so much reject traditional notions of *qualitates occultae* (occult qualities) as such, but the assumption that they were 'hidden' and unknowable by definition: the ambition was to take them out of the 'asylum of ignorance', as famously formulated by Julius Caesar Scaliger, and make them into genuine objects of scientific research.[14] Eventually, traditional examples of occult forces such as gravity, magnetism or electrostatic phenomena have become normal parts of scientific theory and technological practice: any moment we use our cell phone or watch TV, we are making connections by means of an invisible medium – electromagnetic waves – that would most definitely have been seen as occult by pre-Enlightenment generations. Next to these successful cases, other claims of occult causality have taken a long time to lose their scientific prestige. Notably this is true of all kinds of 'ether' theories, which remained part of mainstream scientific theorizing until far into the twentieth century. Many of them were retrospectively written out of the history books, and have ended up in the wastebasket of 'the occult' only after theories such as relativity and quantum mechanics had emerged victorious.[15] But before that happened, the fact that they could serve as a permeable medium between spirit and matter made it possible for them to mediate between religious and scientific concerns as well.

Yet other claims of occult causality, for instance, thought transference or healing at distance, have never managed to gain a serious foothold in mainstream science, and were widely delegated to the domain of the non-scientific occult and dismissed as superstition. The argument was (and remains) that – in contrast to such hidden forces as magnetism or electricity – they could not satisfy the basic requirement of experimental reproducibility and that neither their actual occurrence nor the existence of a relevant causal medium could be conclusively demonstrated. This mainstream perception evoked a reaction already during the nineteenth century, known as psychical research or parapsychology. Some of its representatives have tried to demonstrate that such 'anomalous' phenomena do in fact occur and can be explained in terms of known mechanisms of instrumental causality. Others acknowledge that either the phenomena, or the mechanisms, or both, are difficult or impossible to prove conclusively in those terms, but argue that they are realities nevertheless, which therefore require us to expand our current scientific models. For instance, in a more recent period the English biologist Rupert Sheldrake developed a theory called 'morphic resonance' that postulates the existence of 'morphic fields' and clearly falls under the heading of occult causality.[16] And perhaps the most famous case of a revival of the correspondences model, now defended with partial reference to advanced quantum mechanics, is the theory of synchronicity developed by Carl Gustav Jung in collaboration with the Nobel Prize winning physicist Wolfgang Pauli.[17]

With respect to the basic argument of this chapter – the importance of historical discontinuity and creative innovation in the history of Western esotericism – the point that must be emphasized is that the dominance of instrumental causality since the Enlightenment has resulted in multiple attempts at avoiding its materialist and reductionist implications by developing some new kind of *Naturphilosophie*.[18] The social and discursive authority of modern science is so overwhelming that, whether in esoteric contexts or elsewhere, it almost never gets rejected as such: rather than radical projects of returning to a pre-modern worldview, we therefore encounter complicated attempts at negotiating some kind of compromise between the conflicting options of instrumental causality, occult causality and correspondences (not to mention the spontaneous activity attributed to concepts such as the soul or a 'vital force'). These projects are driven by a sense of religious or spiritual urgency, because it is felt that failure to find a solution will condemn us to a thoroughly disenchanted world; but the very difficulty of finding a solution without sacrificing one's intellect has continued to be an incentive for creativity and conceptual innovation. Much of what has happened in Western esotericism after the Enlightenment is impossible to understand unless one takes these conceptual battles into account.

The expanding horizon of religion

A second crucial transformation concerns the religious and cultural horizon of Western esotericism. Roughly until the eighteenth century, all forms of Western esotericism were solidly Christian in their religious assumptions: the widespread belief in an ancient wisdom handed down from such Oriental sages as the Egyptian Hermes or the Persian Zoroaster was not seen as implying a superiority of paganism but, on the contrary, rested on the assumption that these gentile sources had been inspired by the divine *Logos* and were therefore in profound harmony with Christian doctrine.[19] Some vague references to the Indian Brahmans notwithstanding, the horizon of Platonic Orientalism did not go beyond what we now see as the Middle East. When missionaries and other travellers encountered the religious practices of far-away continents, whether Africa, Asia or the New World, they typically saw them as nothing more than idolatry and pagan error, and certainly not as serious alternatives to the Christian revelation.

This began to change as the Christian churches started to lose more and more of their power and authority during the eighteenth century, while Western scholars became curious about the vast religious literature beyond the borders of the Old World. The revolution that followed has been described quite correctly as a 'new Renaissance'. During the Renaissance of fifteenth-century Italy, humanists had been exploring the sources of Greek and Roman antiquity, including the newly available manuscripts pertaining to 'Platonic Orientalism;' but now, as a new wave of ancient texts became available, scholars began to move the sources of 'Oriental wisdom' much further eastward. This began with the pioneering work of Abraham Hyacinthe Anquetil-Duperron, who went to India in the 1750s and came back with a great number of Avestan, middle-Persian and Sanskrit manuscripts. As formulated by Raymond Schwab in his standard work *The Oriental Renaissance*,

> [W]ith his translation of the Upanishads, [Anquetil] dug an isthmus between the hemispheres of the human spirit and liberated the old humanism from the Mediterranean Basin. . . . Before him, Latin, Greek, Jewish, and Arab writers were the sole sources of knowledge about the distant past of the planet. The Bible appeared as an isolated rock, a meteorite. People believed that text contained the whole universe; hardly anyone seemed to imagine the immensity of the uncharted territories. . . . He cast a vision of countless and ancient civilizations, an enormous mass of literatures into our schools, which to this day arrogantly keep the door shut behind the narrow legacy of the Greek-Latin Renaissance. . . .[20]

During the course of the nineteenth century, the comparative study of religions developed into a new academic discipline closely interwoven with the study of ancient and oriental languages, leading to the widely accepted paradigm of a common 'Indo-European' cultural and linguistic matrix that could be brought to light with the technical methods of comparative philology.[21]

The new wave of fascination with the ancient religions of the Far East was fed by Enlightenment concerns and agendas as well as by Romantic ones. Rationalist sceptics and anti-Christian libertines developed radical theories of myth and symbolism, suggesting that religion in all its forms, including Christianity, had not originated in a divine revelation but had emerged from primitive rituals directed towards the powers of nature, notably the sun ('solar worship'), and the sexual organs ('phallicism'). They argued that the remnants of solar and sexual symbolism could still be discovered everywhere, in Christianity as well as in the religions of India.[22] Romantics, for their part, were impressed by the rich mythology and symbolism of the Oriental religions and by their mystical aspirations. In the wake of Friedrich Schlegel's *Über die Sprache und Weisheit der Indier* (1808), Hinduism came to be perceived in an ideal light, as a noble tradition of great antiquity based upon a universal spiritual wisdom from which Westerners had much to learn. Buddhism took longer to be discovered by Europeans: at mid-century it was still perceived as a 'gloomy religion of negation',[23] but in the wake of the popular success of Sir Edwin Arnold's *The Light of Asia* (1879) and Theosophical ideas of 'esoteric Buddhism' it became a source of inspiration for Europeans and Americans.

This enormous expansion of comparative studies in religion, mythology and ancient languages during the nineteenth century, and the growth of popular fascination with the religions of the Far East, all took place in a political and economic context dominated by European imperialism and colonialism. In the complex dialectics of the Orientalist imagination (famously placed on the agenda by Edward Said), Western audiences defined their own identity with implicit or explicit reference to the 'Otherness' of the East. Negative stereotypes such as the supposed passivity or lasciviousness of the 'oriental mind' could thus be used to suggest the superiority of European attitudes and values; but the latter could be *criticized* in Orientalist terms as well, notably by presenting a country like India as the home of ageless Wisdom and contrasting it to the narrowmindedness of Christian orthodoxy and its obsession with sin, or the shallowness of modern notions of secular progress.

All these elements – the comparative study of religions, the Indo-European model, mythographic theories of phallicism and solar worship, India as the home of ancient wisdom and a superior spirituality, and the dialectics of Orientalism – are of fundamental importance if one wishes to understand the most influential esoteric movement of the nineteenth century, modern Theosophy.[24] Far from being a 'revival of ancient wisdom',[25] as its followers like to claim, it was a radically new synthesis grounded in concerns that are typical of the nineteenth century. Not least by adopting and integrating terms and concepts from Indian religions that had never been a part of Western esotericism before – the notion of karma is a particularly clear example – Theosophy became a force of religious innovation that created essential foundations for much of twentieth-century esotericism. But although it may be the most obvious example of 'orientalization' in this field, it was by no means the only one. In the American context, for example, Transcendentalism became a crucial mediator between Eastern spiritualities and later developments in Western esotericism.[26] Without Theosophy and the 'Metaphysical Religion' of the United States,[27] with its profound debt to Transcendentalist culture, it would be hard to imagine the 'turn towards the East' of the 1960s and the New Age movement that emerged from it.

India may have been particularly popular, but esoteric audiences since the twentieth century have adopted, integrated and (not in the least place!) reinterpreted and repackaged selected elements from other Asian traditions as well. Consider, for example, the popular vogue of the Chinese I Ching, pioneered by Carl Gustav Jung, or of Japanese Zen Buddhism inspired by D. T. Suzuki (and notice that both Jung and Suzuki belonged to the sphere of Eranos, that crucial academic cauldron from which so much of post-war esotericism has taken its cue). Moreover, the process of orientalization in Western esotericism has been followed by one of globalization, as all other parts of the world became potential sources of esoteric inspiration. Interestingly, the impact of African religions on Western esotericism has remained very limited, and one cannot help thinking that this is related to issues of race: participants in the 'cultic milieu' of post-war esotericism have always been, and still remain, overwhelmingly white. In contrast, Native American spirituality and Latin American 'shamanism' have become significant factors leading to esoteric innovation since the 1960s. Both have been seen as 'wisdom traditions' based on deep knowledge of the mysteries of nature, and moreover, both have been crucial to yet another innovative current that may be referred to as 'entheogenic esotericism':[28] the use of natural psychoactive substances (notably peyote, ayahuasca, psilocybin mushrooms) as avenues towards 'higher knowledge' in the context of 'neo-shamanic' mixtures between Western esoteric and indigenous traditions.

Finally, having expanded its horizon from Christian Europe to the mystical East and eventually the rest of the globe, the esoteric imagination has begun casting its gaze even farther away. In earlier phases, the mythical appeal of the Orient reflected a concern with 'orientation':[29] the very meaning of this word points to a need to situate oneself, or define one's position, with reference to some centre or origin (sacred or spiritual in this case) that is 'Other' with respect to oneself. For Europeans this was the East, hence the term orientation. But as all other parts of the globe have been mapped and explored, inevitably losing much of their mystery in the process, even the generation familiar with Google Earth may still feel a need to find a centre of spiritual otherness so as to avoid 'disorientation'. This makes it entirely logical that in much of contemporary esoteric speculation, partly influenced by Science Fiction, the ultimate source of wisdom now tends to be located in some physical location elsewhere in the universe, with Sirius and the Pleiades as popular favourites. Esotericism has definitely come a long way!

Evolution

A third crucial transformation has to do with conceptualizations of time and history in relation to the destiny of humanity. The notion of spiritual progress by means of evolution is extremely familiar to us today, but before the eighteenth century it did not yet exist. On the contrary, as far as esotericism is concerned, the dominant model of the *prisca theologia* implied a process of degeneration from an original state of perfect truth and wisdom, whereas the conception of *philosophia perennis* emphasized that nothing new was to be expected because the truth had always been available and always would be. In Chapter Four, it has been suggested that the emergence of evolution as a spiritual process that takes place in and through history may have been indebted to the 'alchemical paradigm',[30] which had reached the Romantic and German Idealist philosophers through popular currents such as Christian theosophy. An alternative but not necessarily conflicting account of the birth of evolutionism connects it, rather, with the 'platonic paradigm'. In his classic study about the platonic 'Great Chain of Being', already quoted above, Arthur Lovejoy emphasized the fundamental traditional notion of *plenitude*: the assumption that everything that can possibly exist must in fact exist, somewhere in the grand universal hierarchy of existence. In the eighteenth century, Lovejoy explains, this great chain of being began to be understood in terms of temporality: 'The *plenum formarum* [fullness of forms] came to be conceived by some, not as the inventory but as the program of nature, which is being carried out gradually and exceedingly slowly in the cosmic history'.[31] Hence the static model of universal harmony and cosmic order gave way to a dynamic model of gradual unfoldment. Eventually, this led to a doctrine of evolutionary development, which says that new and higher phenomena emerge organically and in orderly fashion from lower ones, guided by some kind of hidden teleological or providential design.

Such evolutionary models were developed by the German Idealists, notably Schelling and Hegel, and were adopted and popularized by Romantic poets and philosophers in many other countries, such as France, England and America.[32] For popular audiences who were worried about the 'meaning of history' (particularly since the Christian story of fall and redemption was losing credibility), and who were getting interested in ideas of spiritual development, Darwin's theory of biological evolution could easily be integrated within such a larger framework: the new super-story said that life had been unfolding over great stretches of time in an upward movement from the lowest and simplest organisms to the birth of the human species, which in turn became the spearhead of further evolution that had moved from the primitive modes of consciousness exemplified by the 'lower races' to the highly civilized consciousness of modern Western man. Within the larger colonialist framework referred to in the previous section, anthropological theories about 'primitive cultures' seemed to give further support to such visions: hence the founder of anthropology Edward Burnett Tylor, and even more clearly James G. Frazer in his enormously popular *Golden Bough* (1900), described the progress of human civilization in terms of an upward development from 'magic' through 'religion' to modern 'science' (see above, pp. 104–5). All these theories of evolution were based on the confident and obviously ethnocentric assumption that the white middle and upper classes of modern Western civilization, and their intellectual and cultural accomplishments, stood at the pinnacle of the evolutionary process. The question was where we were heading next. As is well known, Hegel thought that the historical process through which the Spirit came to self-realization had attained its highest stage in his own philosophy; but many thinkers after him have envisioned a continuing evolutionary process reaching far into the future, through which human consciousness will develop ever higher and more exalted, god-like abilities and superior levels of spiritual understanding.

German Romantic models of evolution were closely linked to contemporary notions of human development and progress such as Gotthold Ephraim Lessing's famous *Education of the Human Race* (1777–80): here history is the story of how humanity grows up from childhood to maturity under the providential guidance of God (in the role of the Father, of course). And like another highly influential eighteenth-century author, Johann Gottfried Herder, they tended to describe history in terms of the achievements of successive 'peoples'. All these tendencies came together in the work of a Tyrolean physician and mesmerist, Joseph Ennemoser: his large *Geschichte der Magie* (History of Magic, 1844) is a model example of esoteric evolutionist historiography in the German Romantic tradition.[33] It is also among the strongest influences on H. P. Blavatsky, whose system of Theosophy is certainly the central nineteenth-century example not just of 'orientalization' and the impact of comparative religion on esotericism (see previous section), but of the popular impact of evolutionism as well. Blavatsky developed an ambitious evolutionary cosmology, full of references to contemporary scientific theorizing, built around the concept of seven 'root races' (each subdivided into seven subraces) that represent the successive stages of humanity's spiritual advancement on earth. She claimed, wholly in line with Ennemoser's emphasis on the 'Germanic people', that we had now progressed up to the fifth 'Teutonic' subrace of the fifth 'Aryan' root race. Much of the traditional 'orientalist' narrative of ancient wisdom was integrated by Blavatsky within the history of this fifth rootrace: the previous subraces had been the 'Hindu', 'Arabian', 'Persian' and 'Celtic', and the next 'Australo-American' subrace would begin to take over in the twenty-first century.

Finally, evolutionist visions of the history of humanity are closely linked, in the context of modern and contemporary esotericism, to ideas about spiritual progress after death. Already Gotthold Ephraim Lessing ended his book on the education of the human race (see above) with references to reincarnation, to the surprise of many readers, but at the time this was still an exception. References to the transmigration of souls can be found in just a few authors before the eighteenth century, such as Giordano Bruno or Franciscus Mercurius van Helmont (who picked it up from Pythagorean or kabbalistic sources); but even far into the nineteenth century, it remained a controversial topic even in esoteric circles.[34] Blavatsky only came out clearly in favour of reincarnation in her second great book, *The Secret Doctrine* (1888), after her trip to India; and her eventual defence of it is inseparable from her evolutionist beliefs and her discovery of karma as a universal and impersonal 'natural law' of moral retribution that should replace Christian notions of sin and punishment.[35] From a notion unconnected to esotericism, during the twentieth century reincarnation has become one of the most universal and widespread beliefs in esoteric milieus. In the context of the New Age movement since the 1960s, it has developed into a core assumption of increasingly science-fictionlike cosmologies, in which the human soul moves through an infinite number of cosmic dimensions as part of a never-ending process of spiritual evolution that ultimately leads us far beyond the boundaries of the planet and the solar system and into the infinite future. If the movement of orientalization, globalization and ultimately 'universalization' described in the previous section has expanded the spatial range of esotericism to its maximum, the emergence of evolutionism has done the same for its horizon in time.

The impact of psychology

A fourth major transformation is concerned with the human mind and its relation to God or the supernatural. That human beings have an inborn capacity of knowing the divine is a core belief in Western esotericism; and we have seen that already the Hermetic writings contain some radical pantheistic suggestions, implying that if the human mind is in God, God himself is in the human mind.[36] Nevertheless, the dominant tendency has been towards a hierarchical concept based on the ontological primacy and superiority of God, with human souls as sparks that have come from the great divine light and are longing to return to their original source. As Platonic and Hermetic concepts were integrated in Christian culture, the hierarchical relation between God and the human soul was further emphasized. The overwhelming assumption has been that not only God, but other spiritual intelligences such as angels or demons as well, are independent entities that exist outside of our own mind.

The development of psychology during the nineteenth century has had the effect of questioning that assumption, even to the point of reversing the hierarchy and suggesting that the fundamental reality is not God but the human soul or mind. This trend is not specific to psychologization alone, but is closely linked to more general philosophical and theological tendencies of questioning traditional Christian metaphysics and exposing the basic dynamics of religious projection. Ludwig Feuerbach's *Das Wesen des Christentums* (The Essence of Christianity, 1841) played a crucial role in that regard, with his basic procedure of 'reversal' or 'inversion', culminating in the radical statement that 'Man made God in his own image' instead of the reverse.[37] Feuerbach became a major influence on the great 'masters of suspicion' (Marx, Nietzsche and Freud), and the once so radical idea that gods and other spiritual realities might be no more than psychological projections of our own hopes and wishes has become a popular commonplace in society today.

These developments, too, have had a very strong impact on how Western esotericism developed during the nineteenth and twentieth centuries. Starting with Mesmerism and somnambulism, the human mind and its hidden potentials became a predominant focus of esoteric practice, speculation and empirical research. But as modern psychology and psychiatry developed out of these very same foundations, the inevitable result was a strong tension between traditional esoteric worldviews and their belief in a superior spiritual reality, on the one hand, and the reductionist implications of 'projection' and 'reversal/inversion' mechanisms, on the other. In the earlier phases of Romantic Mesmerism and its concern with the 'nightside' phenomena of nature and the human soul, this potential remained largely implicit: for example, not too much attention was paid to the puzzling fact that Justinus Kerner's 'Seeress of Prevorst' described not just the physical stars and the moon, but even intelligent spirits and the mystery of the divine source itself, as located in the inner world of her own mind.[38] But as somnambulist descriptions became ever more spectacular, with elaborate descriptions of invisible spiritual realities 'from India to the Planet Mars', including space travels and encounters with spiritual entities and the inhabitants of other planets,[39] it became very difficult even for esoteric enthusiasts to accept it all at face value. In line with the 'mediating' tendencies of esotericism (Chapter Four), some kind of middle position had to be found between the extremes of dismissing such accounts as simple delusions and accepting them as literal truth. As argued by the American scholar Jeffrey J. Kripal, such an ambiguous middle state between acceptance and rejection is essential to understanding how the dimension of 'the paranormal and the sacred' functions in contemporary religious consciousness.[40]

The gradual psychologization of Western esotericism since the end of the nineteenth century can be described in terms of a double dialectics: the increasing psychologization of the sacred is paralleled by an increasing sacralization of psychology. This means that in much of modern and contemporary esotericism, authors and practitioners can talk about divine realities while really meaning their own psyche, and about their own psyche while really meaning the divine. The common tendency of avoiding the term 'religion' in favour of 'spirituality' reflects and facilitates this approach. At the same time, it is strongly related to a shift from theoretical or dogmatic reflection (inspired by a need of justifying to the sceptics) to a pragmatic emphasis on practice: in the end, for many of those who are involved in esotericism today, perhaps it does not matter so much whether those spiritual entities or realities 'out there' really exist in some manner independently from their own mind. More important is *whether it works* to get in contact with them, that is to say, what one gets out of the practice in terms of personal satisfaction.

The psychologizing trend is very common in modern and contemporary esotericism, but certainly not universal. The point is neither that all forms of religion get psychologized and thereby naturalized, nor that psychologization necessarily undermines belief in some larger metaphysical (or metapsychical?) reality. Rather, the birth of psychology has resulted in a new kind of discourse that has room for many shades of interpretation and forms of negotiation between the strongly naturalizing and supernaturalizing poles. For example, evident tendencies of psychologization can be observed already in the occultist magic of the late Victorian age (see its pioneering practices of guided visualization), but while Aleister Crowley's secretary Israel Regardie went on to interpret the rituals of the Golden Dawn from a perspective grounded in Freudian psychoanalysis, Crowley himself ultimately came to insist on the independent metaphysical reality of the entities contacted in magical ritual.[41] Another example is Jungian psychology (one of the most important influences on how esotericism has developed after World War II), where the 'numinous' energies of the collective unconscious are seen as mysterious forces somehow more primary and original than the products of human reflection – including the theories of psychologists. This means that the sacralization of the psyche trumps the reductionist trends of psychologizing the sacred mostly associated with Freud. A final example (but many more could be given) is the contemporary phenomenon of Chaos Magic, which uses radical poststructuralist arguments to dismiss the very distinction between fiction and reality as a modernist myth. As a result, the argument that religion is 'all in the mind' loses its reductionist sting, and such practices as the self-conscious evocation and worship of self-invented gods (e.g. those of H. P. Lovecraft's Cthulhu mythology) becomes no less reasonable than any other kind of religious activity.[42] None of this would have been conceivable in the eighteenth century or before, but it all fits naturally in the changing religious consciousness of Western audiences today.

The religious supermarket

A final transformation is grounded in political and economic revolutions since the eighteenth century. In Europe and the United States of America, the legally enforced separation between church and state made it possible for religious minorities to establish themselves as new organizations or communities next to the traditional Christian churches. The result was a new situation of religious competition in the context of an emerging 'free market' of larger and smaller religions, with citizens in the role of religious consumers who are at liberty to follow their personal preferences in picking and choosing what they like. Moreover, the expanding range of available options did not remain limited to more or less stable religious organizations alone, whether big or small. The emergence of a fluid 'cultic milieu' of spiritual seekers and consumers (or perhaps many overlapping cultic milieus) is based upon the fact that people may now make highly individual choices in matters of religion, combining elements of belief or practice taken from different sources and traditions that happen to appeal to them, without a need to commit themselves to any single group or community to the exclusion of others.

To get an analytic grip on this situation, it may be helpful to distinguish between 'religion', 'religions' and 'spiritualities', as follows:

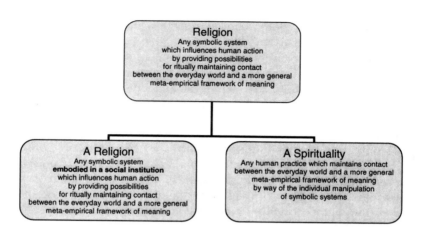

This framework is a further development of the famous definition of religion proposed by the anthropologist Clifford Geertz in 1966.[43] For our present concerns, the point is that it allows us to clarify a major transformation of religion under secular conditions, and of esotericism more specifically. All esoteric systems are examples of 'spiritualities': for example, Marsilio Ficino's Platonic Christianity or Jacob Böhme's Christian theosophy are the result of their own personal, creative manipulation of available symbolic systems (mainly Platonic Orientalism and Roman Catholicism in Ficino's case; Paracelsianism, alchemy, Christian mysticism and Lutheran theology in Böhme's case). But before the separation of church and state, any such spirituality had to be grounded in a specific religion, in this case a Christian one: Ficino was a Catholic with his own peculiar understanding of Christianity, Böhme was a bible-based Lutheran with quite a different way of interpreting the Scriptures. In other words, 'religion' as such took the form of 'religions', or churches; and esoteric forms of religion ('spiritualities') were necessarily embedded within them.

This situation was changed dramatically by the separation of church and state in secular societies. For the first time, it became possible for esoteric spiritualities to *detach* themselves from organized religions and set up shop for themselves: as competing organizations invested entirely in their own esoteric belief system. But moreover, and even more importantly, a more radical perspective now began to dawn as well. It became possible for spiritualities to exist as entirely individual forms of syncretism without *any* organizational structure at all: spiritualities independent from any religions (while still recognizable as forms of religion!). The sociologist of religion Emile Durkheim had begun to perceive that trend in the early twentieth century, and understood that it created problems for his own understanding of religion as a social phenomenon. He mentioned the notion of 'individual religions that the individual institutes for himself and celebrates for himself alone', and even predicted that this new phenomenon might turn out to be the religion of the future: 'Some people today pose the question whether such religions are not destined to become the dominant form of religious life – whether a day will not come when the only cult will be the one that each person freely practices in his innermost self'.[44] Although religious organizations or 'churches' have in fact remained significant factors in Western society, Durkheim's prophecy was largely correct: it is exactly in this direction of radical individualization that religion has developed in the context of the emerging 'spiritual supermarket' after World War II. Much of contemporary esotericism has become entirely independent of any established religion (including esoteric religions such as the Theosophical Society, Rosicrucian Orders, etc.), and manifests itself in the form of ad hoc spiritualities created by individual consumers from whatever they happen to encounter on that market.

In terms of the framework presented above, the current esoteric landscape can therefore be described in terms of three dimensions:

(1) Esoteric religion, that is the sum of all esoteric ideas and practices that are currently available for people to pick and choose from,

(2) Esoteric religions, that is larger or smaller organizations based upon some specific esoteric doctrine,

(3) Esoteric spiritualities, that is individual mixtures of esoteric and other elements that are fine-tuned, so to speak, to the personal needs and interests of the religious consumer.

The supermarket analogy is close and instructive. There has been a time when only one or a few large Internationals monopolized the religious food market: Roman Catholicism provided white grain, Lutheranism brown wheat, and so on, but the choices were very limited (and whatever was available depended largely on the country or city where one happened to be born). Enterprising individuals might bring some variety to the menu by adding ingredients of their own, but they still baked their bread with the flour that everyone was using. Nowadays, in sharp contrast, a stunning variety of foods is available on the new religious supermarket. Much of it comes ready-made for consumption: all kinds of bread are available for us to pick and choose from (we do not need to bake them ourselves, unless we want to), and it may be difficult or even impossible to find out the original ingredients from which they are made. Many kinds of spiritual food are offered with the promise that they are good for our health, will satisfy our hunger and will sustain us through the day. Some of them claim to come from old and hence reliable companies, but others advertise their novelty, or attract customers by promising exotic taste sensations. In any case, no matter how rich or confusing the supply may be, the bottom line is that it is up to us to decide what we put in our trolley at any given time.

This autonomization and individualization of esoteric spiritualities, in contrast to their traditional embeddedness in established religions, is a final innovation that has radically changed the landscape of Western esotericism. Nothing escapes from this new phenomenon, which has been referred to as the 'heretical imperative' (referring to the original Greek meaning of *haeresis*: choice),[45] for even the most traditional and well-established churches are no longer self-evident foundations for how one lives one's life: they, too, have become an optional choice among others, and even many orthodox churchgoers feel free to play with ideas (e.g. reincarnation) that are officially rejected by their community. Finally, the 'supermarket' metaphor is obviously more than just that: it also refers to the fact that esotericism has literally become a multi-million 'market' in the real-world economy. Once again, this is something new for which no parallels exist before the nineteenth century.

As a counterweight against the tendency of seeing Western esotericism as one coherent and unchanging worldview or spiritual perspective, we have been looking at five radical aspects of modernization: the rise to social dominance of instrumental causality, the expansion of the geographical horizon of esotericism, the new theories of evolutionism, the impact of psychology on esotericism and the emergence of a religious supermarket of esoteric religions and spiritualities. Due to all these changes, Western esotericism has changed almost beyond recognition from its pre- and early modern manifestations to its modern and postmodern ones. Nevertheless, as has been argued in Chapters Four and Five, there is still a recognizable pattern of coherence to esoteric worldviews, approaches to knowledge and practices. But as argued in Chapters One and Three, what ultimately keeps the field together as one field of study, in spite of its enormous variety through space and time, is the status of 'rejected knowledge' that it acquired in the wake of the Enlightenment. The modern study of Western esotericism must preserve a delicate balance between interest in what all its manifestations have in common and recognition of the many ways in which they are different from one another.

CHAPTER EIGHT

Between the disciplines

This book opened with an emphasis on the radical trans-disciplinarity of Western esotericism. For historical reasons that were explained in Chapter Three, this field of research became 'academically homeless' after the eighteenth century; and even today, none of the traditional disciplines – not even the study of religion, where it has established itself most clearly over the last two decades – is entirely sufficient as an academic context for studying its development and its manifestations, or analyzing its significance to Western culture. The other side of the coin, of course, is that this situation allows Western esotericism to set up a home base in *any* of the programmes that now exist in the humanities and (to a smaller extent) the social sciences. To further stimulate and assist in such a development, this chapter looks at Western esotericism from the perspective of the most important academic disciplines. The hope is that this will make it easier for students in various fields of study to find their way into this unfamiliar domain.

Religion, philosophy, science

Within the domain of Western esotericism the boundaries between religion, philosophy and science are often extremely fluid and permeable, and this is true particularly for the period before the eighteenth century. When the academic disciplines devoted to these fields of research began to establish themselves in their modern forms, during and after the period of the Enlightenment, they had to define and demarcate their own identities much more sharply than before. Partly they did so by drawing boundaries against one another, and partly by drawing a general boundary against the 'Other' that they shared in common, whether it was referred to as 'heresy', 'superstition', 'the occult' or any other similar term of opprobrium. While theologians, philosophers and scientists have usually (although not always, of course) been willing to accept one another's academic legitimacy as long as each kept in their own domain, they have been quite united in their condemnation of this latter category as being beyond the pale of respectable study.

This process of exclusion has led to alarming levels of academic ignorance about major developments in the history of religion, philosophy and science, and hence to seriously impoverished views of those domains. In all three fields, the core problem is that their histories have been written on the basis of normative distinctions between 'correct' and 'incorrect' religion, philosophy and science. In the case of religion, this has led to multiple histories of Christianity dominated by, and written from the perspective of, the established churches and their doctrinal theologies; in the case of philosophy, it has led to higly selective overviews, some of which suggest, or even state explicitly, that there is not much 'real' philosophy before the time of Descartes; and in the case of science, it has led to historiographies grounded in profoundly anachronistic distinctions between real and 'pseudo' science.[1] In all cases, the pattern is that historians have tended to focus on what *they* considered interesting and important, not on the full complexity of what one actually finds in the historical records. One could say that in their explorations of the garden of history, they have been thinking like gardeners intent on cultivating their own flowers and plants while silently removing the weeds as much as possible.

If we further pursue that metaphor, the 'new historiographies' that have been developing particularly since the 1990s, and of which the study of Western esotericism is a part, look at that same garden of history from the perspective of the biologist: what *they* see is a complex biosystem that deserves attention in its own right. Considered as biological organisms, the weeds or the mushrooms of history are of no less interest or importance than the cultivated plants or flowers. It must be emphasized that from a scientific point of view, the perspectives of the gardener and the biologist represent not just personal opinions: the former is simply incorrect. Whether or not one likes to acknowledge the fact, anybody who cares to take a good look at the garden of history will see that it has always been a fertile breeding-ground for organisms of all kinds. Attempts at cultivation have never been all too successful, and undoubtedly will never be. The illusion that this is otherwise can only be maintained by a deliberate decision to ignore those parts of the evidence that are not congenial to one's own preferences.

Students in the fields of religion, philosophy and science must therefore make up their minds about whether they want to be gardeners or biologists. If they prefer the former, then the study of Western esotericism is not for them. But if they choose the latter, then they must train their awareness and their sensitivity about how strongly, and with how much subtlety, the existing disciplines and their standard programmes of education still tend to confirm the biases of the gardener. The dominant patterns of discourse are changing only slowly, and some deeply ingrained assumptions vanish only with the change of generations. In the meantime, students in religion, philosophy and science are well advised to look at standard textbooks and academic programmes with a healthy dose of suspicion: they should ask themselves continuously what those authoritative conveyors of information might *not* be telling them. In case this advice sounds subversive of academic authority, it is. In line with Immanuel Kant's famous motto of Enlightenment, *sapere aude* (dare to think!),[2] the essence of the academic enterprise is to never believe blindly what one is being told, but have the courage to investigate it critically and independently.

With respect to the study of religion, philosophy and science, there is no need here to go into further detail about the directions into which students might want to look: these should already be evident from the previous chapters. Most of the central figures that were discussed in Chapter Two have been condemned to a kind of liminal state halfway between philosophy and religion, and can be studied fruitfully from both perspectives (preferably both at the same time). With respect to the history of science, the central relevance of *magia naturalis*, alchemy and astrology should by now be obvious; and here too, the boundaries with religion and philosophy are permeable and fluid. For all these cases, some initial bibliographical advice will be given in the next chapter. It should be emphasized that, next to the limited number of famous 'big names' in all these fields, almost limitless amounts of unexplored materials by lesser figures are waiting in libraries and archives for somebody to take an interest in them. Sometimes such research can lead to unexpected new discoveries that provide us with surprising new perspectives on what we already knew, or thought we knew. But what those new horizons will be, we obviously will not know until the research is done first.

The visual arts

Particularly since the early modern period, Western esotericism has generated an extremely rich and impressive production of visual materials. A preliminary impression can easily be gained from many books for the commercial market, such as Grillot de Givry's *Illustrated Anthology of Sorcery, Magic and Alchemy* (Causeway Books: New York 1973), Stanislas Klossowski de Rola's *The Golden Game: Alchemical Engravings of the Seventeenth Century* (Thames & Hudson: London 1988) or, more recently, Alexander Roob's *Alchemy and Mysticism: The Hermetic Museum* (Taschen: Cologne, etc. 1997 and many reprints). The written commentary in such books is often less than reliable, but their illustrations should be sufficient to show the great relevance of esotericism – and more in particular, alchemy – for art historians. To decipher the intricate symbolism of alchemical emblematics and other forms of 'hermetic' art, one obviously needs to combine expertise in this field with experience in the study and analysis of images, and fortunately there are some good examples of such a combination, for instance Barbara Obrist's *Les débuts de l'imagerie alchimique (XIVe–XVe siècles)* (Le Sycomore: Paris 1982), Jacques van Lennep's *Alchimie: Contribution à l'histoire de l'art alchimique* (Crédit Communal: Brussels 1985), Heleen M. E. de Jong, *Michael Maier's Atalanta Fugiens: Sources of an Alchemical Book of Emblems* (1969; Nicolas-Hays: York Beach 2002) or Peter J. Forshaw's forthcoming book on Heinrich von Khunrath. A particularly useful online resource is the enormous alchemy website of Adam MacLean (www.levity.com/alchemy).

In the high art of the Italian Renaissance, the revival of Platonic Orientalism has left many traces, some of which require considerable expertise to decipher. For instance, Ficino's writings have inspired such works as Botticelli's *Primavera*, Raphael's *School of Athens* and several works by Michelangelo.[3] From the seventeenth century, next to the high tide of alchemical imagery during the baroque period, a unique and particularly impressive work of art is the Christian kabbalistic *Lehrtafel* [educational tableau] *of Princess Antonia of Württemberg* (1659–63) in Bad Teinach, Germany, which inspired one of the most important books by the theosopher Friedrich Christian Oetinger.[4] From the next century and after, the enigmatic art of William Blake is an excellent example of how an original and independent mind can create a mythology all of his own under the evident influence of Platonic, gnostic and Swedenborgian forms of speculation.[5] Swedenborg's remarkable influence on nineteenth- and twentieth-century art (as well as on literature and music) is well-documented,[6] and mostly belongs to the idealist tradition in Romanticism. In that context, however, we are faced with problems of interpretation that are quite similar to the case of German Idealism:[7] although the general relevance of Platonic and Christian theosophical models might seem evident even to the casual observer, it is often difficult to demonstrate conclusively, due to a frequent absence of direct and explicit references. The same is true, although to a lesser extent, for the darker stream of 'Gothic' Romanticism and its evident debts to the imagination of 'the occult', in literature but also in art.[8] When we come to the 'decadent' art of the *fin-de-siècle* in France, such hesitations become less necessary: it is well-known that many artists and writers frequented the occultist milieus of Martinism, were flirting with satanism (largely because of the Romantic appeal of Satan as a heroic individualist who dares to rebel against divine authority), and got involved in the various new forms of Rosicrucianism around charismatic figures such as Stanislas de Guaïta and Joséphin Péladan; however, much research remains to be done about the exact nature of how the occultist currents have affected specific visual artists. Although the close relation between occultism and art in this period is impossible to deny, one must beware of over-enthusiastic speculation: not a few art historians have fallen prey to the temptation of seeing hidden 'messages' everywhere, resulting in an esoteric or even paranoid hermeneutics of art based on limitless over-interpretation.[9] Not every cup is an alchemical vessel, and not every arrangement of ten visual elements is a sefirotic tree.

Moving on to the twentieth century, in the case of the surrealist movement around André Breton we are dealing with the highly interesting case of a progressive increase of esoteric influence over the course of several decades, originally focusing on somnambulism and culminating in explicitly esoteric (especially alchemical) art after World War II, but combined with a politically leftist and Freudian approach that sharply rejected supernatural beliefs.[10] As for abstract art, in the mid-1980s a famous exhibition titled *The Spiritual in art* (Los Angeles County Museum of Art, 1986)[11] called attention to the enormous but hitherto ignored importance of esoteric speculation to the emergence of abstraction – much to the dismay of the reigning school of 'formalist' art criticism associated with Clement Greenberg. It is now widely accepted that the well-known pioneers of abstraction (e.g. Malevich, Kandinsky, Mondriaan, Arp, Klee or Duchamp) all saw their work as deeply connected to their spiritual and esoteric aspirations, and the very earliest abstract paintings were in fact made by a previously neglected spiritualist medium, Hilma af Klint. Next to such examples of esotericism as an influence on famous artists, quite some esotericists have developed artistic aspirations as an extension of their spiritual agendas, as in the case of Rudolf Steiner and his Goetheanum, designed as an architectural representation of his anthroposophical worldview. In many other cases, it is hard or impossible to tell the esotericist apart from the artist: among countless examples, one might think of the theosophically inspired landscape paintings of Nicholas Roerich, Niki de Saint-Phalle's Tarot Garden in Toscany (Italy) or even the psychedelic paintings of Alex Grey.

Contemporary art is a veritable fancy-fair of the esoteric and the occult. Joseph Beuys is just one of the better-known examples of an artist who plays subtle games with overt or hidden references to such traditions as alchemy or (in his case) shamanism. In the postmodern context, where anything goes, such allusions do not need to (although they may) imply serious adherence to the beliefs or worldviews of some esoteric tradition or other. One often does not know whether they are meant in earnest or ironically, and this very ambiguity can be the whole point of an artistic statement, as would seem to be the case in Bruce Naumann's neon artwork *The True Artist Helps the World by Revealing Mystic Truths* (1967).[12] In sum, particularly since the twentieth century, esotericism has become one of the indispensable core dimensions of modern art, whether or not it is advertised as such. Its symbolism, imagery and mythical narratives are used and recycled freely, with or without acknowledgement, and with or without a deliberate spiritual agenda. The material for research by art historians is so rich as to be virtually inexhaustible.

Literature

While the esoteric dimensions of visual art have come to be recognized more generally at least in the wake of *The Spiritual in Art*, there have been almost no systematic attempts yet to investigate them for the domain of literature.[13] And yet, the potential here is at least as great, possibly even greater. The basic pattern must begin to sound familiar by now: in countless cases, the role of esotericism in the work of well-known poets and writers has been overlooked or wholly neglected, simply because specialists were unfamiliar or uncomfortable with it, and because they found it difficult (understably enough) to find reliable scholarship that could help them interpret literary references to esoteric ideas or symbolism.

Although we could go back as far as antiquity (with Apuleius' *Metamorphoses*, better known as *The Golden Ass*, as a particularly obvious example of a novel inspired by magical traditions and mystery cults), and the medieval production of chivalric and Grail literature has often been considered as pertaining to esotericism, we will here restrict ourselves to the period starting with the Renaissance. A major title is the *Hypnerotomachia Poliphili* (1499) attributed to Francesco Colonna: famous as one of the most beautiful books ever printed, its hallucinatory story of Poliphilus' 'dream-quest' for his beloved is set in a thoroughly pagan atmosphere that reflects the contemporary revival of ancient religious myth and symbolism.[14] The *philosophia occulta* and its fascination with the ancient sciences is reflected in many other better- or lesser-known writings of the sixteenth and seventeenth centuries, including famous cases such Shakespeare's *Tempest* or Ben Jonson's satirical *The Alchemist*.[15] One of the key texts of Rosicrucianism, *The Chymical Wedding of Christian Rosenkreutz*, is written in the form of an alchemical novel, and the emergence of Rosicrucianism and Freemasonry led to an entire genre of popular novels (almost completely forgotten today) around mysterious secret brotherhoods with benevolent or sinister aims.[16] At the same time, the vogue of hermeticism was reflected in a rich production of alchemical poetry next to (or combined with) the alchemical emblematics referred to in the previous section.[17] A particularly important novel in view of its later influence is Henri de Montfaucon de Villars' *Comte de Gabalis* (1670), which created a fascination with 'elemental beings' that is reflected in literature, art, theatre and even opera through the eighteenth, nineteenth and twentieth centuries.[18]

Many of the Christian theosophers and illuminists of the eighteenth and early nineteenth century (Jacques Cazotte, Johann Heinrich Jung-Stilling, Karl von Eckartshausen, Louis-Claude de Saint-Martin and many others) have written fiction next to their theoretical work.[19] The genre of 'initiatic novels' influenced by esoteric speculation includes famous cases such as Novalis' *Heinrich von Ofterdingen* and *Die Lehrlinge zu Saïs*, and can be traced to the present day. Johann Wolfgang von Goethe is a particularly interesting case, with his enigmatic *Märchen* (Fairy-Tale) about the Green Snake and the Beautiful Lily or, most of all, the two parts of the *Faust* tragedy, which are replete with references to alchemy and the *occulta philosophia* of the Renaissance (with Agrippa as an obvious model of Faust himself). The theme of secret initiations and hidden brotherhoods had an evident potential for thrilling stories, leading to a large genre of novels around such mysterious organizations as the Knights Templar or the Illuminaten and their supposed influence, from earlier cases such as Zacharias Werner's *Die Söhne des Thals* (The Sons of the Valley, 1802–4) through countless occultist novels during the later nineteenth century, and up to modern and contemporary titles such as Umberto Eco's *Foucault's Pendulum* (1988) and extremely popular pulp fiction bestsellers such as Dan Brown's *Da Vinci Code* (2003).

Many occultists have also been enthusiastic novelists, and their production must be highlighted here regardless of its quality, which ranges from mediocre to occasionally quite impressive. Among the countless names and titles, we here mention only the anonymous Mesmerist/occultist novel *Ghost Land* (1876), attributed to Emma Hardinge Britten and very important to the early phase of Anglo-Saxon occultism, and many later fictional works by highly influential esotericists and occultists such as Anna Kingsford, Josephin Péladan, Paschal Beverley Randolph, Charles Webster Leadbeater, Aleister Crowley, Dion Fortune, G. I. Gurdjieff, P. D. Ouspensky or Raymond Abellio. This category of esotericists trying their hand at literature as a vehicle for their beliefs merges almost imperceptibly into that of literary writers influenced by esoteric or occult themes. On this side of the scale, we could mention such names as Honoré de Balzac's Swedenborgian/Illuminist stories (*Louis Lambert*, 1832; *Séraphita*, 1834); influential novels of Edward George Bulwer-Lytton, notably *Zanoni* (1842), *A Strange Story* (1862) and *The Coming Race* (1871); Joris-Karl Huysmans's novels situated in the occult milieus of fin-de-siècle Paris (especially *Là-bas*, 1895); the important oeuvre of Gustav Meyrink, which is wholly permeated by esotericism (*The Golem*, 1914; *The Green Face*, 1916; *Walpurgis Night*, 1917; *The White Dominican*, 1921; *The Angel of the West Window*, 1927);[20] a spiritual writer linked to surrealism such as René Daumal (notably *Mount Analogue*, 1952); nobel prizer winner William Butler Yeats and his involvement with the magic of the Hermetic Order of the Golden Dawn (*A Vision*, 1925); Rainer Maria Rilke's poetry and its debt to contemporary esoteric and occultist milieus;[21] or the greatest Portugese writer and poet, Fernando Pessoa, whose works are permeated by esoteric themes.[22]

It is important to emphasize, in this context, that esotericism can be of great importance to poets and novelists regardless of whether they are sympathetic to its ideas: for example, the basic narratives and symbols of alchemy and grail mythology are used frequently but in characteristic 'ironic' fashion in the great novels of Thomas Mann.[23] Likewise, especially in the post-World War II period, the history and literature of esotericism is used pragmatically as a fertile source of motifs, characters or storylines by countless authors; to give just a few examples, the German writer Helmut Krausser uses Renaissance magic as a central topic in his novel *Melodien* (1993), the Dutch writer Harry Mulisch makes used of alchemical and kabbalistic motifs in many of his works (*Voer voor psychologen* [Food for psychologists], 1974; *De ontdekking van de Hemel* [The Discovery of Heaven], 1992; *De procedure* [The Procedure], 1998) and the American writer John Crowley plays a subtle game with esoteric references and iconic figures such as Giordano Bruno and John Dee in *Little, Big* (1981) and the four volumes of his *Aegypt* cycle (1987–2007). In countless other authors, the medium of literature is used more deliberately to convey some kind of esoteric message, as in the immensely popular novels by Paulo Coelho, or (apparently) as a medium for initiating the reader into some deeper gnosis concerning the human condition, as in the impressive novel *The Chymical Wedding* (1989) by the British writer Lindsay Clarke.

These few names and titles are clearly just the tip of a very large iceberg, most of which remains to be brought to light. So far, scholars of literature have seldom noticed the presence of esotericism in modern and contemporary literature, but it is in fact one of its core dimensions. The case is similar to that of visual art. To do justice to this esoteric dimension – or even just to recognize it – a hasty perusal of some popular studies or Internet sources is insufficient; to pick up the references for what they are, and be able to make sense of them, one needs to study the history of Western esotericism seriously and at length, with reference to the best available scholarship.

Music

It is not by chance that one of the major works of Renaissance esotericism is titled *De harmonia mundi* (Francesco Giorgio da Veneto, 1525): in the context of what we have referred to as the 'Platonic Paradigm', the picture of a cosmos grounded in universal harmony and divine order – whence the famous notion of a 'music of the spheres' – was intimately related to what has been described as 'speculative music'.[24] In terms of the theory of correspondences (see above, p. 124), all parts of that universe resonated with one another like the strings of a great instrument tuned by God (as visualized with perfect literalness in some famous images from Robert Fludd's oeuvre), and their hidden relations could be deciphered by means of pythagorean number symbolism and kabbalistic hermeneutics. The words and letters through which God had created the world could ultimately be reduced to numbers, and numerical relations could be made audible as harmonious (or disharmonious) sounds. Speculative music was intimately related not only to kabbalah and the symbolism of numbers but also to magic, astrology and alchemy in the early modern period;[25] and this relevance of music to the *occulta philosophia* continued straight into the 'scientific revolution' of the seventeenth century.[26] This in itself makes the field of Western esotericism into a fruitful domain of study for musicologists.[27]

As pointed out by Godwin, while the eighteenth century was a high point in Western music, it was a period of decline for musical esotericism, which ran counter to the spirit of Enlightenment rationalism.[28] There are exceptions, however, such as notably the role of Freemasonry in Mozart's *Magic Flute*. The speculative tradition began to revive along with Romanticism, in the work of authors such as Johann Friedrich Hugo von Dalberg, Antoine Fabre d'Olivet, Charles Fourier, Hoëne Wronski, R. F. G. Lacuria, Louis Lucas, Edmond Bailey and Saint-Yves d'Alveydre.[29] A late continuator of the pythagorean tradition who carried it into the twentieth century is Hans Kayser, whose work is continued by his pupils Rudolf Haase and Werner Schulze. Apart from this speculative tradition with its ancient and Renaissance roots, the occultism of fin-de-siècle Paris was attractive not just to painters, poets and novelists, but occasionally to composers as well. A notable example is Erik Satie, who was strongly influenced by Sâr Joséphin Péladan's Rosicrucianism but eventually broke with him and founded an order of his own, called 'Église Metropolitaine d'Art de Jésus Conducteur' (with Satie himself as the high priest and sole member). From these backgrounds emerged piano music on esoteric themes such as Satie's 'Sonneries de la Rose+Croix', 'Le Fils des Étoiles' and a mystical ballet titled 'Uspud'.[30] Spiritual themes were 'in the air' in the decades before and after World War I, and Richard Wagner's great music dramas were sometimes interpreted from esoteric perspectives; but in most cases the present state of research does not allow definitive statements about whether esotericism has exerted a major influence on composers during that period (with a few exceptions, such as, notably, Alexander Scriabin).

The picture becomes clearer when we get to the birth of atonality and the 'dodecaphonic' or 12-tone music of Arnold Schönberg and his pupils, Alban Berg and Anton Webern. In a highly interesting parallel to the birth of abstraction in visual art, esoteric speculation played a decisive role in this breakthrough from late Romanticism to modernity in music. Next to Schönberg's fascination with Jewish kabbalah and Webern's devotion to Goethe's speculative theories of plant morphology and colours, Swedenborg's theory of correspondences was a crucial source of inspiration in the conceptualization of dodecaphony as a universal system for organizing 'musical space'.[31] What made such esoteric sources relevant to composers was the idea that music was grounded in a universal 'law' that structured the whole of reality: music could be imagined as an autonomous world of sound that paralleled the basic laws of the macrocosmos and stood in a relation of exact correspondence with an absolute spiritual reality beyond the world of the senses. The relation of esoteric speculation to the development of dodecaphony towards 'total serialism' after World War II remains virtually uncharted territory, waiting for serious scholars to explore it. At least one of the most important composers to come out of that development, Karlheinz Stockhausen, is an ultimate example of how avant-garde music can be wholly grounded in an esoteric worldview (in this case the neo-gnosticism of a channelled text, the *Urantia Book*).[32]

Similar to the case of visual art, avant-garde music after World War II is full of scattered references to esoteric themes and traditions, but no systematic research has been done from that angle and comprehensive studies are still lacking. The same is true when we move from the 'classical' tradition to that of popular music. The development of rock music since the 1960s coincided with the vogue of alternative spiritualities full of influences from Oriental as well as Western esoteric traditions; but there have been almost no serious and persistent attempts yet to study the role of esotericism in rock lyrics, or investigate such obvious themes as the relation between Crowleyan occultism or Chaos Magic and the heavy metal subculture. Slightly more attention has been given to the spiritual dimensions of contemporary Rave and Festival culture,[33] but hardly from a perspective of esotericism per se. In this domain, too, almost all the groundwork remains to be done.[34]

The social sciences and popular culture

The popular vogue of esotericism during the 1960s and 1970s came somewhat as a surprise for sociologists of religion, who tended to adhere to some version of the Secularization Thesis and expected that the process of rationalization and the spread of scientific knowledge would coincide with a steady decline and marginalization not only of religion but of magical 'superstition' as well. After some early attempts at the creation of a 'Sociology of the Occult',[35] with a focus on the analysis of 'deviant' beliefs and practices, it has eventually become clear that the presence of esotericism and the occult in contemporary culture is not some strange anomaly but a permanent feature of the religious landscape. In Chapter Seven we have already discussed the emergence of a 'Religious Supermarket' with a rich supply of esoteric ideas and commodities, and the fundamental notions of the 'Cultic Milieu' and the complicated phenomenon of contemporary 'Occulture'. These latter terms refer to esotericism as a general dimension of popular culture that now finds expression through a wide variety of media: books, comics, the Internet, DVDs, video gaming, art, music, ad hoc rituals ('shamanic' or otherwise), countercultural festivals such as Burning Man or Boom, etc. Whether all of this can still be covered under the general label 'esotericism' is a moot point: scholars who associate the term primarily with a number of specific historical traditions of older provenance might tend to answer in the negative, while others (including the author of this book) prefer to look at esotericism as an open-ended phenomenon that is continually evolving in new directions. As such, it is a fertile domain of study for scholars in the social sciences as well as in that of popular culture.

Apart from studying the Cultic Milieu or Occulture as such, sociologists of religion have concentrated much of their attention on specific esoteric organizations. It is here that the study of Western esotericism merges imperceptibly into that of New Religious Movements (NRMs), concentrating on the countless larger and smaller religious organizations based on Western esoteric belief systems (from older ones such as the Theosophical Society, the Anthroposophical Society or neo-Rosicrucian movements such as AMORC or the Lectorium Rosicrucianum, to newer and sometimes highly controversial ones such as the Church of Scientology, New Acropolis or the Raelian movement). In this domain, invaluable work has been done by the Italian scholar Massimo Introvigne, in close connection with several other leading experts, such as J. Gordon Melton, Eileen Barker or James R. Lewis, in the study of NRMs.[36] Several of these scholars have created organizations for providing the general public as well as government institutions with reliable information on NRMs, particularly in view of popular anxieties about the perceived dangers of 'cults' or 'sects'.[37] Their commitment to critical research without an apologetic or polemical bias has made them controversial in the circles of the 'anti-cult movement', which tends to reject an attitude of scholarly neutrality because of its default perception of NRMs as 'dangerous cults' that brainwash their members (a thesis that has been thoroughly discredited by academic research but remains popular in the media and among the wider public). In these contexts, scholars should be aware that they may well get themselves involved in highly emotional and politically sensitive debates.

Various methodologies can be used in social scientific research of contemporary esotericism. Most sociological studies tend to be qualitative, but there are interesting cases to show the value of quantitative methods as well.[38] One will find many examples of sociological research into esoteric NRMs in leading academic journals such as *Nova Religio* and the *Journal of Contemporary Religion*. Next to sociology, the anthropology of religion is of great importance to the study of contemporary esotericism. A landmark example of anthropological fieldwork in this regard is Tanya M. Luhrmann's study of ritual magic in England, and another useful model is Michael F. Brown's research of Channeling in New Age milieus.[39] As the study of esotericism has begun to establish itself in academic contexts, particularly since the beginning of the twenty-first century, anthropologists are beginning to discover it as a field of research; and this development may prove particularly fruitful in the study of esoteric 'practice' that was highlighted in Chapter Six.

In sum, there can be no doubt about the relevance of contemporary esotericism to the social sciences and the study of popular culture. However, in order to achieve its full potential, such research should make optimal use of *historical* scholarship about the religious and intellectual traditions in question. As demonstrated, for example, by the American scholar Mary Farrell Bednarowski, already several decades ago, one cannot really understand contemporary New Religions unless one takes their worldviews seriously and places them in a historical context. Only in this manner will it be possible to see how traditional esoteric beliefs have been modified, transformed and put to new uses under the impact of new developments such as modernization or secularization.[40] Such an integrated approach remains somewhat unusual in social scientific studies of esotericism, and will hopefully become more normal as the field develops.

CHAPTER NINE

Sources and resources

Newcomers to the study of Western esotericism tend to have a hard time finding their way through the dense forest of secondary literature and distinguishing reliable scholarship from the many doubtful products of (crypto-) esoteric apologetics or amateur scholarship. The situation is not made easier by the fact that some dilettantish products in this domain are written by academics, whereas some excellent research comes from authors without university credentials. Furthermore, scholarship of superior quality may be hidden away in specialized periodicals that are known only to experts and sometimes do not even appear on the lists of recognized peer-reviewed journals; and in this domain, articles that appear in major scholarly media are not necessarily better than those that do not. Likewise, monographs published by recognized university presses are not necessarily more reliable than books that have appeared with obscure publishers, some of them connected to specific esoteric organizations. Partly this situation is typical of a young field of study that is only in the beginning stage of academic professionalization, and partly it reflects some peculiarities unique to the domain of Western esotericism as such. It is hardly an exaggeration to say that the status of esotericism or the occult as 'rejected knowledge' has given rise to a kind of parallel universe of amateur scholarship, much of which is bad but some of which is very good. One implication is that some of the best publications may be hard or impossible to find in standard university libraries, and sometimes it is necessary to turn to privately owned libraries or archives. Some of the best collections are the creations of devoted connoisseurs who may not necessarily wish, or have the practical means, to make their treasures generally available. With the rise of the Internet this situation has begun to improve, since it becomes easier to publish materials online that would have been hard or impossible to find in the past; but as in so many other fields, it has also created much confusion about what to take seriously and what not.

Scholars and students who are new to the study of Western esotericism should be well aware of these peculiarities. For example, they must realize that standard academic library tools or search machines will not necessarily yield the best results, and it may require considerable persistence to find what one needs – or even know that it is out there. There are no shortcuts or easy solutions, and this chapter does not claim to provide any. What it hopes to do is help readers make their first steps and avoid a few pitfalls, by providing an annotated bibliography of sources and resources as well as some further practical information. In so far as possible without lowering scholarly standards, literature in English is quoted with preference; but as will be seen, many important dimensions of Western esotericism remain simply inaccesible without reading knowledge of French, German and Italian. To keep the overview within reasonable limits, subtitles of books are given only if the main title does not give enough information.

Organizations, libraries, teaching programmes

There are two professional organizations for scholars in the field of Western esotericism: the European Society for the Study of Western Esotericism (ESSWE; www.esswe.org) and the USA-based Association for the Study of Esotericism (ASE; www.aseweb.org). In line with the somewhat different academic cultures that they represent, the former is more consistently oriented towards critical historical and empirical approaches, while the latter is more open to religionist perspectives and shows a greater overlap between scholars and practitioners. Esotericism is also well represented at the conferences of several international organizations in the study of religion, notably the International Association for the History of Religions (IAHR; www.iahr.dk), the European Association for the Study of Religions (EASR; www.easr.eu) and the American Academy of Religion (AAR; www.aarweb.org).

The best scholarly library in the field, particularly for the period prior to the nineteenth century, is the renowned *Bibliotheca Philosophica Hermetica* in Amsterdam (BPH; www.ritmanlibrary. nl). Two other famous collections are the library of the Warburg Institute in London (www.warburg.sas.ac.uk) and the Manly P. Hall Archive owned by the Philosophical Research Society in Los Angeles (www.manlyphall.org). One should be aware that, next to such publicly accessible collections, some good or excellent libraries are owned by Masonic or esoteric organizations, which may or may not restrict access to their own members. And finally there are quite a number of private collections created by wealthy individuals, to which one will usually not be admitted without excellent personal connections.

Worldwide there are now three university chairs for the study of Western esotericism. The first was created in 1965 at the École Pratique des Hautes Études (Sorbonne) in Paris, and offers weekly seminars; the second was created in 1999 at the University of Amsterdam (www.amsterdamhermetica.nl), and provides a four-module programme at the undergraduate level next to a full-time Master programme in English; the third one was created in 2005 at the University of Exeter (www.centres.exeter.ac.uk/exeseso) and provides a distance-learning programme. Next to these specialized programmes, courses in Western esotericism are being offered with increasing frequency at various universities in Europe and the United States.

General literature

By far the most comprehensive reference work in Western esotericism, and the logical starting point for reliable information and bibliographical references, is the *Dictionary of Gnosis and Western Esotericism*, edited by Wouter J. Hanegraaff in collaboration with Antoine Faivre, Roelof van den Broek and Jean-Pierre Brach (Brill: Leiden/Boston 2005; also available online). Since 2001, Brill also publishes the most important academic journal in the field, *Aries: Journal for the Study of Western Esotericism* (www.brill.nl/aries;

see also its predecessor, *ARIES* first series, published by La Table d'Emeraude in Paris from 1985 until 1999) and since 2006 there is a companion monograph series called the 'Aries Book Series' (www. brill.nl/publications/aries-book-series). Another monograph series with a similar focus is called 'Gnostica: Texts and Interpretations' and is published by Equinox (www.equinoxpub.com). A mine of information is the French journal *Politica Hermetica* (L'Age d'Homme: Lausanne), published since 1987; and finally there is the online journal *Esoterica* (www.esoteric.msu.edu).

Several of the available textbook introductions to Western esotericism are dated or unreliable, and none of them is without its problems (for a critical overview, see Wouter J. Hanegraaff, 'Textbooks and Introductions to Western Esotericism', *Religion* 43 [2013]). Nicholas Goodrick-Clarke's *The Western Esoteric Traditions* (Oxford University Press: Oxford/New York 2008) is strongest for the period from the seventeenth through the nineteenth centuries, and mostly reliable as a source of factual information. Readers should be aware of a religionist subtext that implicitly minimizes the importance of historical context, change and innovation in order to present 'the Western esoteric traditions' as one single, enduring worldview or spiritual per-spective, defined by 'intrinsic philosophical and religious char-acteristics' and ultimately grounded, according to the author, in 'spirit and spirituality as an independent ontological reality' (o.c., 4, 12–13). Antoine Faivre's *Western Esotericism* (SUNY Press: Albany 2010) is written by the foremost scholar of his genera-tion, and factually quite reliable. Disadvantages are its extreme brevity and the less-than-satisfactory quality of the English trans-lation (the French original, titled *L'ésotérisme* [4th edn, Presses Universitaires de France: Paris 2006] should remain the first choice for readers who can read the language). Most striking about Faivre's overview is his emphasis on esotericism as a form of 'imaginary' (*imaginaire*) that relies primarily on mythical and symbolical forms of expression; and in line with this emphasis, he gives generous attention to how esotericism appears in litera-ture and the arts. Reflecting an unusual level of erudition, he manages (in spite of the book's brevity) to mention quite some lesser-known figures and references, and this makes his introduc-tion a useful resource for readers who want to throw a glance beyond the obvious 'big names'.

Apart from introductory textbooks, general works devoted to Western esotericism are very rare. Pierre Riffard's early *L'ésotérisme* (Robert Laffont: Paris 1990) is intelligent and erudite, but based upon an extreme form of religionism that makes it incompatible with current approaches. Antoine Faivre's two volumes of collected articles, *Access to Western Esotericism* and *Theosophy, Imagination, Tradition* (SUNY Press: Albany 1994 and 2000), contain general discussions of method and theory, detailed analyses of selected figures and topics (with a strong emphasis on Christian theosophy and Illuminism) and, last but not least, detailed bibliographical guides for research. Wouter J. Hanegraaff's *Esotericism and the Academy* (Cambridge University Press: Cambridge 2012) is a history of how 'Western esotericism' has been imagined and conceptualized in intellectual discourse from the Renaissance to the present, and lays the theoretical groundwork for the perspective on esotericism that is basic to this 'Guide for the Perplexed'.

Some chronological overviews of Western esotericism are available in the form of multi-author volumes. The two chief examples are *Modern Esoteric Spirituality* (eds Antoine Faivre & Jacob Needleman; Crossroad: New York 1992) and *Gnosis and Hermeticism from Antiquity to Modern Times* (eds Roelof van den Broek & Wouter J. Hanegraaff; SUNY Press: Albany 1998). An extraordinary collection of scholarship in three languages (English, French, German) is the large Festschrift for Antoine Faivre, *Ésotérisme, Gnoses & Imaginaire symbolique* (eds Richard Caron, Joscelyn Godwin, Wouter J. Hanegraaff & Jean-Louis Vieillard-Baron; Peeters: Louvain 2001).

The rapid development of research on Western esotericism in recent years is documented by a series of thematic volumes that contain a wealth of scholarship on many different themes and aspects. Notable examples are *Polemical Encounters: Esoteric Discourse and its Others* (eds Olav Hammer & Kocku von Stuckrad; Brill: Leiden/Boston 2007); *Esotericism, Art, and Imagination* (eds Arthur Versluis, Lee Irwin, John Richards & Melinda Weinstein; Michigan State University Press: East Lansing 2008); *Esotericism, Religion, and Nature* (eds Arthur Versluis, Claire Fanger, Lee Irwin & Melinda Phillips; North American Academic Press: East Lansing 2009); *Constructing Tradition: Means and Myths of Transmission in Western Esotericism* (ed. Andreas B. Kilcher; Brill: Leiden/Boston 2010); *Die Enzyklopädik der Esoterik* (eds

Andreas B. Kilcher & Philipp Theisohn; Wilhelm Fink: Munich 2010); and *Hidden Intercourse: Eros and Sexuality in the History of Western Esotericism* (eds Wouter J. Hanegraaff & Jeffrey J. Kripal; Fordham University Press: New York 2011).

Finally, some useful bibliographies are available. Those in Faivre's two monographs of 1994 and 2000 are strongly recommended. A virtually inexhaustible source of titles on 'the occult' up to the beginning of the twentieth century can be found in Albert L. Caillet, *Manuel bibliographique des sciences psychiques ou occultes*, 3 vols, Lucien Dorbon: Paris 1912. A useful short guide through the labyrinth, up to 1970, is Robert Galbreath, 'The History of Modern Occultism: A Bibliographical Survey', *Journal of Popular Culture* 5 (1971), 726–54.

Gnōsis in Hellenistic culture

Gnosticism

The best modern introduction, based on up-to-date scholarship and meticulous study of the complete textual corpus in its original languages, is Roelof van den Broek, *Gnostic Religion in Antiquity* (Cambridge University Press: Cambridge 2013); and a more dated but still very useful monograph is Kurt Rudolph, *Gnosis* (Harper & Row: San Francisco 1977). The most reliable English translation of the gnostic texts is Marvin Meyer, *The Nag Hammadi Scriptures* (Harper One: New York 2008). Of particular importance to the modern debate on 'gnosticism' is a monograph by Michael Allen Williams, *Rethinking 'Gnosticism'* (Princeton University Press: Princeton 1996), which argued that the term itself should be dropped. Karen L. King's monograph *What is Gnosticism?* (The Belknap Press of Harvard University Press: Cambridge, MA/ London 2003) is important for uncovering the theological biases that have kept influencing modern scholarship in this domain.

Theurgy

For two good synthetic introductions, see Gregory Shaw, 'Theurgy: Rituals of Unification in the Neoplatonism of Iamblichus', *Traditio*

41 (1985), 1–28, and Georg Luck, 'Theurgy and Forms of Worship in Neoplatonism', in Luck, *Ancient Pathways and Hidden Pursuits* (University of Michigan Press: Ann Arbor 2000), 110–52. For the Chaldean Oracles, see Ruth Majercik, *The Chaldean Oracles* (Brill: Leiden/New York/Copenhagen/Cologne 1989); and for Iamblichus' views of theurgy, see Iamblichus, *De mysteriis* (eds Emma C. Clarke, John M. Dillon & Jackson P. Hershbell; Brill: Leiden/Boston 2004). Finally, see the fascinating analysis in Sarah Iles Johnston, *Hekate Soteira: A Study of Hekate's Role in the Chaldean Oracles and Related Literature* (Scholars Press: Atlanta 1990).

Hermetism

The best general study of Hermetism in Late Antiquity is Garth Fowden's *The Egyptian Hermes* (Princeton University Press: Princeton 1986). However, the indispensable foundation of all modern scholarship in this domain remains André-Jean Festugières monumental four-volume study *La révélation d'Hermès Trismégiste* (1950; reprinted as one volume by Les Belles Lettres: Paris 2006); and the most important modern counterpart to Festugière is Jean-Pierre Mahé with his two-volume *Hermès en Haute-Égypte* (Presses de l'Université Laval: Quebec 1978/1982). The textual corpus of the philosophical Hermetica is available in a standard edition (facing Greek-French translation) by A. D. Nock and A.-J. Festugière, *Corpus Hermeticum* (4 vols, repr. Les Belles Lettres: Paris 1991–2, 2002). The most reliable English translations are by Brian P. Copenhaver (*Hermetica*, Cambridge University Press: Cambridge 1992) and Clement Salaman et al. (*The Way of Hermes*, Duckworth: London 1999; *Asclepius*, Duckworth: London 2007). For the understanding of Hermetism that is basic to the present volume, see Wouter J. Hanegraaff, 'Altered States of Knowledge: The Attainment of Gnōsis in the Hermetica', *The International Journal of the Platonic Tradition* 2:2 (2008), 128–63. For the medieval and early modern reception of Hermetic literature, see Claudio Moreschini, *Hermes Christianus* (Brepols: Turnhout forthcoming) and the large collection of studies and exhaustive bibliography in *Hermetism from Late Antiquity to Humanism* (eds Paolo Lucentini, Ilaria Parri and Vittoria Perrone Compagni; Brepols: Turnhout 2003).

The secrets of nature: Magic, astrology, alchemy

General works

On the transmission of the ancient sciences to the Islamic world and from there to the Latin middle ages, see David C. Lindberg, 'The Transmission of Greek and Arabic Learning to the West', in Lindberg (ed.), *Science in the Middle Ages* (University of Chicago Press: Chicago/London 1978), 52–90; and David Pingree, 'The Diffusion of Arabic Magical Texts in Western Europe', in Biancamaria Scarcia Amoretti (ed.), *La diffusione delle scienze islamiche nel medioevo europeo* (Accademia Nazionale dei Lincei: Rome 1987), 57–102. An older but still useful analysis of the Islamic corpus is Manfred Ullmann, *Die Natur- und Geheimwissenschaften im Islam* (Brill: Leiden 1972). For the Hermetica in Islamic culture, see now Kevin van Bladel, *The Arabic Hermes* (Oxford University Press: Oxford/New York 2009). For the problematic nature of the term 'occult sciences', see Hanegraaff, *Esotericism and the Academy*, 177–91, and literature cited there. The standard reference for the field as a whole remains Lynn Thorndike's virtually inexhaustible 8-volume opus: *A History of Magic and Experimental Science* (Columbia State University Press: New York 1923–58).

Magic

The scholarly literature on magic is enormous, and any choice can only reveal a very small tip of the iceberg. For the basic problematics of 'magic' as a category and its role in the study of Western esotericism, see Hanegraaff, *Esotericism and the Academy*, 164–77. For antiquity, one of the best modern studies is Matthew W. Dickie, *Magic and Magicians in the Greco-Roman World* (Routledge: London/New York 2001). For the Middle Ages, by far the best starting point is Richard Kieckhefer, *Magic in the Middle Ages* (Cambridge University Press: Cambridge 1989), next to the important collective volumes *Conjuring Spirits* (ed. Claire Fanger; Sutton: Phoenix Mill, etc. 1998) and *Invoking Angels* (ed. Claire

Fanger; Pennsylvania State University Press: Philadelphia 2012). Generally, one should keep checking new titles in the 'Magic in History' series of Pennsylvania State University Press. For those who want to delve deeply into the intellectual discussion of medieval magic in relation to astrology and talismans, a particularly good study is Nicolas Weill-Parot, Les *'images astrologiques' au Moyen Âge et à la Renaissance* (Honoré Campion: Paris 2002). The standard peer-reviewed journal on magic is *Magic, Ritual & Witchcraft* (www.magic.pennpress.org).

Astrology

For general introductions and overviews, see Jim Tester, *A History of Western Astrology* (The Boydell Press: Woodbridge 1987) and Kocku von Stuckrad, *Geschichte der Astrologie* (C.H. Beck: Munich 2003). Two good studies that show how astrology functioned in the early modern period are Patrick Curry, *Prophecy and Power* (Princeton University Press: Princeton 1989) and Anthony Grafton, *Cardano's Cosmos* (Harvard University Press: Cambridge, MA/London 1999).

Alchemy

The literature on alchemy is enormous but of uneven quality. For a reliable short introduction with a particular focus on natural philosophy and early modern science, see Lawrence M. Principe, *The Secrets of Alchemy* (University of Chicago Press: Chicago/London 2012); for a longer overview from a similar perspective, see Hans-Werner Schütt, *Auf der Suche nach dem Stein der Weisen* (C.H. Beck: Munich 2000). A serious problem with almost all the literature interested in the religious dimensions is the influence of non-historical perspectives derived from Carl Gustav Jung or Mircea Eliade and Traditionalism (see Hanegraaff, *Esotericism and the Academy*, 191–207, 289–95, 305–7), which sometimes cause critics to exaggerate in the opposite direction. A complete history by a very good specialist that avoids these pitfalls, but is unfortunately not yet translated into English, is Michela Pereira, *Arcana Sapienza* (Carocci: Rome 2001). For alchemy and early modern science, the 'new historiography' associated with Lawrence M. Principe and William R. Newman is of fundamental importance: see especially Newman, *Gehennical Fire: The Lives of George Starkey, an American Alchemist in the Scientific Revolution* (Harvard University Press: Cambridge, MA/London 1994), Principe, *The Aspiring Adept: Robert Boyle and his Alchemical Quest* (Princeton University Press: Princeton 1998), and William R. Newman and Lawrence M. Principe, *Alchemy Tried in the Fire: Starkey, Boyle, and the Fate of Helmontian Chymistry* (University of Chicago Press: Chicago/London 2002). As for the famous case of Newton, it may be best to begin with chapter 8 of Richard S. Westfall, *Never at Rest: A Biography of Isaac Newton* (Cambridge University Press: Cambridge 1980), continue with Betty Jo Teeter Dobbs, *The Janus Face of Genius: The Role of Alchemy in Newton's Thought* (Cambridge University Press: Cambridge 1991), and visit 'The Newton Project' online (www.newtonproject.sussex.ac.uk). In the field of alchemy it is particularly easy to be led astray by quasi-scholarly literature grounded in esoteric or occultist assumptions. For solid scholarship, see the academic journal *Ambix*, published by the Society for the History of Alchemy and Chemistry (www.ambix.org), and the excellent French *Chrysopoeia* with its associated series of monographs called 'Textes et Travaux de Chrysopoeia', both published by Archè/Edidit under the aegis of the Société d'Étude de l'Histoire de l'Alchimie (www.editionsarche.com).

The Renaissance

General works

Surprisingly, there is no comprehensive, reliable, and up-to-date overview of Renaissance esotericism; and as a result, scholars and the general public tend to keep falling back on a series of famous but now seriously outdated studies. Frances A. Yates' *Giordano Bruno and the Hermetic Tradition* (1964; reprint Routledge: London/New York 2002) is well-written and thoroughly inspiring, but incorrect in some of its most basic assumptions (see Hanegraaff, *Esotericism and the Academy*, 322–34). This is true even more for the extreme whiggishness of Wayne Shumaker's *The Occult Sciences in the Renaissance* (University of California Press: Berkeley/Los Angeles/ London 1972). D. P. Walker's *Spiritual and Demonic Magic from Ficino to Campanella* (1958; reprint Pennsylvania State University Press: Philadelphia 2000) has aged somewhat better, but still belongs to a bygone era of scholarship. Ioan P. Couliano's *Eros and Magic in the Renaissance* (University of Chicago Press: Chicago/ London 1987) is extremely original in its approach, but also highly idiosyncratic. One may learn valuable things from each of these classics, but they must all be read with great caution.

Prisca Theologia/Philosophia Perennis

For the basic Renaissance tradition of *prisca theologia* and *philosophia perennis*, see the two classic articles by Charles B. Schmitt, 'Perennial Philosophy: From Agostino Steuco to Leibniz', *Journal of the History of Ideas* 27 (1966), 505–32, and D. P. Walker, 'The *Prisca Theologia* in France', *Journal of the Warburg and Courtauld Institutes* 17 (1954), 204–59; but compare the recent discussion in Hanegraaff, *Esotericism and the Academy*, chapter 1. An inexhaustible source of information on the Renaissance fascination with 'ancient wisdom' is Michael Stausberg's two-volume *Faszination Zarathushtra* (Walter de Gruyter: Berlin/New York 1998).

Christian Kabbalah

A good modern introduction to Christian Kabbalah in English is sorely missing. A large, recent study in German is Wilhelm Schmidt-Biggemann's four-volume *Geschichte der christlichen Kabbala* (Frommann Holzboog: Stuttgart-Bad Cannstatt 2012). Andreas Kilcher's *Die Sprachtheorie der Kabbala als ästhetisches Paradigma* (J. B. Metzler: Stuttgart/Weimar 1998) looks at the topic from a perspective of literary studies and focuses on the discourse about 'kabbalah' from its Jewish origins to its Christian interpretations and finally its reception in German Romanticism. An older classic is François Secret's *Les kabbalistes chrétiens de la Renaissance* (1964; new rev. edn; Archè/Arma Artis: Milan/Neuilly-sur-Seine

1985). Finally, there are two good collective volumes: *The Christian Kabbalah* (ed. Joseph Dan; Harvard College Library: Cambridge, MA 1997) and *Christliche Kabbala* (ed. Wilhelm Schmidt-Biggemann; Jan Thorbecke: Ostfildern 2003).

Essential figures

For Plethon, see C. M. Woodhouse, *Gemistos Plethon* (Clarendon Press: Oxford 1986) and especially Brigitte Tambrun, *Pléthon* (Vrin: Paris 2006).

For Ficino, the indispensable modern author is Michael J. B. Allen. All his books are highly recommended, but see especially his *Synoptic Art* (Leo S. Olschki: Florence 1998) and his six-volume translation, in collaboration with James Hankins, of the *Platonic Theology* (Harvard University Press: Cambridge, MA/London 2001–6). Two excellent collective volumes are *Marsilio Ficino* (eds Michael J. B. Allen & Valery Rees; Brill: Leiden/Boston/Cologne 2002) and *Laus Platonici Philosophi* (eds Stephen Clucas, Peter J. Forshaw & Valery Rees; Brill: Leiden/Boston 2011). Finally, see the indispensable critical edition and translation by Carol V. Kaske and John R. Clark of Ficino's *Three Books on Life* (Medieval & Renaissance Texts & Studies/The Renaissance Society of America: Binghamton, New York 1989).

On Lodovico Lazzarelli and Giovanni 'Mercurio' da Correggio, see Wouter J. Hanegraaff and Ruud M. Bouthoorn, *Lodovico Lazzarelli (1447–1500): The Hermetic Writings and Related Documents* (Arizona Center for Medieval and Renaissance Studies: Tempe 2005).

The most comprehensive recent studies of Giovanni Pico della Mirandola are Steven A. Farmer's *Syncretism in the West: Pico's 900 Theses (1486)* (Medieval & Renaissance Texts & Studies: Tempe 1998); and Crofton Black's *Pico's Heptaplus and Biblical Hermeneutics* (Brill: Leiden/Boston 2006). An older classic is Chaim Wirszubski, *Pico della Mirandola's Encounter with Jewish Mysticism* (Harvard University Press: Cambridge, MA/London 1989). Apart from Farmer's translation of Pico's 900 theses, most of his other important writings are available in English in Pico, *On the Dignity of Man/On Being and the One/Heptaplus* (Hackett: Indianapolis/Cambridge 1998).

It is surprising that we still have no modern monograph on Johannes Reuchlin and his Christian kabbalah. Unfortunately, the English translation of *On the Art of the Kabbalah* (University of Nebraska Press: Lincoln/London 1983) is unreliable, and one will have to take recourse to the excellent although extremely expensive German translations in Reuchlin's 'Sämtliche Werke' edited by Widu-Wolfgang Ehlers, Hans-Gert Roloff and Peter Schäfer: *Band I,1: De verbo mirifico/Das wundertätige Wort (1494)* and *Band II,1: De arte cabalistica libri tres/Die Kabbalistik* (Frommann-Holzboog: Stuttgart/Bad Cannstatt 1996 and 2010).

The situation concerning Cornelius Agrippa is similarly unsatisfactory. Still the best general monograph, Charles G. Nauert's *Agrippa and the Crisis of Renaissance Thought* (University of Illinois Press: Urbana 1965) is over half a century old; Marc van der Poel's *Cornelius Agrippa, the Humanist Theologian and his Declamations* (Brill: Leiden/New York/Köln 1997) is excellent but focuses on Agrippa's declamations rather than his *philosophia occulta*; and the interpretations of Christopher Lehrich's *The Language of Demons and Angels* (Brill: Leiden/Boston 2003) are rather problematic in terms of their methodology and treatment of sources. Vittoria Perrone Compagni has published an excellent critical editon of *De occulta philosophia libri tres* (Brill: Leiden/New York/Cologne 1992), but anglophone readers are still dependent on James Freake's problematic translation of 1651, published with well-intended but unreliable notes and commentaries by the occultist Donald Tyson: *Three Books of Occult Philosophy* (Llewellyn: St. Paul 1995).

A good monograph is available on Johannes Trithemius and his involvement in magic: Noel L. Brann, *Trithemius and Magical Theology* (SUNY Press: Albany 1999). For the French Christian kabbalist Guillaume Postel, see Yvonne Petry, *Gender, Kabbalah and the Reformation: The Mystical Theology of Guillaume Postel (1510–1581)* (Brill: Leiden/Boston 2004) and Marion Leathers Kuntz, *Guillaume Postel* (Martinus Nijhoff: The Hague 2010). On another important later kabbalist, the younger van Helmont, see Allison P. Coudert, *The Impact of the Kabbalah in the Seventeenth Century: The Life and Thought of Francis Mercury van Helmont (1614–1698)* (Brill: Leiden/Boston/Cologene 1999).

In contrast to figures such as Reuchlin or Agrippa, John Dee has been the topic of a remarkable number of recent monographs. It is best to start with Deborah Harkness' *John Dee's Conversations* with Angels (Cambridge University Press: Cambridge 1999), but see also the important study by Nicholas H. Clulee, *John Dee's Natural Philosophy* (Routledge: London/New York 1988), György E. Szönyi more recent *John Dee's Occultism* (SUNY Press: Albany 2004), and last but not least *John Dee: Interdisciplinary Studies in English Renaissance Thought* (ed. Stephen Clucas; Springer: Dordrecht 2006). Meric Casaubon's exposure, *A True & Faithful Relation of What Passed for Many Years Between Dr. John Dee and Some Spirits* (orig. 1659) is available in a handy facsimile by an occult publisher (Magickal Childe Publishers: New York 1992); but one must be extremely cautious about the countless publications (paper or online) by occultists fascinated by Dee's Enochian language. On this topic, see Egil Asprem, *Arguing with Angels* (SUNY Press: Albany 2012).

As for Bruno: next to countless publications in Italian, often of high quality, an extremely readable biography was published by Ingrid Rowland: *Giordano Bruno* (Farrar, Straus & Giroux: New York 2008). Readers who wish to go deeper into Bruno's philosophy are well advised to seek out the works of Hilary Gatti: *Giordano Bruno and Renaissance Science* (Cornell University Press: Ithaca & London 1999), *Essays on Giordano Bruno* (Princeton University Press: Princeton 2011), and the edited volume *Giordano Bruno* (ed. Hilary Gatti; Ashgate: Aldershot/Burlington 2002). A collection of writings by Bruno that are presented as *Opere Magiche*, with facing Latin/Italian translations, was edited by Michele Ciliberto (Adelphi: Milan 2000). Bruno's Italian dialogues are all available in English, see especially *The Ash Wednesday Supper* (University of Toronto Press: Toronto/Buffalo/London 1995), *The Expulsion of the Triumphant Beast* (University of Nebraska Press: Lincoln/London 1992); *Cause, Principle and Unity, and Essays on Magic* (Cambridge University Press: Cambridge 1998), and *The Heroic Frenzies* (Lorenzo da Ponte Italian Library: Los Angeles forthcoming).

Naturphilosophie and Christian theosophy

General works

As noted above, Antoine Faivre's monographs on Western esotericism (1994, 2000) are largely devoted to this domain, and the second volume contains an extensive introduction to Christian theosophy. Furthermore, an excellent collective volume with contributions in three languages is *Epochen der Naturmystik* (eds Faivre & Rolf-Christian Zimmermann; Erich Schmidt: Berlin 1979). Arthur Versluis' *Wisdom's Children* (SUNY Press: Albany 1999) gives a complete overview of Christian theosophy, but coloured by the author's strong religionist gaze. Two good studies by B. J. Gibbons both carry misleading titles (the term 'occult' is hardly applicable here) but actually count among the best studies of Christian theosophy in English: *Gender in Mystical and Occult Thought* (Cambridge University Press: Cambridge 1996) and *Spirituality and the Occult* (Routledge: London/New York 2001). Andrew Weeks' *German Mysticism from Hildegard of Bingen to Ludwig Wittgenstein* (SUNY Press: Albany 1993) places the same traditions in a larger context going back to medieval mysticism.

Essential figures

Paracelsus has generated a very large scholarly literature, mostly in German. Reliable biographies in English are Andrew Weeks, *Paracelsus* (SUNY Press: Albany 1997) and Charles Webster, *Paracelsus* (Yale University Press: New Haven/London 2008). For those who read French, Alexandre Koyré's chapter on Paracelsus in his *Mystiques, spirituels, alchimistes du XVIe siècle allemand* (Gallimard: Paris 1971) remains one of the most brilliant short syntheses of Paracelsus' worldview. In addition to several multi-volume editions of the German originals, a short selection of fragments was published by Nicholas Goodrick-Clarke as *Paracelsus: Essential Readings* (North Atlantic Books: Berkeley 1999) and a large German-English edition of several writings is now available as *Paracelsus . . . Essential Theoretical Writings* (ed. Andrew Weeks; Brill: Leiden/Boston 2008). As for Paracelsus' reception, there is an enormous literature in German: see, for example, the journal *Nova Acta Paracelsica* (published by Peter Lang) or the many publications by Joachim Telle, including his edited volumes *Parerga Paracelsica* (Franz Steiner: Stuttgart 1991) and *Analecta Paracelsica* (Franz Steiner: Stuttgart 1994). A good volume in English is *Paracelsus: The Man and his Reputation, his Ideas and their Transformation* (ed. Ole Peter Grell; Brill: Leiden/Boston/

Cologne 1998), including a particularly important article by Carlos Gilly, '"Theophrastia Sancta": Paracelsianism as a Religion in Conflict with the Established Churches' (151–85). Allen G. Debus has traced the history of paracelsianism as 'Chemical Philosophy' in a long series of important monographs. With respect to its wider cultural impact, finally, see the impressive French study by Didier Kahn, *Alchimie et paracelsisme en France (1567–1625)* (Droz: Geneva 2007).

Some of the best scholarship on Jacob Böhme is in French, not German: see Alexandre Koyré's classic *La philosophie de Jacob Boehme* (Vrin: Paris 1929) and the perceptive analyses in Pierre Deghaye, *La naissance de Dieu, ou la doctrine de Jacob Boehme* (Albin Michel: Paris 1985). Andrew Weeks' *Boehme* (SUNY Press: Albany 1991) is solid and reliable, but could have been a bit more sensitive to the visionary and symbolic dimensions of Böhme's oeuvre. For English translations we must still turn to the eighteenth-century editions by William Law: modern translations are virtually non-existent. As for later authors in the 'Behmenist' tradition, such as Johann Georg Gichtel and John Pordage (whose writings have survived only in German), see above under 'General Works'. Just a few selected fragments have been translated into English, by Arthur Versluis in his *Wisdom's Book* (Paragon House: St. Paul 2000).

Several key texts of Friedrich Christoph Oetinger are available in excellent critical editions: see especially *Die Lehrtafel der Prinzessin Antonia* (eds Reinhard Breymayer & Friedrich Häussermann; Walter de Gruyter: Berlin/New York 1977, two volumes) and *Biblisches und emblematisches Wörterbuch* (ed. Gerhard Schäfer; Walter de Gruyter: Berlin/New York 1999, 2 vols). Virtually the only scholarly text on Oetinger in English is Wouter J. Hanegraaff, *Swedenborg, Oetinger, Kant* (Swedenborg Foundation: West Chester 2007).

Most scholarship on Louis-Claude de *Saint-Martin* is in French: see especially Nicole Jacques-Lefèvre, *Louis-Claude de Saint-Martin (1743–1803)* (Dervy: Paris 2003). For a biography in English one must still turn to the esotericist Arthur Edward Waite, *The Unknown Philosopher* (Rudolf Steiner Publications: New York 1970). Saint-Martin's main writings are easily accessible in modern French editions, but English translations are rare. The same is true for Franz von Baader, whose *Sämtliche Werke* are conveniently available in a 16-volume edition by Franz Hoffmann (Scientia: Aalen 1963). On Baader's significance in the context of Western esotericism, the chief specialist is Antoine Faivre: see several chapters in English in his two books quoted under 'General Literature', and his French volume *Philosophie de la Nature* (Albin Michel: Paris 1996).

Initiatic societies

Rosicrucianism

The Rosicrucian manifestoes are conveniently combined in one volume edited by Richard van Dülmen: *Fama Fraternitatis (1614), Confessio Fraternitatis (1615), Chymische Hochzeit Christiani Rosencreutz Anno 1459 (1616)* (Calwer: Stuttgart 1973). English translations of the first two manifestoes can be found in the appendix of Frances A. Yates, *The Rosicrucian Enlightenment* (Ark: London/New York 1972), but this famous book itself is over-speculative and must be read with the greatest caution; and for the third one, see *The Chemical Wedding of Christian Rosenkreutz* (trans. Joscelyn Godwin; Phanes Press: Grand Rapids 1991). The leading specialist on early Rosicrucianism is Carlos Gilly, who has spent decades researching the reception of the manifestoes, and whose *Bibliographia Rosicruciana* is eagerly awaited. Everything published by Gilly is strongly recommended; and for the very earliest backgrounds to Rosicrucianism, see his *Adam Haslmayr* (In de Pelikaan: Amsterdam 1994). For an accessible introduction to Rosicrucianism for non-specialists see Christopher McIntosh, *The Rosicrucians* (Samuel Weiser: York Beach 1997). The main French expert Roland Edighoffer has authored a monograph *Les Rose-Croix et la Crise de la Conscience européenne au XVIIe siècle* (Dervy: Paris 1998); and for a particularly good collection of articles in English, German and French, see the volume *Rosenkreuz als europäisches Phänomen im 17. Jahrhundert* (In de Pelikaan: Amsterdam 2002). As for authors who began to see themselves as 'Rosicrucians', see, for example, Hereward Tilton, *The Quest for the Phoenix: Spiritual Alchemy and Rosicrucianism in the Work of Count Michael Maier (1569–1622)* (Walter de Gruyter: Berlin/

New York 2003), who, among other things, warns against the many fanciful myths that trace Freemasonry back to Rosicrucianism with authors like Maier and Fludd as 'mediators' (o.c., 27–9). For the first actual Rosicrucian organization, the *Gold- und Rosenkreuz*, see Christopher McIntosh, *The Rose Cross and the Age of Reason* (1992; repr. SUNY Press: Albany 2011), and Renko D. Geffarth, *Religion und arkane Hierarchie* (Brill: Leiden/Boston 2007). On the many later Rosicrucian organizations, see Harald Lamprecht, *Neue Rosenkreuzer* (Vandenhoeck & Ruprecht: Göttingen 2004).

Freemasonry

On the backgrounds and early history of Freemasonry, see David Stevenson, *The Origins of Freemasonry* (Cambridge University Press: Cambridge 1988), and for a first general introduction to the English development, see John Hamill, *The Craft* (Crucible: Wellingborough 1986). For women and Freemasonry, see Jan A. M. Snoek, *Initiating Women in Freemasonry* (Brill: Leiden/Boston 2012). For an analysis of the ritual dimension in relation to other forms of esotericism, see Henrik Bogdan, *Western Esotericism and Rituals of Initiation* (SUNY Press: Albany 2007). For Freemasonry in America, see Steven C. Bullock, *Revolutionary Brotherhood* (University of North Carolina Press: Chapel Hill & London 1996). Marsha Keith Schuchard's massive *Restoring the Temple of Vision: Cabalistic Freemasonry and Stuart Culture* (Brill: Leiden/Boston 2002) is based on extensive research but over-speculative: see the exhange with Andrew Prescott in *Aries* 4:2 (2004), 171–227. There is an enormous amount of literature on Freemasonry by Freemasons: see especially the journals *Ars Quatuor Coronatorum* (accessible through the Quatuor Coronati Lodge No. 2076, www.quatuor-coronati.com) and *Renaissance Traditionnelle: Revue d'études maçonniques et symboliques* (www.renaissancetraditionnelle.org).

Illuminism

On this important topic, almost all the literature is in French (the exception, David Allen Harvey's *Beyond Enlightenment: Occultism and Politics in Modern France* [Northern Illinois

University Press: DeKalb 2005] is unfortunately derivative and full of errors and omissions). The indispensable and almost inexhaustible classic in this domain is Auguste Viatte, *Les sources occultes du Romantisme*, 2 vols (1928; repr. Honoré Champion: Paris 1979). A further standard reference is René le Forestier, *La Franc-Maçonnerie Templière et Occultiste aux XVIIIe et XIXe siècles*, 2 vols. (repr. La Table d'Émeraude: Paris 1987) and *La Franc-Maçonnerie occultiste au XVIIIe siècle & l'Ordre des Élus Coens* (repr. La Table d'Émeraude: Paris 1987). On the central personality of Willermoz, see the excellent study by Alice Joly, *Un mystique Lyonnais et les secrets de la Franc-Maçonnerie* (1938; Télètes: Paris n.d.). For modern scholarship, see the many writings of Antoine Faivre; and for an encyclopaedic overview, see Karl R. H. Frick, *Die Erleuchteten* (Akademische Druck- und Verlagsanstalt: Graz 1973). On the wider context of French Romanticism, see Arthur McCalla, *A Romantic Historiosophy* (Brill: Leiden/Boston/Cologne 1998).

The modernist occult

General works

On the relation between esotericism and the Enlightenment, Monika Neugebauer-Wölk has done pioneering work in Germany: see her two edited volumes titled *Aufklärung und Esoterik* (Felix Meiner: Hamburg 1999; Max Niemeyer: Tübingen 2008). This kind of research is still virtually unknown in anglophone scholarship, in spite of an occasional publication such as *The Super-Enlightenment* (ed. Dan Edelstein; Voltaire Foundation: Oxford 2010), which shows some awareness of the importance of the topic but not enough familiarity with the relevant scholarship in French and German. As for the nineteenth and early twentieth centuries, James Webb's classics *The Occult Underground* and *The Occult Establishment* (Open Court: La Salle, IL 1974, 1976) remain very useful as introductions. Joscelyn Godwin's *The Theosophical Enlightenment* (SUNY Press: Albany 1994) is extremely well informed and an indispensable foundation for research in this domain. Russia, finally, is a domain all of its own: for the rapidly developing scholarship see *The Occult in Russia and Soviet Culture* (ed. Bernice Glatzer Rosenthal; Cornell University Press: Ithaca/ London 1997) and *The New Age of Russia: Occult and Esoteric Dimensions* (eds Birgit Menzel, Michael Hagemeister & Bernice Glatzer Rosenthal; Otto Sagner: Munich/Berlin 2012).

Swedenborg

The most comprehensive study is now Friedemann Stengel, *Aufklärung bis zum Himmel* (Mohr Siebeck: Tübingen 2011), some major conclusions of which can already be found in Wouter J. Hanegraaff, *Swedenborg, Oetinger, Kant* (Swedenborg Foundation: West Chester 2007). In English, the best biographical treatments are the old but excellent study by Martin Lamm, *Emanuel Swedenborg* (1915; repr. Swedenborg Foundation: West Chester 2000) and Ernst Benz's *Emanuel Swedenborg* (Swedenborg Foundation: West Chester 2002). Probably the best contemporary Swedenborg specialist is Inge Jonsson: see his excellent *Visionary Scientist* and *The Drama of Creation* (Swedenborg Foundation: West Chester 1999 and 2004). Marsha Keith Schuchard's enormous tome *Emanuel Swedenborg, Secret Agent on Earth and in Heaven* (Brill: Leiden/Boston 2011) is extremely erudite but constructs a kabbalistic and esoteric context for which the evidence is missing (see above, Chapter Seven, p. 126 with nt 12)

Mesmerism and somnambulism

The best general histories in English are Adam Crabtree, *From Mesmer to Freud* (Yale University Press: New Haven/London 1993); and Alan Gauld, *A History of Hypnotism* (Cambridge University Press: Cambridge 1992). For the French context, see the impressive study by Bertrand Meheust, *Somnambulisme et médiumnité*, 2 vols. (Synthélabo: Le Plessis-Robinson 1999). Particularly good for the British context is Alison Winter, *Mesmerized* (University of Chicago Press: Chicago/London 1998). Unfortunately, no comparable modern studies exist on German mesmerism. For the development of modern psychology and psychiatry out of Mesmerist roots, the indispensable reference remains Henri F. Ellenberger, *The*

Discovery of the Unconscious (Basic Books: New York 1970). For the lineage towards New Thought, see Robert C. Fuller, *Mesmerism and the American Cure of Souls* (University of Pennsylvania Press: Philadelphia 1982). For the broader development towards American 'Metaphysical Religion', see the standard work of Catherine L. Albanese, *A Republic of Mind & Spirit* (Yale University Press: New Haven/London 2007).

Spiritualism

For Britain, a good standard history is Janet Oppenheim, *The Other World* (Cambridge University Press: Cambridge 1985). For America, R. Laurence Moore's *In Search of White Crows* (Oxford University Press: Oxford/New York 1977) remains a standard reference; but see now Cathy Gutierrez, *Plato's Ghost* (Oxford University Press: Oxford/New York 2009). For France, see John Warne Monroe, *Laboratories of Faith* (Cornell University Press: Ithaca/London 2008). For Germany, the best option is Diethard Sawicki, *Leben mit den Toten* (Schöningh: Paderborn, etc. 2002).

French occultism

An older but still useful introduction is Christopher McIntosh, *Eliphas Lévi and the French Occult Revival* (Rider & Co.: London 1972). Jean-Pierre Laurant's *L'ésotérisme chrétien en France au XIXe siècle* (L'Age d'Homme: Lausanne 1992) is the work of a great specialist but extremely difficult to read. Strangely enough, apart from the old overview by James Webb, mentioned above, it is very hard to find any reliable modern studies on the occultist *fin de siècle* as a whole, or on a central figure such as Papus and the Martinist milieu.

Traditionalism

The best modern monograph is Mark Sedgwick, *Against the Modern World* (Oxford University Press: Oxford/New York 2004); and for the reception history leading to American perennialism, see Setareh Houman, *De la philosophia perennis au pérennialisme américain* (Archè: Milan 2010). For a short popular biography of Guénon in English, see Robin Waterfield, *René Guénon and the Future of the West* (Crucible: Wellingborough 1987), and for a more complete and authoritative French alternative, see Jean-Pierre Laurant, *René Guénon* (Dervy: Paris 2006). An impressive documentation of Guénon's influence in France is Xavier Accart, *Guénon ou le renversement des clartés* (1920–70) (Edidit/Archè: Paris/Milan 2005). For central figures such as Schuon, Nasr or Smith, see Sedgwick and Houman. The best specialist of Evola, Hans Thomas Hakl, has written many contributions in the form of introductions to Evola's works or articles in journals and collective volumes, but no comprehensive monograph.

Modern theosophy

There is no scholarly biography of H. P. Blavatsky, but good monographs exist about most of her successors: see Stephen Prothero, *The White Buddhist: The Asian Odyssey of Henry Steel Olcott* (Indiana University Press: Bloomington/Indianapolis 1996), Gregory Tillett's *The Elder Brother: A Biography of Charles Webster Leadbeater* (Routlege & Kegan Paul: London, etc. 1982) and the older volumes by Arthur H. Nethercot, *The First Five Lives of Annie Besant* and *The Last Four Lives of Annie Besant* (Rupert Hart-Davis: London 1961 and 1963). There is an enormous literature on modern Theosophy (see Michael Gomes, *Theosophy in the Nineteenth Century: An Annotated Bibliography* (Garland: New York/London 1994)), much of it written by Theosophists, but no generally recognized academic standard treatment. A wealth of information can be found in the independent academic journal *Theosophical History* and its associated series of 'Occasional papers' (see www.theohistory.org).

Anthroposophy

Until 2007, almost everything on this topic used to be written by Anthroposophists and permeated by their specific biases, with the relative exception of an isolated older study in English by Geoffrey

Ahern, *Sun at Midnight: The Rudolf Steiner Movement and the Western Esoteric Tradition* (Aquarian Press: Wellingborough 1984). But the indispensable and almost inexhaustible foundation for all future scholarship on Anthroposophy is now Helmut Zander, *Anthroposophie in Deutschland*, 2 vols. (Vandenhoeck & Ruprecht: Göttingen 2007).

Occultist magic

For the pioneer Randolph, the standard reference is John Patrick Deveney, *Paschal Beverly Randolph* (SUNY Press: Albany 1997); and see the closely related volume by Joscelyn Godwin, Christian Chanel and John P. Deveney, *The Hermetic Brotherhood of Luxor* (Samuel Weiser: York Beach 1995). On the Hermetic Order of the Golden Dawn, the indispensably history remains Ellic Howe, *The Magicians of the Golden Dawn* (1972; repr. Samuel Weiser: York Beach 1978); the best contemporary specialist is Robert A. Gilbert, among whose many titles see especially *The Golden Dawn Companion* (Aquarian Press: Wellingborough 1986). For the wider context of occultism in Germany, especially Theodor Reuss, see the classic by Helmut Möller and Ellic Howe, *Merlin Peregrinus* (Königshausen & Neumann: Würzburg 1986). For Aleister Crowley, the best reference is Marco Pasi. See his *Aleister Crowley and the Temptation of Politics* (Equinox: London 2013) and his important article 'Varieties of Magical Experience: Aleister Crowley's Views on Occult Practice', *Magic, Ritual & Witchcraft* 6:2 (2011), 123–62. On the merits of existing Crowley biographies, see Pasi, 'The Neverendingly Told Story: Recent Biographies of Aleister Crowley', *Aries* 3:2 (2003), 224–45. Finally see the new collective volume *Aleister Crowley and Western Esotericism* (eds Henrik Bogdan & Martin P. Starr; Oxford University Press: Oxford/New York 2012).

Gurdjieffianism

For the general history of Gurdjieff and his followers, see James Webb, *The Harmonious Circle* (Thames & Hudson: London 1980); and for a reliable biography of Gurdjieff, see James Moore: *Gurdjieff* (Element: Shaftesbury etc. 1999).

Esotericism after World War II

On the phenomenon of the Cultic Milieu, including a reprint of Colin Campbell's classic article of 1972, see Jeffrey Kaplan and Helène Lööw (eds), *The Cultic Milieu* (AltaMira: Walnut Creek 2002). For general comprehensive discussions of the 1950s and 1960s respectively, see Robert S. Ellwood, *The Fifties Spiritual Marketplace* and *The Sixties Spiritual Awakening* (Rutgers University Press: New Brunswick/New Jersey 1997 and 1994). Steven J. Sutcliffe's *Children of the New Age* (Routledge: London/New York 2003) suffers from needless polemics about questions of definition, but provides a good analysis of the early English 'New Age in a strict sense' (see Hanegraaff, below) and its millenarian aspirations inspired by Alice Bailey. There is much modern scholarship on the role of 'UFO religions' in the 'Proto-New Age' (idem., below) and later: for example, *The Gods have Landed* (ed. James R. Lewis; SUNY Press: Albany 1995) and *UFO Religions* (ed. Christopher Partridge; Routledge: London/New York 203). The most complete attempt at interpreting the New Age movement from a historical perspective, with a focus on its ideas and their backgrounds in Western esotericism, is Wouter J. Hanegraaff, *New Age Religion and Western Culture: Esotericism in the Mirror of Secular Thought* (1996; SUNY Press: Albany 1998), which traces the development from a 'Proto-New Age' through the English/theosophical/millenarian New Age 'in a strict sense' and from there to the New Age 'in a general sense' since the 1980s. A pioneering critical study of modern and contemporary esoteric 'strategies of epistemology' is Olav Hammer, *Claiming Knowledge* (Brill: Leiden/Boston/Cologne 2001). For new and up-to-date approaches to the New Age, see Daren Kemp and James R. Lewis, *Handbook of New Age* (Brill: Leiden/Boston 2007).

Neopaganism has generated an enormous academic literature of uneven quality. The indisputed standard work and starting point for any further research is Ronald Hutton, *The Triumph of the Moon: A History of Modern Pagan Witchcraft* (Oxford University Press: Oxford/New York 1999). A brilliant anthropological analysis is Tanya M. Luhrmann, *Persuasions of the Witch's Craft* (Harvard University Press: Cambridge, MA 1989). For a good collective volume, see *Magical Religion and Modern Witchcraft* (ed. James R. Lewis; SUNY Press: Albany 1996).

A new approach to esotericism in contemporary popular culture is beginning to be outlined in the highly original work of Jeffrey J. Kripal: see especially his *Mutants & Mystics: Science Fiction, Superhero Comics, and the Paranormal* (University of Chicago Press: Chicago/London 2011). This line of scholarship is still in its beginning stages, but one sees its potential for studying the still largely unexplored esoteric dimensions of popular media such as comics, film, videogaming and the Internet. Finally, the need for complementing historical approaches to Western esotericism by scholarly research on what is going on right here and now is rightly emphasized by Egil Asprem and Kennet Granholm (eds), *Contemporary Esotericism* (Equinox: Sheffield 2012).

NOTES

Chapter 1

1 Wouter J. Hanegraaff, *Esotericism and the Academy: Rejected Knowledge in Western Culture*, Cambridge University Press: Cambridge 2012, 334–9; Monika Neugebauer-Wölk, 'Der Esoteriker und die Esoterik: Wie das Esoterische im 18. Jahrhundert zum Begriff wird und seinen Weg in die Moderne findet', *Aries* 10:2 (2010), 217–31.

2 Antoine Faivre, 'Introduction I', in Antoine Faivre and Jacob Needleman (eds), *Modern Esoteric Spirituality*, Crossroad: New York 1992, xv–xx; idem, *Access to Western Esotericism*, State University of New York Press: Albany 1994, 10–15.

3 For a bibliographical list of the main contributions, in chronological order, see Hanegraaff, *Esotericism and the Academy*, 356 nt. 375.

4 Tanya M. Luhrmann, *Of Two Minds: An Anthropologist looks at American Psychiatry*, Vintage Books: New York 2000, 41.

5 See Chapter Seven, p. 124; and Bernd-Christian Otto, *Magie: Rezeptions- und diskursgeschichtliche Analysen von der Antike bis zur Neuzeit*, De Gruyter: Berlin/New York 2011, 349–56.

6 Frances A. Yates, *Giordano Bruno and the Hermetic Tradition*, Routledge & Kegan Paul/University of Chicago Press: London/Chicago 1964. See analysis in Hanegraaff, *Esotericism and the Academy*, 322–34.

7 James Webb, *The Occult Underground*, Open Court: La Salle, IL 1974, ch. 1.

8 Hanegraaff, *Esotericism and the Academy*, 184–8 (with reference to Brian Vickers, 'On the Function of Analogy in the Occult', in Ingrid Merkel and Allen G. Debus [eds], *Hermeticism and the Renaissance: Intellectual History and the Occult in Early Modern Europe*, Folger Books: Washington/London/Toronto 1988, 265–92).

9 For example, Christopher Partridge, *The Re-Enchantment of the West*, 2 vols, T&T Clark: London/New York 2004.

10   For example, Edward A. Tiryakian (ed.), *On the Margin of the Visible: Sociology, the Esoteric, and the Occult*, John Wiley & Sons: New York, etc. 1974 (see especially the contributions by Tiryakian and Marcello Truzzi).

11   For example, Alex Owen, *The Place of Enchantment: British Occultism and the Culture of the Modern*, University of Chicago Press: Chicago/London 2004; Corinna Treitel, *A Science for the Soul: Occultism and the Genesis of the German Modern*, The Johns Hopkins University Press: Baltimore/London 2004.

12   Jeffrey J. Kripal, *Mutants & Mystics: Science Fiction, Superhero Comics, and the Paranormal*, University of Chicago Press: Chicago 2011.

13   Hanegraaff, *Esotericism and the Academy*, 126–7, 149, 295–314.

14   For a more extensive argumentation, see Hanegraaff, *Esotericism and the Academy*, 368–79.

15   Hans G. Kippenberg, Jörg Rüpke and Kocku von Stuckrad (eds), *Europäische Religionsgeschichte: Ein mehrfacher Pluralismus*, 2 vols, Vandenhoeck & Ruprecht: Göttingen 2009.

Chapter 2

1   On 'Hermetism' (referring specifically to the 'philosophical' Hermetica and their commentaries) versus the much broader and vaguer term 'Hermeticism', see Antoine Faivre, 'Questions of Terminology Proper to the Study of Esoteric Currents in Modern and Contemporary Europe', in Antoine Faivre and Wouter J. Hanegraaff (eds), *Western Esotericism and the Science of Religion*, Peeters: Louvain 1998, 1–10, here 4 and 9.

2   Notably Michael Allen Williams, *Rethinking 'Gnosticism:' An Argument for Dismantling a Dubious Category*, Princeton University Press: Princeton 1996.

3   Iamblichus, *De Mysteriis* 96,13–97,9.

4   For the problematic nature of this label, see Wouter J. Hanegraaff, *Esotericism and the Academy: Rejected Knowledge in Western Culture*, Cambridge University Press: Cambridge 2012, 177–91.

5   See Chapter Six, pp. 104–5.

6   David Pingree, 'Hellenophilia versus the History of Science', *Isis* 83:4 (1992), 560; see also Lynn Thorndike, 'The True Place of Astrology in the History of Science', *Isis* 46:3 (1955), 276.

7 William R. Newman and Lawrence M. Principe, 'Alchemy *vs.*
   Chemistry: The Etymological Origins of a Historiographical
   Mistake', *Early Science and Medicine* 3 (1998), 32–65.

8 Michael Stausberg, *Faszination Zarathushtra: Zoroaster und die
   Europäische Religionsgeschichte der Frühen Neuzeit*, 2 vols, Walter
   de Gruyter: Berlin/New York 1998.

9 Wouter J. Hanegraaff and Ruud M. Bouthoorn, *Lodovico Lazzarelli
   (1447–1500): The Hermetic Writings and Related Documents*,
   Arizona Center for Medieval and Renaissance Studies: Tempe 2005.

10 Wouter J. Hanegraaff, 'Better than Magic: Cornelius Agrippa and
   Lazzarellian Hermetism', *Magic, Ritual & Witchcraft* 4:1 (2009),
   1–25.

11 Carlos Gilly, '"*Theophrastia Sancta*": Paracelsianism as a Religion,
   in Conflict with the Established Churches', in Ole Peter Grell
   (ed.), *Paracelsus: The Man and his Reputation, his Ideas and their
   Transformation*, Brill: Leiden/Boston/Cologne 1998, 151–85.

12 The terminology 'occultism of the right'/'occultism of the left' comes
   from Joscelyn Godwin, *The Theosophical Enlightenment*, State
   University of New York Press: Albany 1994, 204.

13 Godwin, *Theosophical Enlightenment*.

14 Colin Campbell, 'The Cult, the Cultic Milieu and Secularization', *A
   Sociological Yearbook of Religion in Britain* 5 (1972), 119–36.

15 Christopher Partridge, *The Re-Enchantment of the West*, 2 vols,
   T&T Clark: London/New York 2004, 62–86.

16 Erik Davis, *TechGnosis: Myth, Magic and Mysticism in the Age of
   Information*, Five Star: London 2004.

17 The term was coined by Victoria Nelson, *The Secret Life of Puppets*,
   Harvard University Press: Cambridge, MA 2003; and see also
   Nelson, *Gothicka*, Harvard University Press: Cambridge, MA 2012.

Chapter 3

1 Olav Hammer and Kocku von Stuckrad, 'Introduction', in Olav
   Hammer and Kocku von Stuckrad (eds), *Polemical Encounters:
   Esoteric Discourse and Its Others*, Brill: Leiden/Boston 2007,
   vii–viii.

2 Compare Jan Assmann, *Moses the Egyptian: The Memory of Egypt
   in Western Monotheism*, Harvard University Press: Cambridge,
   MA/London 1997, 6–22.

3   Tertullian, *De praescriptione haereticorum* 7.9.

4   Arthur Droge, *Homer or Moses? Early Christian Interpretations of the History of Culture*, J.C.B. Mohr (Paul Siebeck): Tübingen 1989, 9.

5   Origen, *Contra Celsum* 5.33, 8.2 (Henry Chadwick [ed.], At the University Press: Cambridge 1953, 289, 454).

6   Eusebius, *Praep. Evang.* I.2.4 (see Droge, *Homer or Moses?* 175).

7   Augustine, *Retractationes* I.1.2.3.

8   Augustine, *De Civitate Dei* VIII.5.9. He did, however, reject Hermes Trismegistus as an idolater: ibid., VIII.23–4.

9   Karen L. King, *What is Gnosticism?* The Belknap Press of Harvard University Press: Cambridge, MA/London 2003, 29–30.

10 As demonstrated in detail by King, *What is Gnosticism?* passim.

11 Weyer, *De praestigiis daemonum* II.3.

12 Wouter J. Hanegraaff, *Esotericism and the Academy: Rejected Knowledge in Western Culture*, Cambridge University Press: Cambridge 2012, 83–6.

13 Mark Pattison, *Isaac Casaubon, 1559–1614*, 2nd edn, Clarendon Press: Oxford 1892, 322.

14 The standard treatment is Sicco Lehmann-Brauns, *Weisheit in der Weltgeschichte: Philosophiegeschichte zwischen Barock und Aufklärung*, Max Niemeyer: Tübingen 2004. For a complete version of the argument in this section, see Hanegraaff, *Esotericism and the Academy*, Chapter Two.

15 Gerhard May, *Creatio Ex Nihilo: The Doctrine of 'Creation out of Nothing' in Early Christian Thought*, T&T Clark International: London/New York 1994.

16 Ehregott Daniel Colberg, *Das Platonisch-Hermetisches Christenthum* . . ., 2 vols, Moritz Georg Weidmann: Frankfurt/Leipzig 1690–1, vol. I, 5.

17 Above, Chapter One, pp. 10–14.

18 Michael Albrecht, *Eklektik: Eine Begriffsgeschichte mit Hinweisen auf die Philosophie- und Wissenschaftsgeschichte*, frommann-holzboog: Stuttgart/Bad Cannstatt 1994.

19 Christoph August Heumann, 'Von denen Kennzeichen der falschen und unächten Philosophie', *Acta Philosophorum* 2 (1715), 209–11.

20 Voltaire, *Treatise on Tolerance and other Writings*, Cambridge University Press: Cambridge 2000, 83; *Dictionnaire philosophique* . . ., Garnier: Paris 1967, 394, 396.

21 Peter Gay, *The Enlightenment: An Interpretation. Vol. II: The Rise of Modern Paganism* (1966), W.W. Norton & Co.: New York/ London 1977.

22 Hans Thomas Hakl, *Eranos: An Alternative Intellectual History of the Twentieth Century*, Equinox: Sheffield 2012.

Chapter 4

1 Clement of Alexandria, *Excerpts of Theodotus* 78.

2 J. D. Salinger, 'Teddy', in Salinger, *Nine Stories*, Signet Books: New York 1954, 122–44, here 138.

3 Wouter J. Hanegraaff, *New Age Religion and Western Culture: Esotericism in the Mirror of Secular Thought*, SUNY Press: Albany 1998, 128–32.

4 Wouter J. Hanegraaff, 'Altered States of Knowledge: The Attainment of Gnōsis in the Hermetica', *The International Journal of the Platonic Tradition* 2 (2008), 128–63, here 139–41.

5 Jan van Rijckenborgh and Catharose de Petri, *De Chinese Gnosis*, Rozekruis Pers: Haarlem 1987, 140–1.

6 See, for example, Yuri Stoyanov, *The Other God: Dualist Religions from Antiquity to the Cathar Heresy*, Yale University Press: New Haven/London 2000.

7 Henrik Bogdan, 'Explaining the Murder-Suicides of the Order of the Solar Temple: A Survey of Hypotheses', and Benjamin E. Zeller, 'The Euphemization of Violence: The Case of Heaven's Gate', in James R. Lewis (ed.), *Violence and New Religious Movements*, Oxford University Press: Oxford/New York 2011, 133–45 and 173–89.

8 Arthur O. Lovejoy, *The Great Chain of Being: A Study of the History of an Idea*, Harvard University Press: Cambridge, MA/ London 1964, 315.

9 Giovanni Pico della Mirandola, 'On the Dignity of Man', in Ernst Cassirer, Paul Oskar Kristeller and John Herman Randall, *The Renaissance Philosophy of Man*, University of Chicago Press: Chicago/London 1948, 225.

10 Plato, *Phaedrus* 246a–257b.

11 Alexander Pope, *An Essay on Man* I.3–18.

12 Marsilio Ficino, 'The Vita Coelitus Comparanda', in Ficino, *Three Books on Life* (Carol V. Kaske and John R. Clark, eds), Medieval

& Renaissance Texts & Studies: Binghamton, New York 1989, 236–393.

13 *Asclepius* 23–4/37–8.

14 Nicolas Weill-Parot, 'Astral Magic and Intellectual Changes (Twelfth-Fifteenth Centuries): "Astrological Images" and the Concept of "Addressative" Magic', in Jan N. Bremmer and Jan R. Veenstra (eds), *The Metamorphosis of Magic from Late Antiquity to the Early Modern Period*, Peeters: Louvain/Paris/Dudley 2002, 167–87.

15 Wouter J. Hanegraaff, 'Better than Magic: Cornelius Agrippa and Lazzarellian Hermetism', *Magic, Ritual & Witchcraft* 4:1 (2009), 1–25.

16 C.H. XI: 20–2.

17 For example, Benjamin Lazier, *God Interrupted: Heresy and the European Imagination between the World Wars*, Princeton University Press: Princeton 2008.

18 Jeffrey J. Kripal, *Esalen: America and the Religion of No Religion*, University of Chicago Press: Chicago/London 2007.

19 Wouter J. Hanegraaff, 'Roberts, Dorothy Jane', in Wouter J. Hanegraaff (ed.), in collaboration with Antoine Faivre, Roelof van den Broek & Jean-Pierre Brach, *Dictionary of Gnosis and Western Esotericism*, Brill: Leiden/Boston 2005, 997–1000.

20 Ferdinand Christian Baur, *Die Epochen der kirchlichen Geschichtsschreibung* (1852), Georg Olms: Hildesheim 1962, 40.

21 Giovanni Pico della Mirandola, 'On the Dignity of Man', 223 (referring to *Asclepius* 6)

22 Compare Lawrence M. Principe, 'Revealing Analogies: The Descriptive and Deceptive Roles of Sexuality and Gender in Latin Alchemy', in Wouter J. Hanegraaff and Jeffrey J. Kripal (eds), *Hidden Intercourse: Eros and Sexuality in the History of Western Esotericism*, Fordham University Press: New York 2011, 209–29.

23 Friedrich Christoph Oetinger, *Biblisches und emblematisches Wörterbuch* (Gerhard Schäfer, ed.), vol. I, Walter de Gruyter: Berlin/New York 1999, 223.

24 For example, Ferdinand Christian Baur, *Die christliche Gnosis oder die christliche Religions-Philosophie in ihrer geschichtlichen Entwiklung*, C.F. Osiander: Tübingen 1835; Ernst Benz, *Schellings theologische Geistesahnen*, Franz Steiner: Wiesbaden 1955; Glenn Alexander Magee, *Hegel and the Hermetic Tradition*, Cornell University Press: Ithaca/London 2001.

25 Hanegraaff, *New Age Religion*, 462–82.

26 Ibid., 482–513.

27 Wouter J. Hanegraaff, *Esotericism and the Academy: Rejected Knowledge in Western Culture*, Cambridge University Press: Cambridge 2012, 266–77.

28 Ibid., 277–95.

Chapter 5

1 Kocku von Stuckrad, *Locations of Knowledge in Medieval and Early Modern Europe: Esoteric Discourse and Western Identities*, Brill: Leiden/Boston 2010, 60–1.

2 C.H. IX:10, and see commentary in Wouter J. Hanegraaff, 'Altered States of Knowledge: The Attainment of Gnōsis in the Hermetica', *The International Journal of the Platonic Tradition* 2 (2008), 128–63, here 134 with footnotes 16–17.

3 Friedemann Stengel, *Erleuchtung bis zum Himmel: Emanuel Swedenborg im Kontext der Theologie und Philosophie des 18. Jahrhunderts*, Mohr Siebeck: Tübingen 2011.

4 Marc van der Poel, *Cornelius Agrippa: The Humanist Theologian and his Declamations*, Brill: Leiden/New York/Cologne 1997.

5 Wouter J. Hanegraaff, *New Age Religion and Western Culture: Esotericism in the Mirror of Secular Thought*, SUNY Press: Albany 1998, 62–76, 113–81.

6 See Chapter Seven, p. 120.

7 For rare exceptions, see Garth Fowden, *The Egyptian Hermes: A Historical Approach to the Late Pagan Mind*, Princeton University Press: Princeton 1986, 105–14; Antoine Faivre, 'Le terme et la notion de "gnose" dans les courants ésotériques occidentaux modernes (essai de périodisation)', in Jean-Pierre Mahé, Paul-Hubert Poirier and Madeleine Scopello (eds), *Les Textes de Nag Hammadi: Histoire des religions et approches contemporaines*, AIBI/Diffusion De Boccard: Paris 2010, 87–112; Hanegraaff, 'Altered States of Knowledge'; idem, 'Gnosis', in Glenn A. Magee (ed.), *The Cambridge Companion to Western Mysticism and Esotericism*, Cambridge University Press: Cambridge 2013.

8 Nag Hammadi Codex VI[6], 57–8 (compare Hanegraaff, 'Altered States of Knowledge', 151–8, here 155).

9 John Walbridge, *The Leaven of the Ancients: Suhrawardī and the Heritage of the Greeks*, State University of New York Press: Albany 2000.

10 Suhrawardī, *Ḥikmat al-ishrāq* II.2.165–6, trans. according to
    Suhrawardī, *The Philosophy of Illumination* (John Walbridge and
    Hossein Ziai, eds/trans.), Brigham Young University Press: Provo,
    Utah 1999, 107–8.

11 C.H. X: 5–6.

12 F. Pfister, 'Ekstase', in *Reallexikon für Antike und Christentum*, 2nd
    edn, Hiersemann: Stuttgart 1970, 944–87.

13 Detailed analysis in Hanegraaff, 'Altered States of Knowledge'.

14 For 'mysticism', see Hanegraaff, 'Teaching Experiential Dimensions of
    Western Esotericism', in William B. Parsons (ed.), *Teaching Mysticism*,
    Oxford University Press: Oxford/New York 2011, 154–69, here 154–8.
    For 'magic', see below, Chapter Six, pp. 104–5. For 'shamanism', see,
    for example, Gloria Flaherty, *Shamanism and the Eighteenth Century*,
    Princeton University Press: Princeton 1992; Ronald Hutton, *Shamans:
    Siberian Spirituality and the Western Imagination*, Hambledon &
    London: London/New York 2001; Andrei A. Znamenski, *The Beauty
    of the Primitive: Shamanism and the Western Imagination*, Oxford
    University Press: Oxford/New York 2007.

15 Imants Barušs, *Alterations of Consciousness: An Empirical
    Analysis for Social Scientists*, American Psychological Association:
    Washington 2003.

16 For a short systematic overview, see Arnold M. Ludwig, 'Altered
    States of Consciousness', in Charles T. Tart (ed.), *Altered States
    of Consciousness*, Anchor Books: Garden City, NY 1972, 11–24,
    esp. 12–15.

17 Clifford Geertz, 'Religion as a Cultural System', in Michael Banton
    (ed.), *Anthropological Approaches to the Study of Religion*,
    Tavistock: London/New York 1966.

18 Plato, *Phaedrus* 249d.

19 Wouter J. Hanegraaff, 'The Platonic Frenzies in Marsilio Ficino', in
    Jitse Dijkstra, Justin Kroesen and Yme Kuiper (eds), *Myths, Martyrs
    and Modernity: Studies in the History of Religions in Honour of
    Jan N. Bremmer*, Brill: Leiden/Boston 2010, 553–67; idem, 'Under
    the Mantle of Love: The Mystical Eroticisms of Marsilio Ficino
    and Giordano Bruno', in Wouter J. Hanegraaff and Jeffrey J. Kripal
    (eds), *Hidden Intercourse: Eros and Sexuality in the History of
    Western Esotericism*, Fordham University Press: New York 2011,
    175–207.

20 Wouter J. Hanegraaff, 'How Hermetic was Renaissance Hermetism?
    Reason and Gnosis from Ficino to Foix de Candale', in Jan Veenstra

(ed.), *Hermetism and Rationalism*, Peeters: Louvain/Paris/Dudley forthcoming.

21 Faivre, 'Le terme et la notion'.

22 Jacob Böhme, *Morgen-Röte im Aufgangk*, chapter 19 (Ferdinand van Ingen, *Jacob Böhme Werke*, Deutscher Klassiker Verlag: Frankfurt a.m. 1997, 336).

23 Ann Taves, *Fits, Trances, and Visions: Experiencing Religion and Explaining Experience from Wesley to James*, Princeton University Press: Princeton 1999.

24 Wouter J. Hanegraaff, 'Magnetic Gnosis: Somnambulism and the Quest for Absolute Knowledge', in Andreas Kilcher and Philipp Theisohn (eds), *Die Enzyklopädik der Esoterik: Allwissenheitsmythen und universalwissenschaftliche Modelle in der Esoterik der Neuzeit*, Wilhelm Fink: Munich 2010, 259–75.

25 Karl Baier, *Meditation und Moderne: Zur Genese eines Kernbereichs moderner Spiritualität in der Wechselwirkung zwischen Westeuropa, Nordamerika und Asien* (2 vols), Königshausen & Neumann: Würzburg 2009.

26 Wouter J. Hanegraaff, 'Entheogenic Esotericism', in Egil Asprem and Kenneth Granholm (eds), *Contemporary Esotericism*, Equinox: Sheffield 2012, 392–409.

Chapter 6

1 Jonathan Z. Smith, *Drudgery Divine: On the Comparison of Early Christianities and the Religions of Late Antiquity*, University of Chicago Press: Chicago/London 1990, esp. 1–35; idem, *To Take Place: Toward Theory in Ritual*, University of Chicago Press: Chicago/London 1987, esp. 96–117.

2 But for the development of ritual studies, see now Jens Kreinath, Jan Snoek and Michael Stausberg (eds), *Theorizing Rituals: Issues, Topics, Approaches, Concepts*, Brill: Leiden/Boston 2006; idem, *Theorizing Rituals: Annotated Bibliography of Ritual Theory, 1966–2005*, Brill: Leiden/Boston 2007.

3 For a detailed and conclusive argument, see Bernd-Christian Otto, *Magie: Rezeptions- und diskursgeschichtliche Analysen von der Antike bis zur Neuzeit*, De Gruyter: Berlin/New York 2011, 1–132. See also Randall Styers, *Making Magic: Religion, Magic, and Science in the Modern World*, Oxford University Press:

Oxford/New York 2004; Wouter J. Hanegraaff, *Esotericism and the Academy: Rejected Knowledge in Western Culture*, Cambridge University Press: Cambridge 2012, 164–77; idem, 'Magic', in Glenn Alexander Magee, *The Cambridge Companion to Western Mysticism and Esotericism*, Cambridge University Press: Cambridge 2013.

4 For these two complementary discourses of exclusion and self-referential acceptance, see Otto, *Magie*.

5 For example, Richard Kieckhefer, *Magic in the Middle Ages*, Cambridge University Press: Cambridge 1989, 56–94.

6 See contributions by Frank Klaassen, Claire Fanger and Michael Camille in Claire Fanger (ed.), *Conjuring Spirits: Texts and Traditions of Medieval Ritual Magic*, Sutton: Phoenix Mill 1998.

7 Kieckhefer, *Magic in the Middle Ages*, 151–75.

8 Stephen Clucas, 'John Dee's Angelic Conversations and the Ars Notoria' (2006), repr. in Clucas, *Magic, Memory and Natural Philosophy in the Sixteenth and Seventeenth Centuries*, Ashgate/ Variorum: Farnham/Burlington 2011.

9 Thérèse Charmasson, 'Divinatory Arts', in Wouter J. Hanegraaff (ed.), in collaboration with Antoine Faivre, Roelof van den Broek & Jean-Pierre Brach, *Dictionary of Gnosis and Western Esotericism*, Brill: Leiden/Boston 2005, 313–19.

10 Joscelyn Godwin, *The Theosophical Enlightenment*, SUNY Press: Albany 1994, 169–86.

11 Francesco Cattani da Diacceto, *De pulchro* (in *Opera Omnia*, 45–6), here quoted according to the translation of D. P. Walker, *Spiritual and Demonic Magic from Ficino to Campanella*, The Warburg Institute: London 1958, 32–3.

12 Frances A. Yates, *The Art of Memory*, University of Chicago Press: Chicago 1966.

13 Alex Owen, *The Place of Enchantment: British Occultism and the Culture of the Modern*, University of Chicago Press: Chicago/ London 2004, 1, 156–7, and *passim*.

14 Tanya M. Luhrmann, *Persuasions of the Witch's Craft: Ritual Magic in Contemporary England*, Harvard University Press: Cambridge, MA 1989, 191–202.

15 Henry Corbin, '*Mundus Imaginalis*, or the Imaginary and the Imaginal', in Corbin (Leonard Fox, ed.), *Swedenborg and Esoteric Islam*, Swedenborg Foundation: West Chester 1995, 1–33.

16 Henri F. Ellenberger, *The Discovery of the Unconscious: The History and Evolution of Dynamic Psychiatry*, Basic Books: n.p. 1970.

17 Iamblichus, *De Mysteriis* 12.

18 Claire Fanger, 'Medieval Ritual Magic: What it is and why we need to know more about it', in Fanger, *Conjuring Spirits*, vii–xviii, here vii.

19 Ibid., viii–ix.

20 John Patrick Deveney, *Paschal Beverly Randolph: A Nineteenth-Century Black American Spiritualist, Rosicrucian, and Sex Magician*, State University of New York Press: Albany 1997, 104.

21 Chris Griscom, *Ecstasy is a New Frequency: Teachings of the Light Institute*, Simon & Schuster: New York 1987, 82.

22 Wouter J. Hanegraaff, *New Age Religion and Western Culture: Esotericism in the Mirror of Secular Thought*, SUNY Press: Albany 1998, 23, nt. 2.

23 See Wouter J. Hanegraaff, 'Teaching Experiential Dimensions of Western Esotericism', in William B. Parsons (ed.), *Teaching Mysticism*, Oxford University Press: Oxford/New York 2011, 154–69, here 154–8.

24 For a good summary, see Colleen Shantz, *Paul in Ecstasy: The Neurobiology of the Apostle's Life and Thought*, Cambridge University Press: Cambridge 2009, 79–87 (with primary reference to the work of Eugene d'Aquili and Andrew Newberg).

25 See Chapter Four, pp. 78–9.

26 Wouter J. Hanegraaff, 'Altered States of Knowledge: The Attainment of Gnōsis in the Hermetica', *The International Journal of the Platonic Tradition* 2 (2008), 128–63, here 146–8.

27 Jean Houston, *The Possible Human: A Course for Extending your Physical, Mental, and Creative Abilities*, J. P. Tarcher: Los Angeles 1982, 186.

28 Alice Joly, *Un mystique Lyonnais et les secrets de la Franc-Maçonnerie: Jean-Baptiste Willermoz, 1730–1824* (1938), Éditions Télètes: Paris n.d.

Chapter 7

1 On the notion of 'intellectual sacrifice', see Max Weber, 'Wissenschaft als Beruf', in Max Weber, *Wissenschaft als Beruf 1917/1919, Politik als Beruf 1919* (Wolfgang J. Mommsen and Wolfgang Schluchter, eds), J.C.B. Mohr (Paul Siebeck): Tübingen 1994, 1–23.

2 Martin Mulsow (ed.), *Das Ende des Hermetismus: Historische Kritik und neue Naturphilosophie in der Spätrenaissance. Dokumentation und Analyse der Debatte um die Datierung der hermetischen Schriften von Genebrard bis Casaubon (1567–1614)*, Mohr Siebeck: Tübingen 2002.

3 Wouter J. Hanegraaff, *Esotericism and the Academy: Rejected Knowledge in Western Culture*, Cambridge University Press: Cambridge 2012, 295–314.

4 Plotinus, *Ennead* IV.4.32 (and compare IV.4.41–2).

5 Hanegraaff, *Esotericism and the Academy*, 189–91 with note 139; 294–5.

6 For example, Eugenio Garin, *Medioevo e rinascimento: Studi e ricerche*, Gius. Laterza & Figli: Bari 1954, 154 (English trans. in Hanegraaff, *Esotericism and the Academy*, 330); Michel Foucault, *Les mots et les choses: Une archéologie des sciences humaines*, Gallimard: Paris 1966, ch. 2 ('La prose du monde').

7 Brian Vickers, 'On the Function of Analogy in the Occult', in Ingrid Merkel and Allen G. Debus, *Hermeticism and the Renaissance: Intellectual History and the Occult in Early Modern Europe*, Folger Books: Washington/London/Toronto 1988, 265–92.

8 Carol V. Kaske and John R. Clark, 'Introduction', in Marsilio Ficino, *Three Books of Life*, Medieval & Renaissance Texts & Studies/Renaissance Society of America: Binghamton, New York 1989, 1–90, here 48–53.

9 Pinella Travaglia, *Magic, Causality and Intentionality: The Doctrine of Rays in al-Kindī*, Sismel – Edizioni del Galluzzo: Florence 1999.

10 Ficino, *De Vita* III.3.31–3 (Kaske and Clarke, eds), 256–7).

11 Weber, 'Wissenschaft als Beruf', 9.

12 Wouter J. Hanegraaff, *Swedenborg, Oetinger, Kant: Three Perspectives on the Secrets of Heaven*, The Swedenborg Foundation: West Chester 2007; and on the kabbalistic interpretation, see idem, 'Emanuel Swedenborg, the Jews, and Jewish Traditions', in Peter Schäfer and Irina Wandrey (eds), *Reuchlin und seine Erben: Forscher, Denker, Ideologen und Spinner*, Jan Thorbecke: Ostfildern 2005, 135–54. Essentially the same conclusions are drawn in the comprehensive study by Friedemann Stengel, *Aufklärung bis zum Himmel: Emanuel Swedenborg im Kontext der Theologie und Philosophie des 18. Jahrhunderts*, Mohr Siebeck: Tübingen 2011.

13 Tanya Luhrmann, *Persuasions of the Witch's Craft: Ritual Magic in Contemporary England*, Harvard University Press: Cambridge, MA 1989, 274–82.

14 Keith Hutchison, 'What happened to Occult Qualities in the Scientific Revolution?' *Isis* 73 (1982), 233–53.

15 Egil Asprem, 'Pondering Imponderables: Occultism in the Mirror of Late Classical Physics', *Aries* 11:2 (2011), 129–65.

16 Fraser Watts, 'Morphic Fields and Extended Mind: An Examination of the Theoretical Concepts of Rupert Sheldrake', *Journal of Consciousness Studies* 18, nrs. 11–12 (2011), 203–24.

17 Carl Gustav Jung and Wolfgang Pauli, *The Interpretation of Nature and the Psyche*, Pantheon Books: New York 1955.

18 Wouter J. Hanegraaff, *New Age Religion and Western Culture: Esotericism in the Mirror of Secular Thought*, SUNY Press: Albany 1998, 62–70.

19 Hanegraaff, *Esotericism and the Academy*, 5–76.

20 Raymond Schwab, *The Oriental Renaissance: Europe's Rediscovery of India and the East, 1680–1880*, Columbia University Press: New York 1984, 6.

21 For example, Eric J. Sharpe, *Comparative Religion: A History*, Duckworth: London 1986; Hans G. Kippenberg, *Discovering Religious History in the Modern Age*, Princeton University Press: Princeton 2002.

22 Joscelyn Godwin, *The Theosophical Enlightenment*, State University of New York Press: Albany 1994, esp. chapters 1–4.

23 Ibid., 266.

24 See in particular Godwin, *Theosophical Enlightenment*.

25 For example, Bruce F. Campbell, *Ancient Wisdom Revived: A History of the Theosophical Movement*, University of California Press: Berkeley/Los Angeles/London 1980.

26 Arthur Versluis, *American Transcendentalism and Asian Religions*, Oxford University Press: Oxford/New York 1993.

27 Catherine L. Albanese, *A Republic of Mind and Spirit: A Cultural History of American Metaphysical Religion*, Yale University Press: New Haven & London 2007.

28 Wouter J. Hanegraaff, 'Entheogenic Esotericism', in Egil Asprem and Kenneth Granholm (eds), *Contemporary Esotericism*, Equinox: Sheffield 2012, 392–409.

29 Jeffrey J. Kripal, *Mutants & Mystics: Science Fiction, Superhero Comics, and the Paranormal*, University of Chicago Press: Chicago and London 2011, 31–69.

30 See above, p. 83.

31 Arthur O. Lovejoy, *The Great Chain of Being: A Study of the History of an Idea*, Harvard University Press: Cambridge, MA/ London 1964, 242–87, here 244.

32 Frederick William Conner, *Cosmic Optimism: A Study of the Interpretation of Evolution by American Poets from Emerson to Robinson*, University of Florida Press: Gainesville 1949.

33 Hanegraaff, *Esotericism and the Academy*, 266–77.

34 Helmut Zander, *Geschichte der Seelenwanderung in Europa: Alternative religiöse Traditionen von der Antike bis Heute*, Wissenschaftliche Buchgesellschaft: Darmstadt 1999.

35 Hanegraaff, *New Age Religion*, 470–82.

36 See above, pp. 70–1.

37 See Jeffrey J. Kripal, *The Serpent's Gift: Gnostic Reflections on the Study of Religion*, University of Chicago Press: Chicago/London 2007, 59–89; and some critical reservation in Wouter J. Hanegraaff, 'Leaving the Garden (in Search of Religion): Jeffrey J. Kripal's Vision of a Gnostic Study of Religion', *Religion* 38:3 (2008), 259–76, here 265–8.

38 Justinus Kerner, *Die Seherin von Prevorst: Eröffnungen über das innere Leben des Menschen und über das Hereinragen einer Geisterwelt in die unsere*, Reclam: Leipzig n.d., 220–49, esp. 227–8.

39 Théodore Flournoy, *From India to the Planet Mars: A Case of Multiple Personality and Imaginary Languages* (orig. 1899), Princeton University Press: Princeton 1994.

40 Jeffrey J. Kripal, *Authors of the Impossible: The Paranormal and the Sacred*, University of Chicago Press: Chicago/London 2010, 1–35.

41 Marco Pasi, 'Varieties of Magical Experience: Aleister Crowley's Views on Occult Practice', *Magic, Ritual & Witchcraft* 6:2 (2011), 123–62, esp. 143–60.

42 Wouter J. Hanegraaff, 'Fiction in the Desert of the Real: Lovecraft's Cthulhu Mythos', *Aries* 7:1 (2007), 85–109.

43 Clifford Geertz, 'Religion as a Cultural System', in Michael Banton (ed.), *Anthropological Approaches to the Study of Religion*, Tavistock: London 1966, 1–46. For the complete argument, see Wouter J. Hanegraaff, 'Defining Religion in Spite of History', in Jan

G. Platvoet and Arie L. Molendijk (eds), *The Pragmatics of Defining Religion: Contexts, Concepts & Contests*, Brill: Leiden 1999, 337–78; and idem, 'New Age Spiritualities as Secular Religion: A Historian's Perspective', *Social Compass* 46:2 (1999), 145–60 (repr. in Bryan S. Turner [ed.], *Secularization*, vol. 4, Sage: London 2010, 121–36).

44 Emile Durkheim, *The Elementary Forms of Religious Life* (orig. 1912; Karen E. Fields, trans.), The Free Press: New York 1995, 43–4.

45 Peter L. Berger, *The Heretical Imperative: Contemporary Possibilities of Religious Affirmation*, Doubleday: New York 1980.

Chapter 8

1 Wouter J. Hanegraaff, 'The Dreams of Theology and the Realities of Christianity', in J. Haers and P. de Mey (eds), *Theology and Conversation: Towards a Relational Theology*, Leuven University Press/Peeters: Louvain 2003, 709–33; idem, *Esotericism and the Academy: Rejected Knowledge in Western Culture*, Cambridge University Press: Cambridge 2012, 127–52, 314–34.

2 Immanuel Kant, 'What is Enlightenment?' in Margaret C. Jacob, *The Enlightenment: A Brief History with Documents*, Bedford/ St. Martin's: Boston/New York 2001, 202–08.

3 Marieke J. E. van den Doel, *Ficino en het voorstellingsvermogen: Phantasia en Imaginatio in kunst en theorie van de Renaissance*, PhD dissertation, University of Amsterdam 2008.

4 Otto Betz, *Licht vom unerschaffenen Lichte: Die kabbalistische Lehrtafel der Prinzessin Antonia in Bad Teinach*, Sternberg Verlag: Metzingen 1996; Friedrich Christoph Oetinger, *Die Lehrtafel der Prinzessin Antonia*, Reinhard Breymayer and Friedrich Häussermann (eds), 2 vols, Walter de Gruyter: Berlin/New York 1977.

5 William Blake, *The Complete Illuminated Books* (David Bindman, introduction), Thames & Hudson: London 2000; Jos van Meurs, 'William Blake and his Gnostic Myths', in Roelof van den Broek and Wouter J. Hanegraaff (eds), *Gnosis and Hermeticism from Antiquity to Modern Times*, State University of New York Press: Albany 1998, 269–309.

6 See, for example, various contributions to Robin Larsen, *Emanuel Swedenborg: A Continuing Vision. A Pictorial Biography & Anthology of Essays & Poetry*, Swedenborg Foundation: New York 1988.

7   See above, p. 83.

8   Victoria Nelson, *Gothicka*, Harvard University Press: Cambridge, MA 2013.

9   Umberto Eco, with Richard Rorty, Jonathan Culler and Christine Brooke-Rose, *Interpretation and Overinterpretation*, Cambridge University Press: Cambridge 1992.

10 Tessel M. Bauduin, *The Occultation of Surrealism*, PhD dissertation, University of Amsterdam 2012.

11 Maurice Tuchman (ed.), *The Spiritual in Art: Abstract Painting 1890–1985*, Abbeville: New York 1986. See also the massive catalogue *Okkultismus und Avantgarde* (based on an exhibition in the Schirn Kunsthalle in Frankfurt), Edition Tertium: Ostfildern 1995.

12 See, for example, the representative catalogue of an ambitious exhibition *Traces du Sacré*, Centre Pompidou: Paris 2008, here 16.

13 An exception, although focused on a limited period, is Alain Mercier, *Les sources ésotériques et occultes de la poésie Symboliste (1870–1914)*, A.-G. Nizet: Paris 1969.

14 Francesco Colonna, *Hypnerotomachia Poliphili: The Strife of Love in a Dream* (trans. Joscelyn Godwin), Thames & Hudson: London 1999; compare Joscelyn Godwin, *The Pagan Dream of the Renaissance*, Thames & Hudson: London 2002.

15 For a useful list, see Antoine Faivre, *Western Esotericism: A Concise History*, State University of New York Press: Albany 2010, 51.

16 References in Hanegraaff, *Esotericism and the Academy*, 222, nt. 258.

17 For example, Robert M. Schuler (ed.), *Alchemical Poetry 1575–1700, From Previously Unpublished Manuscripts*, Garland: New York/London 1995.

18 Hanegraaff, *Esotericism and the Academy*, 222–30, and literature quoted there.

19 See list in Faivre, *Western Esotericism*, 67.

20 Hartmut Binder, *Gustav Meyrink: Ein Leben im Bann der Magie*, Vitalis: Prague 2009; Theodor Harmsen, *Der magische Schriftsteller Gustav Meyrink, seine Freunde und sein Werk*, In de Pelikaan: Amsterdam 2009.

21 Gísli Magnússon, *Dichtung als Erfahrungsmetaphysik: Esoterische und okkultistische Modernität bei R.M. Rilke*, Königshausen & Neumann: Würzburg 2009.

22 Marco Pasi, 'The Influence of Aleister Crowley on Fernando Pessoa's Esoteric Writings', in Richard Caron, Joscelyn Godwin, Wouter J.

Hanegraaff & Jean-Louis Vieillard Baron (eds), *Ésotérisme, gnoses & imaginaire symbolique: Mélanges offerts à Antoine Faivre*, Peeters: Louvain 2001, 693–711, esp. 694–9 and literature in nt. 4.

23 Wouter J. Hanegraaff, 'Ironic Esotericism: Alchemy and Grail Mythology in Thomas Mann's "Zauberberg"', in Caron, Godwin, Hanegraaff & Viellard-Baron, *Ésotérisme*, 575–94.

24 Joscelyn Godwin, 'The Revival of Speculative Music', *Musical Quarterly* 68 (1982), 373–89. See also the useful anthology by Godwin (ed.), *Music, Mysticism and Magic: A Sourcebook*, Arkana: New York/London 1986.

25 See many examples in Laurence Wuidar (ed.), *Music and Esotericism*, Brill: Leiden/Boston 2010.

26 For example, Penelope Gouk, *Music, Science and Natural Magic in Seventeenth-Century England*, Yale University Press: New Haven/London 1999.

27 For general overviews and literature suggestions, including the roots of Renaissance musical speculation in antiquity and the Middle Ages, see Albert de Jong, Mariken Teeuwen, Penelope Gouk and Joscelyn Godwin, 'Music I–IV', in Wouter J. Hanegraaff (ed.) in collaboration with Antoine Faivre, Roelof van den Broek & Jean-Pierre Brach, *Dictionary of Gnosis and Western Esotericism*, Brill: Leiden/Boston 2005, 808–18. See also D. P. Walker, *Music, Spirit and Language in the Renaissance* (Penelope Gouk, ed.), Variorum: London 1985; and Gary Tomlinson, *Music in Renaissance Magic: Towards a Historiography of Others*, University of Chicago Press: Chicago/London 1993.

28 Joscelyn Godwin, 'Music IV: 18th Century to the Present', in Hanegraaff, *Dictionary*, 815–18, here 816.

29 Joscelyn Godwin, *Music and the Occult: French Musical Philosophies, 1750–1950*, University of Rochester Press: Rochester 1995.

30 Recorded on CD by Reinbert de Leeuw in 2011 (KTC 1427, 2 CDs; www.etcetera-records.com).

31 Wouter J. Hanegraaff, 'The Unspeakable and the Law: Esotericism in Anton Webern and the Second Viennese School', in Wuidar, *Music and Esotericism*, 329–53.

32 Joscelyn Godwin, 'Stockhausen's *Donnerstag aus Licht* and Gnosticism', in Roelof van den Broek and Wouter J. Hanegraaff

(eds), *Gnosis and Hermeticism from Antiquity to Modern Times*, State University of New York Press: Albany 1998, 347–58.

33 For example, Robin Sylvan, *Trance Formation: The Spiritual and Religious Dimensions of Global Rave Culture*, Routledge: New York/Oxon 2005.

34 See, however, Christopher Partridge, *The Re-Enchantment of the West*, T&T Clark: London/New York 2004, vol. 1, 143–84.

35 Edward A. Tiryakian (ed.), *On the Margin of the Visible: Sociology, the Esoteric, and the Occult*, John Wiley & Sons: New York, etc. 1974.

36 Massimo Introvigne, *Il cappello del Mago: I nuovi movimenti magici, dallo spiritismo al satanismo*, Sugarco: Carnago 1990 (unfortunately not yet translated) and countless other titles on specific organizations; J. Gordon Melton, *Encyclopedic Handbook of Cults in America*, Garland: New York/London 1992, and many large encyclopedic reference works; Eileen Barker, *New Religious Movements: A Practical Introduction*, HMSO: London 1992; James R. Lewis, *The Oxford Handbook of New Religious Movements*, Oxford University Press: Oxford/New York 2004, and again many other encyclopedic reference works.

37 See especially Introvigne's CESNUR (Center for Studies on New Religions) and its extremely useful website www.cesnur.org; and Barker's INFORM (Information Network on Religious Movements), www.inform.ac.

38 For example René Dybdal Pedersen, 'The Second Golden Age of Theosophy in Denmark: An Existential "Template" for Late Modernity?' *Aries* 9:2 (2009), 233–62.

39 Tanya M. Luhrmann, *Persuasions of the Witch's Craft: Ritual Magic in Contemporary England*, Harvard University Press: Cambridge, MA 1989; Michael F. Brown, *The Channeling Zone: American Spirituality in an Anxious Age*, Harvard University Press: Cambridge, MA/London 1997.

40 Mary Farrell Bednarowski, *New Religions and the Theological Imagination in America*, Indiana University Press: Bloomington/Indianapolis 1989.

NAME INDEX

SUBJECT INDEX